THE PASTOR'S
COMPLETE GUIDE
◇────── TO ──────◇
PERSONAL
FINANCIAL
PLANNING

H. L. BERT AKIN

OLIVER
NELSON

THOMAS NELSON PUBLISHERS
Nashville

To
All my pastor friends

For God is not unjust to forget your work
and labor of love
which you have shown toward His name,
in that you have ministered to the saints,
and do minister.

Hebrews 6:10

PUBLISHER'S NOTE: This book is intended only for general financial information and guidance. Readers are urged to consult a financial planner to determine personal strategies for specific goals and situations.

Copyright © 1993 by Herbert Lindsey Akin

Published in Nashville, Tennessee, by Oliver-Nelson Books, a division of Thomas Nelson, Inc., Publishers, and distributed in Canada by Lawson Falle, Ltd., Cambridge, Ontario.

Unless otherwise noted, the Bible version used in this publication is THE NEW KING JAMES VERSION. Copyright © 1979, 1980, 1982, Thomas Nelson, Inc., Publishers.

Printed in the United States of America.

Library of Congress Cataloging-in-Publication Data

Akin, H. L., 1926–
    The pastor's complete guide to personal financial planning / H.L. Bert Akin.
        p.   cm.
    Includes index.
    ISBN 0-8407-9635-8 (pbk.)
    1. Clergy—Finance, Personal.   I. Title.
BV4397.A55   1993
332.024′2—dc20   92-34640
                                                           CIP

1 2 3 4 5 6 — 98 97 96 95 94 93

CONTENTS

PREFACE

What This Book Will Do for You

This book will help you, a clergyperson, stretch your dollars by showing the following:

- How to set up your pay package properly
- How to set up your housing allowance for maximum tax savings
- How to use the magic word *reimbursement* for expenses
- How to buy a home with no down payment
- How to buy a retirement home
- How to decide whether or not to opt out of Social Security
- How to decide what investments you should make
- How to make sure your children go to college
- How to retire with enough money to have fun
- How to know which retirement plan to buy
- How to choose the right kind and amount of life insurance
- How to discuss these ideas with your church board
- How to get out of debt and stay out
- How to keep the IRS happy with you and your church
- How to choose a professional tax preparer for clergy

This book is aimed specifically at clergypersons and their special needs. Many CPAs shy away from clergy tax preparation because of the complexities involved.

For many years I have conducted seminars for clergypersons. Often I hear the same laments: "I never learned *any* of this in seminary!" and "Where were you twenty-five years ago?" I have included in this book some answers to the concerns I hear repeatedly from professional clergypersons.

My hope is that seminary students as well as pastors in the field will find this book informative and profitable over the years.

INTRODUCTION

The information and suggestions in this book are based on experience, the recommendations of responsible professionals, and hours of research.

The author and the publisher realize that each pastor has a unique situation. Therefore, we disclaim any and all responsibility for any adverse consequences resulting from the reader implementing the suggestions contained here.

This book is not intended to be used as a complete guide to prepare your income tax records. It is designed to show you *why you should seek professional help* from tax preparers who are knowledgeable about church and clergy tax laws. If the services of a qualified tax preparer are not readily available in your area, this book should provide much information for you to share with a professional who may not be familiar with some of the ideas and those portions of tax law that are helpful specifically to clergypersons. Then, the tax preparer can confirm and implement some of the procedures suggested. Our prayerful hope is that these ideas may stretch your dollars and help you accomplish your financial goals. Please remember, the primary audience of this book is *clergypersons,* not the general public.

The author has heard the lament of many clergypersons over the years, telling of having their income tax forms completed by persons who were not familiar with their tax status as members of the clergy. Having income tax records done incorrectly can be very costly to ministers.

We strongly suggest that you do not take any action on your own, based on the information in this book, without seeking the counsel of a *competent* professional tax preparer, CPA, tax attorney, or investment counselor.

Even more important for you to understand is the need for ongoing financial planning throughout your ministry. If you haven't started because you think you can't afford to set funds aside, I urge you to reconsider and begin now at any level no matter how small you think it is. Here are the items most clergypersons need and the ones that must be planned for:

- income replacement for your family if you die prematurely
- college costs
- a home now and for retirement
- retirement income
- disability income

Some explanations are in order for sources mentioned in the text. The Internal Revenue Code (IRC) refers to the revenue laws of the federal government as passed by Congress. Regulations are official decisions made and published by the Treasury Department to interpret, implement, and enforce the Internal Revenue Code. Revenue Rulings are official publications issued by the IRS to apply the IRC, regulations, and court decisions to specific situations.

Material quoted extensively from governmental publications is noted in two ways: with quotation marks or with a different typeface from the main body of the text. A reference to the specific publication will be provided in each case. You will occasionally find brackets used in this quoted material; that information has been added by the author or publisher to clarify a point or to refer you to a section in *this* book. For example, [see 1-11] means to turn to point 11 in chapter 1, which discusses "What Are Sacerdotal Duties?"

The Paradox of Clergy Compensation

1-1 How to Be Certain Whether You're Self-Employed or an Employee

The Bible says that Satan is the author of confusion, but the Internal Revenue Service (IRS) would probably be voted a close second by many taxpayers. The answer to the following question should be simple, but it is not: Are clergypersons considered to be employees, or are they self-employed? Although many ministers may be able to complete their own income tax forms, most would be wise to seek competent individual tax counsel from professionals who *specialize* in clergy tax returns.

1-2 The Dual Nature of Your Tax Status

Many ministers have experienced the frustration of consulting with a tax preparer only to discover that the person knew nothing of the dual tax status of clergypersons, not to mention the complexities of housing allowance and special retirement plans available only to employees of tax-exempt employers. I have heard many ministers say, "I had to tell my tax adviser what to look up, and he did it wrong and still sent me a bill." Unfortunately, that is a common lament. You must understand the dual nature of your tax status to follow through with the proper setup of your pay package.

Most clergypersons are considered to be self-employed for Social Security purposes, but they are considered to be employees for income tax purposes. As a self-employed clergyperson, you will have to report your earnings for Social Security purposes unless you have taken a vow of poverty or you are opposed to accepting *any* public protection because of matters of conscience or religious principles.

1-3 Should Your Church Give You a Form W-2?

Prior to 1980, the law was unclear about the income tax status of clergypersons. As of 1980, the IRS attempted to clarify this question further by enacting Revenue Ruling 80-110, 1980-16, 10, but such may not have been the case. This ruling seemed to be aimed at establishing the tax status of *most* ministers as employees, which meant that *most* churches must give out W-2 Forms to *most* ministers. It meant that *most* ministers must file income tax returns as employees, not as self-employed persons, for income tax purposes. But even though the ministers received a Form W-2, they were still considered to be self-employed for Social Security tax purposes.

1-4 How to Report Honoraria

One of the many causes for confusion in determining the tax status of pastors is that they have more than one stream of income. Aside from salary and total pay packages, most pastors receive honoraria for conducting weddings, baptisms, and funerals. This money is not salary; it is self-employment income.

1-5 Why the Rules of Common Law Are so Important to You

A quick test to determine whether you are an employee or are self-employed is to ask, Can I be hired or fired or told where to live by anyone, including my congregation or my denominational headquarters? At first glance you may think that is a simple question, but consider this: many ministers are assigned to their churches by denominational edict but are paid by the congregation. Are such ministers employees or self-employed? Who is the employer: the congregation or the denomination?

If you are still convinced that you are self-employed for income tax purposes, I suggest that you refer to Revenue Ruling 87-41, which outlines twenty specific tests for you to answer. They are not listed here because almost all qualified interpreters of the tax law agree that most ministers are considered to be employees when tested by common law rules.

1-6 Who Is the Minister's Boss?

Some uncertainty can be lifted by determining who is in control of the minister's daily life. Is it the minister, or is it someone or some organization who has the authority to supervise the minister? To what extent does the minister have to submit to such authority? Can the minister refuse such attempts to control his or her work?

That is the key question. Even if the higher authority does not use its power to control the minister, the fact that it has such power is enough to settle the issue. A minister in such a situation is considered to be an employee.

The question of control can be different with each denomination or independent church. In the Presbyterian Church, USA, for example, a minister cannot be fired by the congregation.

1-7 Taking Tax Advice from Amateurs Can Be Costly to You

Unfortunately, it is not always simple to determine which minister is an employee and which one is self-employed. Very often at meetings, ministers will tell other ministers how they handle their tax records, and the listeners will follow that advice. In most cases, it will probably be wrong to some extent. The biblical admonition to test all things is especially important in regard to advice from amateurs! If you are audited and some well-meaning friend gave you incorrect advice, the possible extra taxes and penalties are almost sure to exceed the cost of seeking professional tax counsel in the first place.

1-8 Giving Financial Advice Can Be Costly to You

You should be very careful in giving financial advice to friend and foe alike. We would all like to think that no minister would sue another minister. But you should know that you can be sued for any financial advice or tip that you might pass on to another person. That might sound extreme, but actual court cases have involved one person passing on an investment tip to a friend at lunch. The "friend" acted on the tip, made an investment that went sour, and then sued his friendly "adviser." The "friend" won the case. It's best to leave financial advice to professionals who probably have professional liability insurance to cover such hazards.

1-9 Are You an Employee, or Are You Self-Employed?

Most tax advisers agree that *most* ministers should be considered to be employees for income tax purposes and that the trade-off of advantages and disadvantages is favorable to ministers.

You must report your salary as income for Social Security purposes if you are under the control of a congregation or denominational authority. You are considered to be a common-law employee. You must pay the self-employment tax rate for Social Security purposes, but you are considered to be an employee for income tax purposes. Any honoraria you receive—such as fees for weddings, funerals, and baptisms—are considered to be self-employment income and not salary.

1-10 Who Is a Minister?

Just who is this person governed by such complex tax laws? Who is considered to be a minister in the eyes of the government? Who is *not* a minister? In IRS Publication 517, a *minister* is defined as follows:

Ministers are individuals who are duly ordained, commissioned, or licensed by a religious body constituting a church denomination. They are given the authority to conduct religious worship, perform sacerdotal functions, and administer ordinances or sacraments according to the prescribed tenets and practices of that church or denomination.

If a church or denomination ordains some ministers and licenses or commissions others, anyone licensed or commissioned must be able to perform substantially all the religious functions of an ordained minister to be treated as a minister for Social Security purposes.

1-11 What Are Sacerdotal Duties?

Ministers of music, cantors, Christian education directors, organists, and other full-time church employees are *not* considered to be ministers of the gospel unless they have been ordained, licensed, or commissioned and perform the sacerdotal duties on a regular basis. These duties include the following:

• Conducting a worship service on a regular basis
• Officiating at weddings
• Conducting funerals
• Officiating at baptisms
• Conducting Communion
• Conducting church administrative affairs
• Teaching

These duties are essential to keep in mind, especially in regard to housing allowance, which is discussed thoroughly in chapter 2.

1-12 The Sacredness of Your Call

There is biblical precedent for the proper support of ministers. In both the New Testament and the Old Testament, God's man or woman who leads people is to be supported by those who are served.

Moses declared, "You shall not muzzle an ox while it treads out the grain" (Deut. 25:4). Was Moses speaking of oxen? Yes, of course. However, he was making a point that applied to the spiritual leaders and their support by the people.

In 1 Timothy 5:17–18 we read, "Let the elders who rule well be counted worthy of double honor, especially those who labor in the word and doctrine. For the Scripture says, 'You shall not muzzle an ox while it treads out the grain,' and, 'The laborer is worthy of his wages.'"

Paul was talking about people. He was referring specifically to those who minister in word and doctrine. In other words, he gave guidelines for the pay packages of ministers of the gospel in today's world. Somewhere along the way, however, the idea of paying ministers double wages seems to have fallen by the wayside.

1-13 Why Your Church Should Have a Pastoral Support Group

Most ministers will not push for additional money. Most believe they should attempt to live on whatever the congregation chooses to pay them. Usually, only extreme financial pressure will cause ministers to share their needs with their congregations. More often than not, the spouse and children put increasing pressure on the minister when finances are inadequate. It is truly a dilemma.

I suggest that you have a special committee with whom you can meet periodically and share your needs. Many ministers suffer in silence unnecessarily, assuming that their needs should be obvious to the congregation, or they may be too embarrassed to mention their financial position. Periodic meetings throughout the year afford ongoing opportunities for communication. Such sharing can be risky, to be sure, but the positive reasons seem to outweigh the negatives.

A person called of God to be a minister has a rare calling and a heavy responsibility. Fortunately or unfortunately, most ministers depend on the generosity of their parishioners for their salaries and fringe and retirement benefits. Even ministers whose denominational executives set their salaries depend ultimately on the donations of the parishioners.

CHAPTER 2

Housing Allowance—Fabulous Tax Advantage

I recommend that whether you live in your own home, a parsonage, or an apartment, you read the homeowner's section first. It contains most of what you need to know as a parsonage dweller or renter. Further on in this chapter I will explain ways to buy a home and how to set up a home equity fund. Housing allowance that is spent, within the allowable limits of Section 107 of the Internal Revenue Code (IRC), is reported on your Form W-2 or Form 1099 not for income tax purposes, only for Social Security purposes.

2-1 How a Homeowner May Get a Double Deduction of Taxes and Interest

Under Section 107 of the Internal Revenue Code, a "minister of the gospel," as defined in chapter 1, may buy a home and deduct up to the "fair rental value plus utilities" as a housing allowance "to provide a home" *if* it is actually spent to provide a home. In addition, interest and taxes itemized on the minister's income tax form may be deducted a *second* time. It is a double deduction.

A little history is in order here. Revenue Ruling 62-212, which allowed the double deduction, was the law of the land for many years. Then, in 1983, that ruling was revoked by Revenue Ruling 83-3, 1983-1, 10 (IRC Section 265; also IRC Sections 107, 162, 163, 164, and 7805), requiring home-owning ministers to use a formula to determine how much interest and taxes they could deduct over and above the amounts deducted in their housing allowance. Fortunately, that law was rescinded shortly thereafter, and refunds were made to ministers who were affected during that period of time when their double deductions were limited. That put home-owning ministers back where they started. They were and still are eligible to double deduct the interest and taxes connected with the home: once in their housing allowance and once on their tax forms as itemized deductions.

2-2 How to Calculate the Fair Rental Value of Your Home

As a homeowner, you must calculate the maximum housing allowance for which you are eligible. There is one way and only one way to do this as outlined in Section 107 of the IRC.

You must determine what your furnished home would rent for, exclusive of the cost of utilities. That figure is called the fair rental value: the amount of money you would be willing to accept if you rented your furnished home to a person who would be willing to pay that amount of rent. Furthermore, it must be a rental amount that would be affirmed by local real estate appraisers. Both the landlord and the renter must be satisfied with the price. That rental value sets the maximum you may have as your housing allowance. *Do not include utilities in housing allowance.* They're listed separately in your pay package, and there is no maximum attached to utilities. Whatever you spend is deductible.

Section 107 has three elements: (1) the fair rental value of your home, (2) the fair rental value of your furniture, and (3) the cost of utilities. You cannot deduct more than the fair rental value of your furnished home no matter how much you spend on your home. You *can* deduct your utilities. Probably the most accurate way for you as a homeowner to determine the fair rental value of your furnished home would be to call in two real estate appraisers and obtain written appraisals. They should know the local values better than anyone.

Another method used by lending institutions is the 1 percent rule. Multiply the market value of your furnished home by 1 percent. That is the amount of monthly rent you might reasonably charge if you were going to rent your home to someone. For example, 1 percent of a home valued at $80,000 is $800. Assuming the value of the furniture and furnishings is an additional $20,000, you could add another $200 to the monthly rent, making the total fair rental value of your furnished home $1,000 per month. Utilities are always in addition to that.

This method doesn't always prove to be accurate. It is not a law or a revenue ruling; it is simply a benchmark sometimes used by lending institutions. But lacking any other method, it is something with which to start.

You must determine the fair rental value, furnished, to properly ascertain your maximum housing allowance. Denominations sometimes use other methods, but there is only one correct way to do it for homeowners.

Many denominations use a percentage of salary to determine housing allowance. It is incorrect to do so in determining the maximum housing allowance available to a homeowner. Denominations use the percentage-of-salary method of determining housing to decide on Social Security taxes or pension deposits, primarily for parsonage dwellers. For the homeowner, the total actual amount spent "to provide a home," subject to the maximum fair rental value, furnished, is the correct amount plus utilities.

For example, two pastors earn the same salary—$30,000. The denomination has set the rental value of the parsonage at 25 percent of salary or $7,500 ($30,000 × 25 percent = $7,500). That assumes the parsonage would rent for $625 per month. Pastor 1, the parsonage dweller, must report $37,500 as total compensation for Social Security purposes. Of course, he reports only $30,000 for income tax purposes. Pastor 2, the homeowner, receives the same $30,000 in cash salary. If the denomination's 25 percent limitation were imposed on Pastor 2, she would be limited to a housing allowance of $7,500. But Pastor 2's actual expenditures are much higher than that. The home would rent for $1,000 per month, furnished. A maximum housing allowance of $12,000 could be claimed if spent. All Pastor 2 has to do in her pay package is to lower the cash salary to $25,500, thus making room for the $12,000 housing allowance. Now Pastor 2 is free to spend and deduct up to $12,000, the legitimate maximum to which she is entitled. The bottom line is the same $37,500.

The concept of nontaxable housing first came about because Congress saw the need to provide for persons who "lived at the convenience of the employer," which included military personnel, caretakers, security guards, and college presidents. Persons in such categories received their benefits under Section 119 of the Internal Revenue Code. They did not have to report their housing as income for income tax purposes.

In the early days of America, ministers and priests lived in parsonages, churches, or rectories, the latter a practice that continues today. So, Section 107 was signed into law to allow ministers who bought homes to have an equal tax advantage with the parsonage dwellers who did not have to report their free housing as income. They "lived at the convenience of the employer."

You, as a minister, will live in a parsonage, a rectory, an apartment, or your own home "at the convenience of the employer." Many ministers may live in all of the above at some time during their careers. No matter where you may live, you will not have to report the value received, and spent, for housing as income for federal income tax purposes if you have set up your housing allowance in accordance with the law (August 16, 1954, c 736, 68A Stat. 32) and if you are eligible for the housing allowance. You *will* have to report the housing allowance as income for Social Security tax purposes.

2-3 How to Prepare for Calculating Your Maximum Housing Allowance

Once you have determined the fair rental value, furnished, of your home, that figure represents the maximum possible housing allowance that may be available to you plus utilities. However, you must keep other parameters in mind:

- Is your home your principal residence? It must be for you to qualify for housing allowance. A summer home will not qualify unless it is your principal home.
- After calculating your housing allowance, is there enough left in your cash salary on which to live? Your income from your church must stand on its own. You cannot lump spousal income into this calculation. It is a gray area, and you would be wise to seek specific tax counsel on this question. It is widely held, however, that there must be enough left to live on after the housing allowance is deducted from your pay package. That is a judgment call. You must be prepared to prove to the IRS that you can live on the cash salary left over after housing allowance is deducted.

  Honoraria and all other nonsalary streams of income may not be included as compensation when calculating cash salary and housing allowance.
- How much is your annual pension deposit? Your pension deposit cannot exceed 25 percent of your cash salary. Most denominations multiply your compensation by a percentage to determine your pension contribution. In so doing they usually include housing allowance along with your cash salary as compensation. If you

have a very high housing allowance and, consequently, a very low cash salary, you must be sure that your pension deposit does not exceed 25 percent of that cash salary. Even though you are eligible for a high housing allowance, you may have to adjust it downward because of this pension deposit limitation.

• Do you own a tax-sheltered annuity (TSA)? If you do, that might limit the amount of housing allowance you may have. Anything withheld from your salary and sent to an annuity company is treated as an exclusion from income. Your salary will be lowered on your income tax records, and the TSA deposit will not be included in your W-2 Form. Insofar as the government is concerned, that money does not exist. It's in a tax-sheltered or tax-deferred account.

There is a limitation on how much you can place in a tax shelter. You're allowed from $16^2/_3$ to 20 percent of your cash salary, depending on your years of service. (See details in chapter 3.) For our purposes here, you must be aware that your TSA deposits reduce your cash income and thereby affect the total available as housing allowance. If you have deposited so much money into your TSA to cause the amount left over after housing allowance to be less than enough on which to live, you will have to raise your cash salary and lower your TSA deposit to comply with this requirement. You must be sure that there is always enough left on which to live as you calculate your TSA and housing allowance.

• What is the total bottom line amount of your pay package? You may use the total gross income you receive, including what many people refer to as allowances, such as car allowance, Social Security offset, and benefits. However, unlike housing allowance, these so-called allowances and benefits are usually income and are subject to income tax. These items will be discussed in detail later. For our purposes in this chapter, recognize that you should include as much as legally permissible in your base salary to have as high a housing allowance amount as possible.

2-4 How to Calculate Your Maximum Housing Allowance

1. Market value of your home $_____
2. Replacement value of furniture and furnishings $_____
3. Total of (1) and (2) $_____

4. Cost of utilities $_____
5. Fair rental value of your home $_____
6. Fair rental value of your furniture and
   furnishings $_____
7. Total of (5) and (6) $_____

8. Cost of utilities $_____
9. Your present housing allowance $_____
10. Your present allowance for furniture
    and furnishings (if listed separately) $_____
11. Present utilities $_____
12. Total of (9) and (10) $_____

Is line 12 as high as line 7? If not, your housing allowance may be too low. If line 12 is greater than line 7, it is probably too high. As you can see, the utilities are ignored in these calculations because there is no limit on the deduction of utilities. They're noted on this worksheet to show they are not to be included in housing allowance but are to be itemized separately.

Lacking any other method of determining the fair rental value of your furnished home, multiply 1 percent of line 3 to come up with a monthly rental value. Then ask yourself if it's a fair figure. Remember, be as sure as possible about this figure. Getting appraisals from realtors is usually best.

Now that you've calculated the maximum possible eligible housing allowance, determine if the amount of salary left over is enough on which to live. This will vary from family to family. Be forewarned that if the IRS suspects you have misrepresented your total income, the agency has the power to come into your home and "net worth" you. That is, IRS agents total up the value of everything you own to determine if you could have purchased all the items with the income you reported.

2-5 What Deductions May Be Included in Housing Allowance?

According to the IRS, you may include in your housing allowance "anything to provide a home," except food and the cost of a cleaning person. The mortgage payment, fire and casualty insurance (not mortgage life insurance or any other personal life insurance payable to a beneficiary chosen by the pastor; only group life insurance premiums may be deducted under certain circumstances, which will be discussed in chapter 10), taxes, upkeep, grass seed and shrubs, any lawn mower including a riding tractor, furniture, drapes, carpets, pictures on the wall, television sets, hanging baskets, a down payment, garage, paneling for the basement, sidewalks, special assessments, lawyer's fees, a new roof, appliances large and small, you name it. If it is to "provide a home," it is probably includible as a deduction in your housing allowance, up to your allowable limit. If in doubt, check with your tax adviser.

2-6 Who Is Eligible for Housing Allowance?

The IRS uses the phrase "minister of the gospel" to include any Protestant, Roman Catholic, or Jewish clergypersons, including cantors, who are ordained, licensed, or commissioned by a religious organization. *Gospel* means "good news." They must also be able to conduct substantially *all* the sacerdotal duties as prescribed by their churches, synagogues, or denominational guidelines (*M. H. Tanenbaum,* 58 TC 1, Dec. 31, 32.7). Any other religious bodies should ask the IRS about their status in regard to "ministers of the gospel."

The sacerdotal duties are as follows:

- Conducting a worship service on a regular basis
- Officiating at weddings
- Conducting funerals
- Officiating at baptisms
- Conducting Communion
- Conducting church administrative affairs
- Teaching

All three categories (i.e., ordained, licensed, and commissioned) must have essentially equal authority to perform the religious duties of their governing body. All duly qualified clergypersons in a church are eligible for housing allowance. However, they must be employees and earn income from that church.

2-7 Who Authorizes Housing Allowance?

Many ministers and laypersons assume that the local church body or the denominational executives are the ones who authorize and set the amount of housing allowance. None other than the Congress of the United States authorizes housing allowance.

2-8 Who Is Responsible for Setting the Amount of Your Housing Allowance?

Contrary to popular belief, the responsibility for setting the minister's housing allowance belongs primarily to the minister. Of course, the minister must meet with the church board and work out the total pay package, which must be approved by the board. But once the total bottom line figure is agreed on, the minister may raise or lower the housing allowance to fit specific needs each year. If the housing allowance is raised, the cash salary is lowered by a like amount, thus keeping the bottom line the same. Let's look at an example.

Example. Suppose Pastor Jones agrees to a total pay package of $30,000 that includes a cash salary of $22,000, a housing allowance of $7,000, and other miscellaneous items totaling $1,000. On the very day his pay package is approved, Jones's refrigerator suddenly expires so he buys a new one costing $1,000. This amount represents an expense not anticipated at the time he set his housing allowance. He can deduct the cost of that refrigerator subject to the following conditions:

1) He should make sure his fair rental value, furnished, is high enough to raise his housing allowance from $7,000 to $8,000. That is, would his furnished home rent for $8,000? This is offset by lowering the cash salary from $22,000 to $21,000.

2) He should ask his church treasurer to change the pay package accordingly. The bottom line remains the same. The change will not cost the church an additional penny. But it will save Pastor Jones some tax dollars. Neither will it change Jones's Social Security payment or pension deposit if he is enrolled in a denominational pension plan. Most denominations and the IRS include salary and housing allowance as compensation. In one denomination, compensation includes utilities as well. In the case of the homeowner, the actual fair rental value should be used instead of a percentage of salary.

3) Jones should ask the treasurer to write him a letter on church stationery detailing his pay package, line by line. He should save that letter in a folder labeled Housing Allowance for many years along with his receipts showing what was spent "to provide a home."

Only the minister and family know what they will need each year in housing costs. They are the ones to determine what is to be done to their home or what furniture to buy and when. The minister will answer to the IRS if an audit occurs. The minister can never say, "See my board. They set my housing allowance." It is the minister's responsibility to set the amount and to justify the spending. If the minister deducts more than the fair rental value, the IRS will disallow the overage. If the church board insists on a housing allowance that is lower than the maximum eligible amount, the minister will simply pay more income tax than is required. The church will not save any money. Therefore, ministers must set their housing allowances so long as they stay within the agreed-on bottom line of the pay package.

Unconstitutional Actions?

It may well be unconstitutional for a church board to prevent a minister from setting the housing allowance. Church board members should know that it is the minister's call once the bottom line of the pay package is agreed on.

2-9 How to Treat Excess Housing Allowance Dollars Left Unspent

Any unspent housing allowance is reportable as income for income tax purposes, on line 22 of Form 1040 on the Worksheet for Form 2106, at the end of the year. Since anticipating your total needs in housing expenditures is sometimes difficult, it is a good idea to set the housing allowance somewhat higher than you think will be necessary, so long as you never set it higher than your fair rental value, furnished. On the other hand, if you experience unexpected housing expenditures in excess of your stated housing allowance for that year, but still less than the furnished fair rental value, you will lose out on some deductions you could have if you had stated a higher figure "ahead of time."

2-10 How to Help Your Church Board Learn About Housing Allowance

There is no reason to expect church board members to know all about housing allowance and clergy pay packages. But there is no reason why they should not inform themselves if they have that responsibility. The results can be considerable savings for the minister.

Unfortunately, many churches still are not aware of the housing allowance privilege. And many board members believe that the housing allowance is, somehow, wrong. Since they don't understand it, they fear it. Since they fear it, they often reject it, even though they don't have the actual authority to do so. However, so long as they believe they have the power and so long as the minister believes they have the power, they do, indeed, have the power. Church board members change frequently, so there is the problem of educating and reeducating board members as they come and go. Of course, many ministers simply will not speak up for themselves in the face of uninformed, unfounded, and unfair resistance.

Church board members need to know they cannot hinder a minister's lawful right to set the amount of housing allowance. No one may prevent any individual in the United States of America from taking all the tax deductions that may be legally claimed.

In short, the best way for ministers to educate their boards is to call a board meeting, state immediately that the subject for discussion will not cost the church a penny, and then explain that it is the minister's responsibility, under the law, to set the housing allowance. Furthermore, the board members should know that if the minister is audited, the board is not responsible for the correctness of the housing allowance maximum; only the minister is. It should be clear to the board members that the bottom line, as originally agreed on, is the same.

2-11 When Should the Amount of Housing Allowance Be Determined?

The law states that the housing allowance must be set "ahead of time." That means it should be set before any expenditure is deducted.

Obviously, the best time to set the housing allowance is just prior to the annual salary review or at the first of each calendar or fiscal year. The minister should anticipate purchases such as appliances or furniture far enough in advance to determine unusual housing needs prior to the annual salary review so they can be included in the housing allowance.

2-12 Can Housing Allowance Be Made Retroactive?

No. The law states that the housing allowance must be declared "ahead of time." That is, it must be stated in writing in your official church board minutes before you spend money "to provide a home." Only then can your costs be deducted. Once again, it does not have to be stated at salary review time or by January 1, although those are the logical times to do it.

Many pastors learn about housing allowance and how to calculate the maximum at seminars during the summer months. They can return home, call a board meeting, and work with their board members to determine the proper amount of housing allowance for the balance of the year. However, if their allowances have been too low and they have missed out on some deductions in the prior months, they *may not* recover those lost deductions retroactively. (See 2-13 to learn how to be ready for an audit of your housing allowance.)

2-13 How to Be Ready for an Audit of Your Housing Allowance

After you have arrived at a figure representing your fair rental value, furnished, you have a responsibility to comply with the IRS rules and to keep proper records. I suggest that you get a folder and label it Housing Allowance. Then do the following:

- Obtain a letter from a local realtor indicating the appraised rental value, furnished, of your home. This letter should be updated every two or three years. Remember, the fair rental value, furnished, determines the maximum you may spend and deduct.
- Enter into the official board minutes the specific amount of your housing allowance "ahead of time." Do not include utilities in your housing allowance. If this notation is not made in the board minutes and you get audited, the IRS may disallow the deductions you take, declare your past deductible amounts as ordinary income, and charge you with back taxes and penalties. It does not matter if you can clearly show canceled checks and receipts proving that you spent the money on your home. The housing allowance must be included in your official church board minutes "ahead of time." Show utilities on a separate line.
- Ask your church treasurer each year for a letter on church stationery, dated and signed, detailing your pay package, line by line.
- Save all your receipts. Save the entire contents of your Housing Allowance folder for eternity!

IRS agents can check your tax records back as many years as they wish if they suspect fraud. On the other hand, they allow you only three years to rectify a mistake.

2-14 Thirteen Things You and Your CPA Need to Consider Before Calculating Your Housing Allowance

1) Do you own your home?
2) Is that home your principal residence?
3) How much would your home rent for, furnished?
4) If you claim your maximum housing allowance, is there enough left over in your pay package on which to live?
5) How much is your pension deposit?
6) If you are enrolled in a qualified pension plan and you claim the maximum housing allowance, will your pension deposit exceed 25 percent of your cash salary? (It *cannot* exceed 25 percent of your cash salary.)
7) What do your utilities cost per year?
8) Does your spouse work outside the home?
9) Do you file a joint income tax return?
10) Do you have an Individual Retirement Arrangement (IRA), Keogh plan, or tax-deferred annuity (TDA)?
11) Who pays it?
12) What is your total yearly deposit going into all those plans?
13) Are you in the Social Security program?

If this sounds complicated, it is. Understanding the details of how the housing allowance works requires time and effort, but it's worth it, whether you live in your home or in a parsonage.

I strongly recommend that you seek qualified professional help, someone who knows the details of tax laws that affect clergypersons. Such a person may well save you enough money each year to pay the necessary fee.

We will discuss the impact of housing allowance on the parsonage dweller or renter later. But first, let's discuss the definition of a *church* as set by the Internal Revenue Service. Why is this important? Because the legality of your housing allowance depends on the legal position of your church.

2-15 Four Tests the IRS Uses to Define a Church

Even the IRS cannot define a church in simple all-inclusive terms. The guidelines are found in IRS Publication 557, *Tax-Exempt Status for Your Organization,* but they cannot cover each and every variable in defining a church. The IRS looks at each group claiming to

1818 18

1818

18 18

1818

be a church on its individual merits. For most, however, the following group structures would qualify as churches and, therefore, as tax-exempt groups:

1) A church is an inter-church organization of local units of a church, a convention or association of churches, or an integrated auxiliary of a church. Section 501(c)(3) organizations that are operated, supervised, or controlled by one or more churches, integrated auxiliaries, or conventions or associations of churches, and. . . .
2) An exclusively religious activity of any religious order. Specifically a religious order that is not opposed to insurance. An organization formed before December 31, 1950.
3) A mission society sponsored by or affiliated with one or more churches or church denominations, more than one-half of the activities of which society are conducted in or directed at persons in, foreign countries.
4) A school below college level affiliated with a church or operated by a religious order, even though it is not an integrated auxiliary of a church.

2-16 Eight Tests that Qualify an Institution as an Integral Agency

To qualify as an integral agency (not a church) under IRS Rev. Ruling 72-606, an institution must meet the following tests:

1) The institution must be incorporated by the religious organization.
2) The corporate name of the integral agency must exhibit a church relationship.
3) The religious organization must maintain, manage, and control the integral agency.
4) The integral agency's directors and trustees must be approved by the religious organization.
5) The religious organization must have the power to remove the directors and trustees.
6) The integral agency must submit annual reports of financial status and overall operations to the religious organization.
7) The records should indicate whether the church contributes to the support of the integral agency.
8) If the institution is discontinued, all assets must be transferred to the religious organization.

The key issue is control. The religious organization must be in control, and the integral agency must be accountable to it. In the past, when many colleges and universities were first formed, there was a close, controlling relationship with religious organizations. With the passage of time, this control has been relinquished, and many institutions no longer qualify as truly integral agencies.

2-17 How to Enter the Housing Allowance Designation for the Homeowner into the Official Church Board Minutes

Suggested wording might be as follows:

This is to acknowledge that Pastor _____ is entitled to a housing allowance under Section 107 of the Internal Revenue Code as part of his/her total compensation. The law provides that Pastor _____ is allowed up to the "fair rental value plus utilities" as a maximum housing allowance. Such allowance is not subject to federal income tax but is reportable as income by Pastor _____ for Social Security purposes. Under the law, Pastor _____ may set his/her housing allowance at any level up to that maximum. He/she has requested that, for 19__, the housing allowance, including utilities, be designated as $_____. A motion was made by _____ and seconded by _____ to provide $_____ for housing allowance, including utilities, for 19__. The board passed and adopted the motion, which is hereby made a part of these official board minutes dated _____.

Signed_____
Chairperson of the Board
Any Legal Church

2-18 Can a Church Ordain All Its Members?

In isolated cases, churches have attempted to ordain everybody, erroneously believing that all of them would be able to deduct their housing costs under Section 107 of the IRC. As a general rule, in addition to being ordained, licensed, or commissioned, only if people actually receive income from the church as legitimate employees, in return for performing the sacerdotal duties, can they be eligible for housing allowance.

2-19 Is Housing Allowance Taxable Income?

In chapter 1, I make the point that most clergypersons are self-employed *and* employees. You need to know this to understand your eligibility for housing allowance. You are self-employed for Social Security purposes, but you are considered to be an employee for income tax purposes. Both salary and housing allowance are taxable for Social Security purposes, whereas housing allowance is *not* reportable for income tax purposes.

2-20 How the Parsonage Dweller or Renter Can Deduct Most Expenditures Used "to Provide a Home"

Just as homeowners may deduct the fair rental value, furnished, plus utilities, so may parsonage dwellers and renters enjoy certain deductions. In the case of a parsonage, the rental value is usually set by the church. The minister receives no money but receives the value by living in the parsonage. That rental value is reportable as income for Social Security purposes but not for income tax purposes. It is also included as compensation in calculating a pension deposit. Therefore, if the fair rental allowance is low, the corresponding Social Security and pension benefits will be low. If it is high, the opposite is true.

The furniture is another matter because the pastor usually owns it. It has rental value. If the pastor moves out of the parsonage and the church offers to rent the furniture if the pastor will leave it behind, it has a fair rental value. That value constitutes the maximum amount of money the pastor can spend on furniture and furnishings in one year and deduct from income tax. To be clear, from now on I will use the term *furniture and furnishings* to indicate the parsonage dweller's and renter's portion of housing allowance that may be spent and deducted.

2-21 How the Parsonage Dweller or Renter Calculates Furniture and Furnishings Allowance

1) Replacement value of furniture and furnishings $_____
2) 1 percent of that value $_____

Example 1.

1) Replacement value of furniture and furnishings $20,000
2) 1 percent of that value $ 200

This minister could have $200 per month or $2,400 maximum furniture and furnishings allowance in one year. It *must* be spent "to provide a home" to qualify as a deduction. Any unspent excess must be reported as income that year.

Remember, the 1 percent rule is only a benchmark. The best way to determine the fair rental value of your furniture and furnishings is to obtain appraisals from qualified real estate persons.

Example 2. Ministers often understate the true fair rental value of their furniture. To assure proper motivation for determining the fair rental value, let's consider an example.

Suppose Pastor Jane Doe's church offers her an opportunity to go overseas for a one-year sabbatical. Church members suggest that she could leave her furniture in the parsonage and that they will employ a young minister from a nearby seminary for that year. Then, when she returns, she will move back into the parsonage to resume her ministry there, and the young seminarian will graduate and get a church of his own somewhere else. She thinks it is a fine arrangement but feels somewhat guilty about charging a seminarian rent for her furniture. However, the members of the congregation assure her that they will gladly pay the rent. And so she looks forward to her sabbatical with great excitement.

Shortly thereafter, at a prearranged time, she looks out her parsonage window and sees a station wagon pulling into her driveway. To her horror, she sees four little children leap from the car and begin racing around her front yard. All four children clutch suckers dripping from their mouths or hands. She cries out as a little boy plows through her beloved rose garden, knocking down her favorite rose bush. Suddenly, she envisions what may happen to her piano, her new organ, and some of the beautiful antiques passed down from her family. Almost panicked, she considers canceling her sabbatical. Now she is in the proper frame of mind to calculate the fair rental value of her furniture and furnishings!

2-22 What Deductions May Be Included by Parsonage Dwellers and Renters?

The IRS says "anything to provide a home" may be included as deductions in the housing allowance for the parsonage dweller and renter as well as the homeowner. Any furniture, decorations, appliances small or large, improvements to the parsonage inside or out, lawn care, lawn mowers, curtains, carpets, and television sets for children's rooms may be included as deductions in your furniture and furnishings allowance. Just as with the homeowner, you cannot deduct the cost of food or a cleaning person, and you cannot express your allowance higher than its fair rental value.

Quite often pastors will make improvements on parsonages, spending their own money. If they do, they can deduct the cost, whether or not it is a permanent improvement, so long as they do not exceed allowable limits. One of the many myths regarding this question has been that only if the improvement is permanent can pastors include the cost as a deduction in housing allowance (furniture and furnishings allowance). But they must save receipts and keep a record of expenses for housing.

2-23 Who Sets the Parsonage Dweller's Furniture and Furnishings Allowance?

In the past the church has set the rental value of the parsonage. In fact, it has been done that way for such a long time that the practice usually is not questioned. The routine method to determine the rental value has been to multiply a percentage of salary, such as 25 or 30 percent. That amount is then used to determine both Social Security taxes and pension contributions. But more often than not, pastors have not included the fair rental value of their furniture as a means of establishing their furniture and furnishings allowance as a part of their total housing allowance. Remember, Section 107 of the Internal Revenue Code has three elements: the fair rental value of the home, the fair rental value of the furniture and furnishings, and the cost of utilities.

Regulation 1.107-1(b) states, "The designation of an amount as rental allowance may be evidenced in an employment contract, in minutes of or in a resolution by a church or other qualified organization or in its budget, or in any other appropriate instrument evidencing such official action."

To set their maximum possible furniture and furnishings allowance each year, pastors must calculate the fair rental value of their furniture and include a separate line item in the pay package entitled Furniture and Furnishings.

If your church has not done this in the past, simply add a line in your pay package entitled Furniture and Furnishings and lower the Cash Salary line by the same amount that you show as Furniture and Furnishings. The bottom line of your pay package will remain the same. Make sure it is approved by your board and is entered into the official board minutes of your church.

2-24 How Parsonage Dwellers and Renters Treat Unspent Furniture and Furnishings Allowance

At the end of the year, if you have not spent all of the furniture and furnishings allowance, report it as income and pay taxes on that unspent amount. It is shown as income on line 22 of Form 1040, the Worksheet for Form 2106.

2-25 When and How Should Parsonage Dwellers' and Renters' Furniture and Furnishings Allowance Be Determined?

Most pastors do it at salary review time or the first of each year. The law says that the establishing of the housing allowance must be "ahead of time," that is, prior to deducting the cost of any expenditure "to provide a home."

The pastor and spouse should plan ahead in anticipation of meeting with the finance committee or church board. They should tell the committee how much they wish to have each year as a furniture and furnishings allowance. Often, there are special needs, such as large appliances. Or perhaps they might wish to purchase a piano or an organ of their own.

Section 119 of the Internal Revenue Code requires that the appraisal value of the parsonage be made annually by independent appraisers instead of having the church or the pastor set an arbitrary rental value. The church is to pay for the appraisal unless the cost is nominal. The church board must approve the final allowance and enter it in the official board minutes.

2-26 How Unordained Employees May Receive Tax-Free Housing

Section 119 also provides nontaxable housing to unordained employees who meet the qualifying tests:

* You must live in your employer's property.
* It must be for your employer's convenience.
* You must be on continuous call twenty-four hours per day.

2-27 Can Parsonage Dwellers' and Renters' Furniture and Furnishings Allowance Be Retroactive?

No. As in the case of the homeowner, housing allowance (and therefore, furniture and furnishings allowance) cannot be retroactive. If you have lost the deduction because your allowance was not set up properly at the time you spent money for furniture or furnishings, you have lost it forever.

2-28 What About Utilities?

Clearly, the cost of utilities of a church-owned parsonage is not includible as income to the pastor for income tax purposes. However, this is another gray area. Most churches pay the utilities and do not report the cost as income to the pastors for income tax or Social Security tax. Some do include the cost in calculating compensation for pastors to determine Social Security tax and/or pension contributions. Each pastor should seek competent tax advice on this question.

As for the telephone, you must keep records showing which calls are personal and which are "church" calls. You must pay for your personal calls.

2-29 How and Where Ordained, Licensed, and Commissioned Parsonage Dwellers and Renters Report Housing Allowance

Since you are considered to be an employee for income tax purposes by the IRS, you must comply with Regulation 31.3401(c)-1, which classifies you as a "common law employee." Therefore, you must receive a W-2 Form from your employer, but you do not report the furniture and furnishings allowance for income tax purposes.

However, since you are considered to be self-employed for Social Security tax purposes according to Section 1402(a)(8), you must use

Schedule SE, Form 1040, Social Security Self-Employment Tax, to determine your Social Security tax liability. You must include your housing allowance as income for this purpose.

2-30 How to Find a Housing Allowance within the Church Budget

Once you decide to buy a home, you have to answer several immediate questions:

- Do you want to buy the parsonage if it is available?
- Is the congregation willing to sell it to you?
- Or do you want to buy a home at a different location?
- Is your congregation willing for you to buy a home away from the church's immediate location?

A congregation willing for you to vacate the parsonage and buy a home must decide whether to hire an assistant and house the person in it, sell the parsonage, or let it remain empty. Sometimes, when the pastor wishes to buy a home, the church converts the parsonage into additional Sunday school rooms or some other additional church use. If the church is not willing to cooperate with your desire to purchase a home, you may want to wait until you move to another church. Otherwise, your purchase could cause a serious disagreement within the congregation.

The congregation could sell the parsonage and invest the money, passing on the yield from that investment, plus the other costs being paid, to you as part of your housing allowance. It might work in this manner:

Sell parsonage for $80,000, invest at 8% yielding $6,400 annually, or monthly	$533
Monthly cost of utilities	200
Monthly cost of real estate taxes	100
Monthly cost of insurance	50
Monthly cost of maintenance	100
Total available for monthly housing allowance	$983

Much would depend on the value of real estate in your area. Obviously, the congregation must be sympathetic to your long-term need for a home in retirement as well as for the present. Owning a home might result in some rising equity accruing to you and your family.

The only thing the congregation gives up is the possible increase in equity of the parsonage. But it is generally agreed that the church's primary mission is not one of profit making, hence the tax-exempt status. On the other hand, there is no guarantee to the pastor that real estate values will continue to increase. However, owning a home will generate important tax advantages to the pastor and will cost the church essentially the same as if the pastor lived in a parsonage.

2-31 How to Purchase a Home with No Down Payment

If you don't have a down payment and *if* you would like to stay with your church and *if* your congregation wants you to stay, here is one method you might want to consider.

Your church can loan you the down payment with a proper written agreement if such a procedure is allowed in your state. Not all states allow such loans. You should check out the idea first if you are discussing a loan from your church. And the church must charge a proper rate of interest (or the IRS may take a dim view of the transaction). These loans can become complex, so you would be wise to seek proper legal counsel before entering into such an arrangement with your church. Special rules apply if a church loans a minister $10,000 or more.

Once you have determined that your down payment is legal and properly set up, you can then obtain a traditional first mortgage through a bank or savings and loan company. It is advantageous to you to repay the church loan over a period of years so that the repaid amount of your down payment each year is included in your housing allowance. As stated earlier, whatever is includible in your housing allowance, up to a maximum of the fair rental value, including furnishings, is deductible in the year it is spent. Usually, a down payment is more than can be included as a deduction in one year, so it must be spread out over a period of years to enjoy deductibility.

Caution! The church must charge the minister the fair market value for the home. Otherwise, the IRS may consider the compensation "unreasonable," possibly resulting in the minister having to report the overage as income, perhaps with penalties. In addition, parishioners might be denied the right to deduct their contributions, and the church itself might be in danger of losing its tax-exempt status.

It would be in order for you to have a life insurance policy to cover the loan to the church in the event of your death. If the church is the owner, beneficiary, and premium payer, you have no income tax liability. If you own the insurance and you name someone other than the church as beneficiary, the payment of the premium is your responsibility, and you *cannot* deduct the cost by including it in your housing allowance. In the latter instance, you cannot deduct it for any reason.

2-32 How One Minister Deducted the Entire Cost of a House and Had No Down Payment

This minister awakened one morning at age fifty-five with the sudden realization that he did not have a retirement home and had only ten years to do something about it. He had been employed by his church for many years, and he fully expected to finish his active ministry there. He enjoyed a very good relationship with the congregation, and they fully expected him to stay with them. He shared his concern with the church leaders who agreed with him that it would be the right thing to do to sell him the parsonage. But he had no down payment.

The parsonage was paid for and had a market value of $60,000 at the time. A legal agreement was drawn providing for a loan of $60,000 to the minister and allowing him to receive a housing allowance of $6,000 per year plus enough extra for furniture and furnishings. Ownership was transferred to the minister. Each year the church paid the minister a housing allowance of $6,000 that he did not have to report as income for income tax purposes. Each year the minister repaid the church $6,000, plus an interest charge, toward the $60,000 loan. The church purchased a mortgage life insurance policy for $60,000, paid the premium, and named itself as beneficiary. The cost of the premium was not charged to the minister as income. At the end of ten years, the church had received the full amount of the loan plus market-rate interest, and the minister owned the house free and clear. In addition, the minister had deducted the entire cost of the house! It is one of the best tax advantages a minister is privileged to have.

2-33 One Way to Pay Off a Thirty-Year Mortgage in Fifteen Years

There is a way to save thousands of dollars in interest payments. It works best if you have a mortgage running thirty years or longer. This plan doesn't work for all ages and all mortgages, but it is worth investigating. When most people assume a mortgage, they buy a decreasing term life insurance policy to cover the mortgage. Then they begin the long, arduous process of monthly repayments. Most people think they have no other choice. Some know the wisdom of paying double mortgage payments, but apparently, most people cannot afford to do that. You may want to count the cost of paying over a period of thirty years. The following examples show the total amount you would repay on a thirty-year mortgage of various amounts, assuming an interest rate of 9 percent:

Amount of Mortgage	Monthly Payment	Amount Paid in 30 Years
$ 30,000	$241.39	$ 86,894
40,000	321.85	115,864
50,000	402.31	144,834
60,000	482.77	173,803
80,000	643.70	231,728
100,000	804.62	289,668

Each example shows that you would have to repay almost three times the amount you borrowed.

How much less would you have to pay if the mortgage were paid off at the end of fifteen years?

Amount of Mortgage	Amount Saved
$ 30,000	$ 43,450
40,000	57,933
50,000	72,405
60,000	86,896
80,000	115,860
100,000	144,832

How is this accomplished? Rather than buy a term mortgage life insurance policy, with nothing accruing to you if you live, you buy an interest-sensitive universal life (ISL) policy. Such a policy pays off the mortgage with tax-free dollars to your beneficiary if you die. And if you live, it builds up enough cash value (in the examples below) to retire your mortgage in fifteen years. It is similar to the idea of paying double mortgage payments, but there are important advantages in using the life insurance policy.

The ISL policy can have a waiver-of-premium rider for pennies per month. It provides for the payment of the premiums if you become disabled. The values in the policy continue to rise the same as if you were paying the premiums. In the event of permanent disability (as determined by a doctor), you would never have to pay the premiums again. In the event of disability for a period of two years, for example, the premiums would be waived during that two-year period; then you would resume the payments but would not owe for the waived premiums. Most life insurance companies require a waiting period of six months in the event of disability before premiums are waived, during which time the insured continues the payment of the premiums. After that, the company usually refunds the amount representing six months' premium if the disability continues beyond six months.

If you had no disability and continued paying the premiums until your death, the death benefit would be payable, tax-free, to your beneficiary. For example, if you died during the first month of coverage, the total amount of coverage, not just the amount of the mortgage, would be payable to your beneficiary. Having a higher death benefit than the mortgage amount is necessary because the death benefits shown below are the precise amounts necessary to produce enough cash value in fifteen years to pay off the remaining mortgage.

At the end of fifteen years, assuming the projected interest rate on the policy had continued at the same average level, you could withdraw the cash value and pay off the mortgage, in which case there would be no more life insurance in force. You would be liable for taxes on any amounts over and above the cost basis (the amount you paid in) of the policy. However, the cost of the term insurance over a period of fifteen years exceeds the taxable cost of the universal life, comparing both the 15 percent and the 28 percent tax brackets. Furthermore, the term insurance produces no cash values.

In the following projections, the guaranteed level annual premiums and the guaranteed death benefit in each of these interest-sensitive universal life policies are the amounts necessary to provide enough cash value to pay off the balance of the mortgage in fifteen years:

Amount of Mortgage	Death Benefit	Monthly Payment	Cash Value in 15 Years	Unpaid Balance in 15 Years
$ 30,000	$ 85,021	$ 94.71	$23,000	$23,798
40,000	117,296	129.04	31,731	31,732
50,000	146,625	160.23	39,665	39,666
60,000	175,954	191.41	47,599	47,599
80,000	234,596	253.77	63,463	63,463
100,000	293,254	316.15	79,331	79,331

Double payments would pay off each of these examples in about seven years. But that is not practical for most people, especially pastors, for two reasons. First, income limitations probably preclude double payments. Second, pastors are eligible for housing allowance, giving them a double deduction of interest and taxes so long as they have their mortgages. There is no big advantage for them to pay off a mortgage too early. In fact, many pastors whose mortgages are paid off have taken out new mortgages or home equity loans to enjoy the advantages of the housing allowance.

Here, then, are the advantages of buying an interest-sensitive universal life policy to pay off your mortgage:

1) Your mortgage may be paid off in half the time.
2) If you become disabled, your premium will be paid.
3) Your cash value accrues in a tax-sheltered account.
4) Your beneficiaries will always receive more than enough tax-free dollars to pay off your mortgage if you die.
5) You can always borrow from your cash value account at a very low net interest rate.
6) You avoid paying for term insurance that pays nothing unless you die. Furthermore, the final net cost of term is higher if you live than using the universal life plan.
7) Paying universal life premiums is much less than paying double mortgage payments.

If you decide *not* to withdraw your cash value at the end of fifteen years, you can keep your policy until retirement and draw monthly retirement income from it for life. You may, for example, decide to live in parsonages and wait to buy a home when you retire. The funds in your policy will be available for you then from each of these same examples, projected as follows:

Death Benefit at Age 65	Cash Value at Age 65
$ 85,021	$ 96,236
117,296	132,768
146,625	165,966
175,954	199,163
234,596	265,540
293,254	331,936

At death, the larger of the two amounts is paid.

2-34 Housing Allowance and Some Other Classifications of Ministers

The first rule to remember is that ministers must be ordained, licensed, or commissioned to perform the sacerdotal duties and must derive their income from a legal church to qualify for a housing allowance. What about some other classifications?

* *Unordained workers* usually do not qualify for housing allowance unless they actually live on the employer's premises to be available twenty-four hours a day at the employer's convenience and do not have the option of receiving cash instead of lodging.
* *Widows of retired ministers* do not qualify for housing allowance (Revenue Ruling 72-249, 1972-1 CB 36).
* *Old age home employees* cannot exclude housing allowance even if ordained, unless the institution is controlled by a church denomination (Revenue Ruling 72-606, 1972-2 CB 78).
* *Ministers of Education* cannot qualify for housing allowance unless ordained, licensed, or commissioned and can perform the sacerdotal duties (*R. D. Lawrence,* 50 TC 494, Dec. 29, 002).
* *Ministers of Music* cannot qualify for housing allowance unless ordained, licensed, or commissioned and can perform the sacerdotal duties (Revenue Ruling 59-270, 1959-2 CB 44).
* *College faculty* may be eligible for housing allowance if they are ordained, licensed, or commissioned and can perform the sacerdotal duties, if the college is operated by a denominational or religious group that is tax-exempt, and if a housing allowance is paid as a portion of the total pay for teaching in a seminary controlled by a denomination.

Very often, ordained college professors are also employed by small churches as part-time ministers to perform their sacerdotal duties. College faculty members who may be unsure of their status would be wise to seek professional counsel prior to taking any action in this area. The college administrators should already be well versed in this regard. But if there is any doubt, seek counsel, including a visit to the Internal Revenue Service office.

- *Veterans' hospital chaplains,* who are usually civilians, may not exclude the housing allowance (Revenue Ruling 72-462, 1972-2 CB 76).

- *Theological students* may not exclude housing allowance from income tax, even if they are serving as pastors, *unless* they are ordained, licensed, or commissioned and can perform the sacerdotal duties (*Your Federal Income Tax 1975,* IRS Publication 17, page 39).

- *Retired ministers* may be eligible to receive a housing allowance via their pension incomes if they meet certain qualifications. The church must designate part of the minister's pension plan as housing allowance. The minister must actually be retired, and the pension must be paid for the minister's past services (Revenue Ruling 75-22).

- *Traveling evangelists* are eligible for housing allowance if they are ordained, licensed, or commissioned and can perform all sacerdotal duties (Revenue Ruling 64-326, 1964-2 CB 37). They must, however, operate out of their private homes and evangelize in churches certifying, in advance, that some of the evangelists' pay will be for housing allowance (Revenue Ruling 64-326).

- *Parochial school employees* are eligible if they are ordained, licensed, or commissioned and can perform the sacerdotal duties and if they are employed by institutions controlled by religious organizations (Revenue Ruling 62-171, 1962-2 CB 39; Revenue Ruling 70-549, 1970-2 CB 16).

- *Cross-denominational eligibility* means that ministers who are ordained, licensed, or commissioned by one denomination can qualify for housing allowance if they serve a different denomination, provided they can perform the sacerdotal duties as a "minister of the gospel."

2-35 Advantages and Disadvantages of Owning Your Home

Advantages

• You have an opportunity to build equity.
• You and your spouse can choose your own decor.
• You can buy a home anywhere you wish.
• You will probably stay longer at each church.
• You can take your equity with you if you move.
• You will have a retirement home or the equity to buy one someplace else.
• You will probably take more interest in local issues, such as real estate taxes and assessments, and perhaps understand your parishioners better.
• The church parsonage committee can disband.

Disadvantages

• You will have to fix everything yourself.
• If and when you have to move, you will have to make all the arrangements for selling your home. The parsonage dweller can simply pack up and move. It is a two-edged sword.

The advantages of a housing allowance far outweigh the disadvantages. The housing allowance law is one that all ministers should take the time to fully understand and implement.

Once again, I cannot emphasize enough the importance of using qualified income tax professionals, particularly to help you with obtaining the maximum housing allowance each year. Find one who understands *all* the laws affecting you as a clergyperson. You should save money as a result. That's simply good stewardship.

2-36 How to Set Up a Home Equity Fund for Your Retirement Home

This fund is not to be confused with a home equity loan. The *home equity fund* is an account that ministers can set up, funded by themselves or by their churches or by a combination of both, to have enough money to purchase a home in retirement. It can become an important part of your salary package negotiations each year with each church that employs you.

Far too many ministers reach retirement age without a home of their own to live in. Many denominations require their ministers to live in parsonages, and many ministers actually prefer living in them. But someday you will need a place to live in retirement. Many ministers believe they will simply keep on ministering and die with their boots on. Certainly, many will do that. However, many more will not enjoy good health and may not feel like continuing to minister. Nevertheless, each and every minister who actually retires will need a place to live.

It is too easy to let time slip by with no thought of retirement housing. It is equally easy to do something about it if you start early enough in your career. It is equally wrong to make no attempt to save for this goal or to attempt to save too much out of the current budget. If the magic of compound interest has enough time to work, you may be surprised at the amount you can save for a retirement home.

Let's look at some examples of compound interest at work. They show the results of savings plans invested at 7 percent, beginning at various ages with various amounts:

Age	Yearly Deposit	Accumulation at Age 65
25	$ 300	$64,083
30	480	70,999
35	600	60,644
40	900	60,909
45	1,500	65,798
50	2,000	53,776
55	3,500	51,743
60	5,000	30,766

These are straightforward compound interest results for illustrative purposes only. Obviously, you would not use a savings account to build a home equity fund. The tax-sheltered annuity and the IRA would be excellent vehicles for this purpose. They would provide tax-sheltered accounts until retirement whereas a savings account or almost any other type of investment would be taxable each year.

The disadvantage would be the comparative inaccessibility of the funds. This so-called disadvantage is probably a disguised advantage because the early withdrawal penalty discourages persons from invading their tax-sheltered plans. In most instances, any funds withdrawn from a TSA or an IRA are income taxable and also subject to a 10 percent additional tax if the funds are withdrawn prior to age 59$\frac{1}{2}$. (This subject is treated in detail in chapters 4 and 5.)

How can you set up a home equity fund plan? Begin it yourself, or talk it over with your church board. If you are living in a parsonage, explain to them that as time passes, you are not building up any equity of your own for a retirement home. You can discuss the subject at salary review time. You may be hesitant to discuss it with your board members, but over a period of time, many of them will come to realize that you have a serious need.

Pastors who have been long-time employees of one church have an especially good chance of receiving a home equity fund. Generally, the pastor must bring up the subject. Board members come and go and often aren't aware of the pastor's long-term needs, such as retirement and retirement housing. Don't hesitate to bring up the subject each and every year. The worker is worthy of hire.

Ministers rarely stay with one church during their entire careers. Most ministers will have been with two to eight churches during a working lifetime. For this reason, ministers who are accumulating a home equity fund must bring it to the attention of each church board they negotiate with. There is no question that church boards are quicker to agree to continue the funding of such a plan if it is in the form of an IRA or TSA rather than an amount set aside for a vague future purchase of a home. Most church board members are not ready for the latter approach. In our society, ministers have been expected to live in the parsonage. The idea of contributing to a home equity fund is comparatively new and requires continual education of church board members.

The other possible disadvantage of the home equity fund approach is that you may become hard-pressed financially and feel that you must invade your home equity fund accumulation prematurely. Financial emergencies are a part of life and, perhaps, occur more often with clergypersons than others with the same educational and experiential levels because of the difference in income. It is a fact of clergy life. Therefore, it might well be best to use the IRA or TSA as your home equity fund vehicle, thus tying up your funds until age 59½. You will pay dearly in taxes and penalties if you invade those funds prematurely.

2-37 What Are the Specific Advantages of a Home Equity Fund Funded with Permanent Life Insurance?

• It's portable. You take it with you from church to church.
• It's tax-sheltered. There is nothing to report to the IRS during all the years your account is growing.
• It's highly tax-favored when withdrawn. Because you pay income taxes on the front end, only the amount over and above your deposits is taxable when withdrawn.
• It's vested; you own it immediately.
• If you die prior to retirement, even one day after your home equity fund plan is approved, your beneficiary is then guaranteed to receive tax-free the price you select now for a home.
• If you become disabled, your home equity fund annual deposits are waived (if waiver of premium is included in your policy), yet your home equity fund continues to grow each year thereafter the same as if you were paying the premium.
• After nine to twelve years in most life insurance companies, you have an option to stop your deposits, commonly called the vanishing premium date. It is often possible to stop paying any further premiums, yet your death benefit can remain in force, and your equity may continue to accumulate if the interest rate stays at an adequately high level. All such life insurance company accumulations are expressed as projections based on *current* interest rates and are not guaranteed. A lower interest rate is usually expressed as well. You would be wise to pick a company that is financially sound and has always paid the same amounts projected or more.

Assuming the current interest rate stays at an adequate level, the policy would remain in force, continuing to grow in value, until retirement age. However, there would not be nearly so much equity at retirement age as there would be if you paid your premium or home equity fund amount each and every year until retirement age. With the steady rise in inflation, almost any long-range projection may miss the mark by a wide margin. The more you can set aside, the more options you will have at retirement age.

• Anytime during your lifetime, even before retirement age, you may decide to cash in the available amount and use it for a down payment on a home. That is always an option.
• Anytime during your lifetime, even before retirement age, you

may wish to borrow your home equity fund. You may do so. Furthermore, the interest costs to you are usually much lower than if you borrowed the money from a bank or savings and loan institution. Loans from most life insurance policies (those not considered to be modified endowments) are not considered to be income and therefore are not taxable unless you borrow your cash value and then cancel a policy from which you derive a profit (i.e., you receive more than your deposits).

Your cash values are always available for emergencies, and you never have to repay the loan so long as you pay the interest. You can repay your life insurance loan on your own schedule.

- Your home equity fund, invested in permanent life insurance, will almost always earn current market interest rates.
- If you decide to discontinue your home equity fund prior to retirement, the entire cash value belongs to you to do with as you see fit.
- At retirement, you may withdraw the cash value and buy your home, or you may elect monthly payments for life to pay mortgage payments.

The tax status of the home equity fund is based on current law. There is no guarantee that these laws will not change in the future. The home equity fund idea remains one of the best ways to insure that the minister and spouse will have a retirement home. In addition, anytime death occurs to the minister, the tax-free funds are paid to the beneficiary providing immediate funds for the purchase of a home.

2-38 A Warning About Including Home Equity Loan Interest in Your Housing Allowance

The home equity loan is a fairly recent innovation of lending institutions. It has released millions of dollars into the economy. Many home-owning ministers whose homes are paid for have taken out a home equity loan, using their homes as collateral. This option became especially attractive when the IRS took away the borrowing public's privilege of deducting interest on loans for automobiles and other goods. After that tax law change, the home equity loan became the primary source of deductible loan interest. People began borrowing money in this manner for many purposes other than remodeling their homes. They began borrowing on their homes to pay cash for new automobiles, thus enjoying lower interest rates and gaining deductibility of their interest once again. The lending institutions send out an annual report indicating the total interest paid by the borrower and, therefore, making it easy to distinguish the total interest available for deduction on income tax forms.

Clergypersons, be forewarned that you are allowed to include in your housing allowance only that amount of interest allocable "to provide a home." Once again, remember that nothing can be included in your housing allowance unless money is actually spent.

CHAPTER 3

How to Get the Most Out of Your Retirement Plans

As of 1992, statistics show that for every one hundred people starting careers between ages nineteen and twenty-two, by the time they would have become age sixty-five,

- Twenty-five will be dead.
- Twenty will have annual incomes under $6,000.
- Fifty-one will have incomes between $6,000 and $35,000.
- Four will have incomes over $35,000.

Because of the increase in inflation, you can hardly decide to start later. You should begin where you are at present and lay away something on a regular basis.

Even if you have a pension plan, you should make several basic decisions prior to retirement age. You must fully understand your pension plan and the options that will be available to you. Let's start with your pension plan.

3-1 Understand Your Denominational Pension Plan

Now is the time to make sure you understand your pension plan. You literally cannot afford to wait until retirement. You should monitor and adjust your retirement goals every year or so just to keep up with inflation. Many ministers become too involved with the problems of their parishioners and forget their own needs in this regard. You must consider your retirement needs as a top priority, beginning as early as possible in your career.

3-2 Four Ways to Choose Your Monthly Income at Retirement Age

Most denominations send an annual report to each minister. These pension reports usually show a projected monthly income at age sixty-five, assuming the annual contribution remains the same, and sometimes project an increasing percentage of annual contributions from the current year to the employee's age sixty-five.

One of the most important items for you to understand now is the monthly retirement income option displayed. Six or seven options are available in most pension plans that determine the amount of monthly retirement income you will receive. These are the most common:

1) *Life only* pays the highest income per month, but when you die, no further amounts are paid to anyone, even if you die one month after receiving your first check.

2) *Ten years certain with life thereafter* pays you, the annuitant, for as long as you live, guaranteed, no matter how long. If you die within the first ten years after beginning to receive your monthly income, your beneficiary receives the remainder of the initial ten-year period and no further income after that. If you die after you have received the monthly income for a period of ten years, your beneficiary will not receive any further income. This option is popular and pays a fairly high monthly amount.

3) *Twenty years certain with life thereafter* pays in the same manner as the ten-years-certain option except that income is guaranteed for a period of twenty years either to the annuitant or to the beneficiary. Of course, the income is guaranteed to the annuitant for life. This option generates slightly less monthly income than the ten-year option.

4) *Joint and survivor* options include the following:
   a) Joint and 50 percent to the survivor provides some retirement income to the annuitant and the survivor for as long as either of them lives. This option pays less than the others already mentioned.
   b) Joint and 66⅔ percent to the survivor offers the same terms as (a). It pays less income than (a) per month.
   c) Joint and 75 percent to the survivor offers the same terms as (b) but pays less income per month than (b).
   d) Joint and 100 percent to the survivor offers the same terms as (c) but pays less income than (c).

Notice that the longer the guaranteed period, the lower the monthly income. In the same manner, the higher the percentage of income guaranteed to the survivor, the less the amount of that monthly income to both the annuitant and the survivor.

Here's an authentic example of the monthly incomes one sixty-five-year-old male retiree was offered from a specific pension plan:

Options	Amount Paid Per Month
Life only	$1,698.00
Ten years certain	1,554.70
Twenty years certain	1,397.90
Joint and 100% to survivor	1,354.00
Joint and 66⅔% to survivor	1,468.70

Let's look at the total amounts that would be paid by each of these options after ten and twenty years:

Options	10 Years	20 Years
Life only	$203,760	$407,520
Ten years certain	186,564	373,128
Twenty years certain	167,748	335,496
Joint and 100% to survivor	162,480	324,960
Joint and 66⅔% to survivor	176,244	352,488

Obviously, the highest monthly income comes from the life-only option. But if the annuitant in this example died after receiving $1,698 for only one month, the rest of the money would be forfeited to the annuity company. On the other hand, if the annuitant lived to be ninety-five, the annuity company would have to pay a total of $20,376 per year for thirty years. That would result in a total payment of $611,280.

There is a safe way to choose the life-only option if you start early enough in life. Before I tell you about that, though, you need to understand the pension trap because such a trap can be avoided by using this safe method.

3-3 How to Avoid the Pension Trap

What is the pension trap? Let's suppose you have been receiving your annual pension statement every year. Let's further suppose that you have been unaware that the option illustrated was the life-only option. You have been unaware that if you retired and began receiving your monthly income, nothing further would be paid to your beneficiary after your death. This is known as the pension trap. As unlikely as this situation may sound, it is true in far too many cases.

Since the life-only option generates the highest monthly retirement income projections, most employers use it for illustrative purposes on the annual pension report. The reasons vary, but one is that it tends to hold employees longer. It's somewhat of a best-foot-forward approach.

Now is the time to check with your pension department if you are in a denomination or with your financial adviser if you are an independent. You may be counting on a higher monthly income than you will finally choose. Don't wait until it's too late. Once you choose an option and begin receiving your retirement income, the monthly amount usually cannot be changed. Most plans will allow a choice of options up to a few weeks prior to actual retirement.

There is a way to enjoy the highest income by choosing the life-only option. Notice in the example in 3-2 that the monthly income from the life-only option is $1,698.00 whereas the monthly income from the twenty-years-certain option is $1,397.90. That's a difference of $300.10 per month.

Let's suppose you are one of the unfortunate persons who lives to retirement age without knowing about the different retirement options. Over the years you have assumed your monthly pension income would be $1,698. After all, each year you have received your annual pension report that always showed the life-only option producing the highest monthly income. It has been a comfort to you to receive the report each year.

Then when you reach retirement age, you sit down with your denominational pension person who explains the differences in retirement income and survivor's benefits. You realize *for the first time* that when you die, even if during the first month of retirement, your beneficiary will get nothing further. You are devastated and ready to panic. It seems to be such a cruel dilemma. After surviving the shock, you choose the twenty-years-certain option that will pay you $1,397.90 per month because you want survivor's benefits. That is especially true if your spouse is much younger than you. You even feel fortunate to have finally discovered this new information. You congratulate yourself for having asked enough questions prior to choosing a retirement option because the pension adviser told you that options cannot be changed after payment has begun.

But stop and think what you have done. You have chosen survivor's benefits. Survivor's benefits are, by definition, nothing more than life insurance. By choosing the lower monthly retirement income, you have been trapped into choosing survivor's benefits. You have been trapped into buying life insurance at age sixty-five for $300.10 per month for the rest of your life! By giving up $300.10 per month of retirement income at age sixty-five in return for the assurance that if you die prematurely, your spouse will continue to receive that income for the balance of the guaranteed period (in this example, twenty years), you have, in effect, paid $300.10 per month for that insurance. You are a victim of the pension trap. But you can avoid it if you learn about it early enough in your career.

Rather than pay $300.10 per month for life insurance at age sixty-five, if you put that many premium dollars into the new generation of life insurance plans available today, early enough in life, you can choose the life-only option in your pension plan. If you live, you enjoy the highest monthly income. *When* you die, not *if*, the proceeds in your life insurance contracts pass tax-free to your beneficiaries.

3-4 How to Use Interest-Sensitive Life Insurance to Avoid the Pension Trap

In selecting the proper life insurance product to accomplish your goal of avoiding the pension trap, you have several options. You could purchase universal life, whole life, interest-sensitive life, or term insurance. Using a conservative approach, let's look at the results of paying $300 per month into an interest-sensitive life (ISL) insurance product with a *guaranteed* annual premium and a *guaranteed* death benefit. A universal life (UL) product would allow you to pay less per month for the same amount of death benefit, but it would not generate nearly as much retirement income. The two guarantees mentioned make the ISL approach conservative. Since most pastors cannot afford to invest $300 per month in their younger years, let's start with age forty-five, when there is still time to plan against the pension trap, and show the results of this $300 per month allocation to ISL insurance:

Age	Death Benefit	Death Benefit at 65	Accumulated Cash at 65	Accumulated Cash at 70	Monthly Retirement Income at 65	Monthly Retirement Income at 70
45	$189,333	$189,333	$139,567	$227,904	$1,238.00	$2,155.97
50	149,285	149,285	88,724	150,331	668.00	1,292.61
55	114,516	114,516	46,851	86,426	308.00	691.06
60	86,228	86,228	20,003	45,050	65.23	289.03

If you have purchased an ISL or a UL product at age forty-five, you can choose the life-only option from your pension plan and begin receiving $1,698 per month at age sixty-five. Then you have the assurance of starting to receive your pension income and, all the while, knowing that your beneficiary will receive $189,333 additional tax-free dollars when you die. However, if your health is good at age sixty-five and your forebears lived to very old age, you can choose to elect the monthly retirement income from your insurance at age sixty-five instead of letting the death benefit stay in force. Your policy would pay $1,238 per month *for life* and to your survivor for the balance of ten years. Now you have the best of both worlds. Your total monthly retirement income at age sixty-five under these circumstances would be $1,698 plus $1,238, or $2,936—for the rest of your life.

From your insurance program alone, at the rate of $1,238 per month beginning at age sixty-five, you would receive $148,560 in ten years, $222,840 in fifteen years, $297,120 in twenty years, and $371,400 in twenty-five years. This amount is in addition to your income from the pension plan.

Your contract with any life insurance company offering a ten-years-certain option guarantees your monthly income for as long as you live once you start receiving it.

In addition to all the other retirement income options afforded by life insurance companies, you can choose the interest-only option, which pays only the interest income from your cash value and leaves your principle intact. For example, in the case of the forty-five-year-old above, his policy generates $139,567 of cash value at age sixty-five. The interest-only option of most companies would pay this person from $750 to $850 per month for at least thirty years, beginning at age sixty-five. This choice is very attractive at age sixty-five if your health is good and your family enjoys a history of longevity.

Of course, you can always choose to receive your accumulated life insurance or annuity cash values in a lump sum instead of a monthly income, but that would eliminate the choice of a guaranteed life income. It would also cause you to pay income taxes on the amount over and above your cost basis, that is, the amount you have deposited over the years. (Cost basis is discussed in detail in chapter 5.) With the assumption that your primary need is to produce a monthly retirement income at retirement age, I won't dwell further on the lump-sum option here.

3-5 How to Use Universal Life to Avoid the Pension Trap

Now let's look at a universal life product that has the same death benefit at each issue age as shown in 3-4 but calls for less premium at each age. In the UL plan, the interest rate, the death benefit, the cash value, and the premium can vary. In the ISL plan, usually the cash value and the death benefit are guaranteed whereas the interest rate can always vary. The UL plan has a projected accumulated value, in addition to the cash value, which is tied to the projected interest rate. That accumulated value will vary as the interest rate varies. You would be wise to learn the difference between projections and guarantees in all plans in all companies.

Assuming an 8.05 percent interest rate in this UL plan, the following results are projected:

Age	Death Benefit	Death Benefit at 65	Accumulated Cash at 65	Accumulated Cash at 70	Monthly Retirement Income at 65	Annual Premium
45	$189,333	$189,333	$111,471	$139,338	$892	$3,004
50	149,285	149,285	68,307	91,076	546	2,993
55	114,516	114,516	34,073	62,748	273	2,911
60	86,228	86,228	13,631	29,774	238	2,751

Obviously, the ISL plan's guarantees make it attractive while the UL plan costs less, assuming interest rates continue to be stable. For purposes of backing up your choice of the life-only option in your pension plan, the UL plan would cost you less than the ISL plan.

3-6 What About Using Term Insurance to Avoid the Pension Trap?

The cost of term insurance in the first year is enticingly low, but in the older ages it is usually prohibitive. Here are some examples of the cost of annual renewable term at various ages, assuming males who are nonsmokers and preferred risks:

Age	Death Benefit	Annual Premium	Premium at 65	Premium at 70	Premium at 75	Premium at 80
45	$189,333	$350	$2,507	$3,965	$6,454	$10,000
50	149,285	352	2,164	3,132	5,094	8,230
55	114,516	374	1,526	2,408	3,914	6,319
60	100,000*	460	1,336	2,106	3,421	5,521

*The minimum amount available at age sixty in most companies. Note: Smokers and impaired risks pay higher premiums.

The total outlay for term insurance in these examples would be:

Age	Death Benefit	Total Premium to 65	Total Premium to 70	Total Premium to 75	Total Premium to 80
45	$189,333	$26,590	$44,174	$70,963	$114,353
50	149,285	17,936	31,039	52,189	86,530
55	114,516	10,531	20,612	36,865	62,836
60	100,000	5,136	13,954	28,162	51,207

These prices are competitive in the marketplace, yet when most people realize the high cumulative cost, they are unwilling to pay such premiums in their later years. They may well find themselves uninsured in their older ages. Then the cost of buying UL or ISL insurance will be even higher.

3-7 How to Avoid the High Cost of Term in Your Later Years and Still Elude the Pension Trap by Electing the Vanishing Premium Option

One important advantage these new generation plans (interest-sensitive life and universal life) have over term insurance is that they offer a vanishing premium option. That allows you to stop premium payments after nine or ten years. The policy then stays in force until death if the interest rate holds an average as indicated in the initial projections at time of issue. In addition, if you decide to cash in the ISL and/or the UL policies, you usually get most of the money back after nine or ten years. All term premiums are gone with no return unless the term plan pays dividends. In that case, all the term premiums would be considerably higher than those shown in the examples in 3-6 since none of them pay dividends.

In chapter 10, we will discuss in detail the use of term plus an investment versus universal life. For now, in discussing the pension trap, I will simply show what seems to be the best way to insure the highest retirement income to an annuitant and the annuitant's family, whether the annuitant lives a long time into retirement or dies soon after retiring.

3-8 How to Integrate All Retirement Income with Social Security

How to get information from the Social Security office. It really isn't necessary to visit your local Social Security office to make an inquiry. In most larger metropolitan areas the Social Security offices have toll-free WATS lines. You can obtain the number by calling information at 1-800-555-1212. Tell the personnel you want to make sure your account is in order. Occasionally, such inquirers are told that there is no record of their name in the Social Security files. Contacting that department early in your life is important so that if there is a problem with your account, you can get it straightened out. Never wait until you're ready for retirement to make your first inquiry of the Social Security department. They will send you a form or, in some cases, will simply input your Social Security number into their computer and send you a printout of your account, showing how much you paid into Social Security each year you have worked. There is no charge for these services.

How to work and still draw Social Security. Let's suppose you reach age sixty-five and decide to retire or, more correctly, semiretire. Let's say you have a pension of $800.00 per month and are eligible to receive $695.00 per month from Social Security. Your spouse is eligible to receive half your Social Security monthly benefit, or $347.50 at age sixty-five. Those three items total $1,842.50 per month payable to you as follows:

Your monthly Social Security retirement amount	$ 695.00
Your spouse's monthly Social Security amount	347.50
Your monthly pension	800.00
Total	$1,842.50

Suppose you want to keep working part-time. Under present law, you would be allowed to earn an additional $10,200 in 1992 (if you are sixty-five or older) and still draw your full Social Security payments each month. The limit is $7,440 for those between ages sixty-two and sixty-five. Even if you earn more than $9,720, you can continue drawing your Social Security, but the Social Security office will take away $1 for every $3 over $10,200 you earn. You must keep in touch with the Social Security office if you feel your *earned* income may be too high. Or if your earned income varies from month to month, you must stay in touch with them so they can monitor your account.

If you are overpaid at the end of the year, your monthly income is adjusted the next year. If you are underpaid by Social Security, you receive the balance of what you should have received in April of the following year. It's easy to monitor if your earned income is steady, but if you are working on commission, the calculation is more difficult. If you are overpaid by Social Security, you *do not* have to repay the amount. The agency simply delays starting your next year's payments if you anticipate a similar amount of earned income the next year.

Notice the importance of the word *earned.* Only earned income is counted in determining taxable income for Social Security purposes. Of course, all income must be reported for income tax purposes. There is no limit to the amount of unearned income (i.e., investment income) you can receive and still draw your full Social Security income. Even if you have millions of dollars in investments, the income from those investments is not earned income and, therefore, is not subject to Social Security tax.

Should you draw Social Security at sixty-two, sixty-five, or seventy? You can begin receiving retirement income from Social Security as early as age sixty-two and still earn limited amounts of income, $7,440 in 1992. This amount has been going up each year. Check with the Social Security office to get the current amount you can earn.

At age seventy, there is no limit to the amount of money you can earn and still draw full Social Security retirement benefits. As you approach age sixty-two, you would be well advised to compare your monthly Social Security retirement income at that age with the age sixty-five monthly income. If you have the option to retire at age sixty-two, you would enjoy three years of Social Security income that would take many years to make up if you waited for a larger monthly income to begin at age sixty-five. You would receive a significant amount of money between age sixty-two and age sixty-five. Discuss this question with Social Security personnel.

3-9 What Happens to Your Retirement Income If You Die?

If you are drawing a monthly amount from a pension plan, Social Security, and/or a monthly retirement income, either from an annuity or the proceeds of a life insurance policy, your beneficiary may or may not receive any further payments. That's why it is imperative to understand your options. Let's discuss Social Security first.

At retirement age, most people will be in one of the following categories: married, single and never married, a widow, a widower, divorced, or separated. If you are married and the Social Security office begins your monthly retirement income at age sixty-five based on your earnings, your spouse will receive half your monthly retirement amount in addition if the spouse is also age sixty-five, or less if the spouse is under age sixty-five. For example, if you and your spouse are over sixty-five, and your monthly retirement amount is $1,000, your spouse will get an additional $500 per month, thus making a total of $1,500.

If you are single and never married, your retirement income benefit will be based on your own earnings. If you are divorced or separated at retirement age, I would suggest you seek help from the Social Security office regarding the specifics of your situation.

If you die while receiving Social Security retirement income based on your earnings as the primary worker, your spouse will then begin receiving the same amount per month that you would have received by yourself. That is, if you and your spouse were receiving $1,500 total retirement income per month from Social Security prior to your death, your spouse will begin receiving $1,000 per month after you die for as long as the person lives.

There are rules for special situations such as those governing divorced former spouses, unmarried children under age eighteen, unmarried children age nineteen if they are still in school, children who were disabled prior to age twenty-two, and spouses who are caring for children under age sixteen or children who were disabled prior to age twenty-two. You would be wise to seek clarification from the Social Security office.

If you die while receiving monthly retirement income from your pension plan, an annuity, or life insurance, the amount your survivor receives depends on the options you chose prior to retirement.

In 3-2, I explained the various options available in most retirement plans, including pensions, annuities, and life insurance. But I will briefly list them again here:

1) *Life only* means there are no further payments after death.
2) *Ten years certain with life thereafter* pays for the life of the annuitant with the certainty that your beneficiary will receive the balance of ten years' payments if you die prior to receiving the income for at least ten years.
3) *Twenty years certain with life thereafter* is the same as the ten-years-certain option but with the balance of twenty years guaranteed to the survivor.
4) *Joint and survivor* means that you and/or your spouse receive income for life with a percentage, such as 50 percent, 75 percent, or 100 percent, going to the survivor at the death of either spouse.

Two other options are worth mentioning: lump-sum settlement and interest-only settlement. Most people have retirement plans to receive a guaranteed income for life, not a lump sum at retirement. Only through the various options is such a guarantee available.

3-10 What to Do If Your Retirement Income Is Discontinued

Fortunately, the law requires that all qualified retirement plans become vested, generally speaking, after five years of eligible service for an employer. The employee must have nonforfeitable rights to the accrued funds in the retirement account. An increasing percentage of vesting begins with 20 percent after three years of employment.

Sad to say, many persons are terminated prior to the time their retirement plans would be vested. If they have no other retirement income possibilities, they have a huge problem. Because of inflation, many denominational pension plans won't provide adequate retirement income. Ministers who work for independent, nondenominational churches have an even bigger problem. Interim ministers have still a bigger problem, since many congregations feel it's unfair to have the sole responsibility for interim ministers reaching retirement age in their churches. Even if a church is willing to pay into an interim minister's annuity prior to retirement, such a minister's salary is usually low. The percentage paid into the annuity is correspondingly low because it's based on a percentage of salary. These are some reasons it is so important to start a supplementary retirement plan as early in life as possible. The tax-sheltered annuity (TSA), discussed thoroughly in chapter 4, is such a plan.

3-11 What About a Housing Allowance After You Retire?

If a residence and utilities are furnished to you in retirement by your church as part of your compensation for past services, "you may exclude the rental value of a residence, plus utilities," from gross income, or the "portion of your pension that was designated as a rental allowance." However, that does not extend to a surviving spouse unless said spouse personally performed such services (IRS Publication 517, *Social Security for Members of the Clergy and Religious Workers*).

In the following chapters, the TSA, the IRA, and other retirement vehicles will be discussed in detail.

CHAPTER 4

The Tax-Sheltered Annuity (TSA)

4-1 What Is a Tax-Sheltered Annuity?

The tax-deferred annuity (TDA), also known as the tax-sheltered annuity (TSA), is authorized by the U.S. government in Section 501(c)(3) and Section 403(b) of the Internal Revenue Code. These sections granted by Congress allow persons employed by tax-exempt organizations to have a tax-sheltered retirement program. I will be quoting extensively from IRS Publication 571, *Tax-Sheltered Annuity Programs for Employees of Public Schools and Certain Tax-Exempt Organizations*. As you study this chapter, remember that clergypersons qualify under Section 403(b) of the Internal Revenue Code.

I will emphasize how the TSA affects clergypersons who work for churches, synagogues, or temples. However, I will also include the details of how to treat tax-sheltered annuities for employees of other tax-exempt employers because many clergypersons, and clergy spouses, may have been employed by tax-exempt employers other than churches during their careers. The contributions to annuity accounts are subject to maximums and other limitations, and accumulations and withdrawals must be recorded and monitored throughout your career. Other eligible categories include teachers, counselors, college presidents, and some bookstore employees. Generally, the TSA is available only through public schools and certain tax-exempt organizations. Clergypersons are often employed by religious schools or universities or have dual employment by churches and some other organizations such as counseling services.

In the past when Congress has changed the tax laws, more often than not it has "grandfathered" plans that were already in place prior to the date of the change.

4-2 Who Pays for the Tax-Sheltered Annuity?

The law allows two ways to make contributions into a TSA. The most common way is for the church to withhold money from the minister's salary and send it to the annuity company. None of the church's funds are involved. There is no legitimate reason for any church to prevent its employees from purchasing a TSA. The other way is for the church to pay for the annuity in addition to the minister's salary. Most of the remarks in this chapter will be aimed at explaining the most common way: having the church withhold money from the minister's salary. The minister and other church employees will be making the entire contribution out of their salaries.

4-3 How the Tax-Sheltered Annuity Works

The TSA offers a method for employees of public schools and certain tax-exempt organizations, such as churches, to accumulate funds in a tax-sheltered account until retirement. The IRS allows the employer to withhold money from the employees' salary and forward it to an annuity company. Those funds are excluded from the employee's income up to certain limits discussed in sections 4-19 and following. The funds grow tax-free until the employee withdraws the funds, usually at retirement time. The usual arrangement is for the annuity company to pay the annuitant an income for life or for some guaranteed time to the annuitant and survivors. The principal advantage of the TSA is the postponement of income tax liability on your employer's contributions until retirement when you should be in a lower income tax bracket.

First, I will give an overview of how to set up a TSA and answer the most frequently asked questions. Then, I will give detailed explanations of every stage of making contributions or withdrawing funds. At first glance the TSA appears to be simple, but it is very complex in its entirety. Since it is a government program, it is to be taken seriously.

4-4 Who Controls the Tax-Sheltered Annuity Plan?

The *employee* is the sole owner of the TSA. It is the employee's money. Even if the church decides to pay the entire amount into the annuity for an employee, it is the employee's property as soon as the money is deposited into the employee's account. If the employee resigns the day after the employer deposits money into the employee's account, the entire fund goes with the employee.

4-5 Can the Church Buy the Minister a TSA in Lieu of Giving a Raise?

Yes. More often than not, however, when ministers first learn of the advantages of the TSA, they usually shop the annuity market and then buy an annuity on their own. The law prohibits an individual from sending in a personal check for the purchase of a TSA, so the church has to be notified prior to the actual purchase and appropriate forms have to be completed. Then, usually at a future annual salary review date, the church has the option of taking over the payment of the TSA in lieu of a raise. The result is to give the minister a nontaxable raise. The raise does not have to be reported as income for Social Security, federal, state, or local income tax purposes.

4-6 The TSA Account Remains Tax-Sheltered While Growing

All the time funds are invested in a TSA, those funds are exempt from income tax liability. There is no form to submit each year to the Internal Revenue Service. The church treasurer does not report the deposits as income received by the minister. There is nothing to report because the deposits are *excluded* from income.

4-7 What If the Minister Quits the Ministry?

Even if the minister quits the ministry, all the money that has already been deposited into the TSA can remain there tax-sheltered as it grows. No additional deposits can be made unless the minister finds employment with another tax-exempt employer.

4-8 Funds Taxable When Withdrawn

Only when the funds are withdrawn from a TSA are they subject to income tax. The idea is to defer the payment of income tax on the fund until retirement age when the minister's income tax bracket should be lower. *Any time the funds from a tax-sheltered annuity are withdrawn, they are to be reported as ordinary income.* But the government imposes no other penalty if the money is withdrawn *after* age 59¹/₂. If the funds are withdrawn *prior* to age 59¹/₂, there is an additional 10 percent penalty for early withdrawal. Some annuity companies allow loans from their TSA accounts.

4-9 Advantages of the Tax-Sheltered Annuity

The maximum allowable income tax exclusion is up to 20 percent of cash salary, depending on the number of years of service for *one* employer and the amount of cash salary. Current law allows almost any pastor who has been employed within one denomination the full 20 percent of cash salary as an exclusion allowance if the pastor has been employed for many years. There are specific formulas to determine the maximum allowable deposit for a tax shelter, all of which will be discussed in detail. But it is probably fair to say that any pastor with ten years' service may tax-shelter the full 20 percent of includible compensation in a TSA.

Formerly, the law required that the pastor had to remain employed by one local church to qualify for the maximum exclusion allowance. Under a prior law, even if a pastor had qualified for the full 20 percent and then changed local churches, the pastor might have to settle for something less than 20 percent of salary as a maximum deposit. Now the government treats the denomination as one employer if it has control, as defined by the government, over the work of the pastor. Thus, an independent pastor would still be guided by the old rules for determining the maximum exclusion allowance. Each time an independent pastor moves from one church to another, the exclusion allowance maximum could be less than 20 percent. But the percentage increases each year until, after about ten years, the full 20 percent of includible compensation is allowed. Includible compensation is usually limited to cash salary and all other allowances except housing allowance and authorized, reimbursed expenses.

Determining what is includible compensation can be confusing. Some denominations define compensation as salary, housing, and utilities. That is done primarily to determine compensation for pension deposit purposes. Defining includible compensation for purposes of determining the maximum allowable deposit into a TSA is quite different, and the difference must be kept in mind.

4-10 How to Earn Up to 50 Percent, and More, Safely and Legally on Your Tax-Sheltered Annuity

You might well question the reliability of an investment situation that results in a 50 percent yield in one year. However, the TSA, a very safe investment, can develop such numbers.

For example, Pastor Jane Doe decides to invest $200 per month in a TSA. She completes the proper application and salary reduction agreement. Each month the church withholds $200 from her salary and sends it to the annuity company. There is no front-end load or annual service fee on most annuities. The assumptions are that Doe is participating in the Social Security program and that she is an employee of a church. Remember that the funds being withheld from her salary and sent to the annuity company are excluded from federal, state, local, and Social Security taxes. The church does not include the $200 on her Form 1040 or Form 1099. Here's how to arrive at the 50 percent figure:

Amount withheld from salary		$200.00
Federal income tax savings	@ 28.0%	$ 56.00
State income tax savings	@ 6.0%	12.00
Local income tax savings	@ 2.0%	4.00
Social Security income tax savings	@ 15.3%	30.60
Total income tax savings	51.3%	$102.60
Add to that interest earned	@ 7.5%	15.00
Total savings plus earnings	58.8%	$117.60

If Pastor Doe had received the $200 as income, she would have had to pay 51.3 percent or $102.60 in income taxes. This way, she can exclude the $200 from income tax and place it in a tax-sheltered annuity, thus building her deferred retirement income on a very favorable basis.

To duplicate this with almost any other investment, Pastor Doe would have had to earn a gross amount of $391 that, after taxes, would produce net income to her of $200!

Let's look at the annual picture:

Amount withheld in one year at $200 per month	$2,400.00
Federal income tax savings at 28%	$ 672.00
State income tax savings at 6%	144.00
Local income tax savings at 2%	48.00

Social Security tax savings at 15.3%	367.20
Total tax savings in one year	$1,231.20

What other safe investment can produce such a yield?

Now let's look at the lifetime results that might be produced for Pastor Doe if she starts making deposits into her annuity at age thirty-five and decides to retire at age sixty-five:

Amount withheld from age 35 to age 65	$ 72,000.00
Federal income tax savings at 28%	$ 20,160.00
State income tax savings at 6%	4,320.00
Local income tax savings at 2%	1,440.00
Social Security tax savings at 15.3% (This will probably increase much more.)	11,016.00
Total income tax savings	$ 36,936.00
Total value of the TSA at age 65	$258,128.86

To see the tremendous effect of taxes compared to tax shelter, let's suppose Pastor Doe had inherited $72,000 in cash and she decided to invest in certificates of deposit (CDs) instead of the tax-sheltered annuity. Here is what might happen:

Total amount invested in CDs	$72,000.00
Annual yield at 7.5%	$ 5,400.00
Federal income tax at 28%	$ 1,512.00
State income tax at 6%	324.00
Local income tax at 2%	108.00
Social Security tax at 15.3%	826.20
Total income tax liability per year	$ 2,770.20
Total net annual yield after taxes	$ 2,629.80

The gross annual yield of 7.5 percent diminishes to 3.65 percent after taxes!

Now, just for purposes of an apples-to-apples comparison, consider the difference between investing $72,000 in CDs versus the TSA, or any annuity for that matter, beginning at age thirty-five:

Total value of CDs at age sixty-five, invested at 3.65 percent = $211,063

versus

Total value of a TSA at age sixty-five, invested at 7.5 percent = $630,358

The annuity accrues three times as much as the CDs! So if Pastor Doe invests in the TSA instead of CDs, our example shows that she would be $47,065.86 ahead at age sixty-five.

For self-employed persons, such as pastors, the high total tax percentage they have to pay can ruin almost any non-tax-sheltered investment they make. Even if Pastor Doe earned 10 percent, gross before taxes, the net left to her would be slightly less than 50 percent. She would have to earn 15 percent steadily from ages thirty-five to sixty-five to keep 7.5 percent net after taxes.

There is, however, one equally important reason that Doe should choose the TSA in preference to CDs if the primary investment goal is a lifetime retirement income. The TSA offers a lifetime guaranteed retirement income. CDs do not.

Let's follow through with our example of Pastor Doe depositing $200.00 per month from ages thirty-five to sixty-five and earning 7.5 percent interest throughout that time. We noted that she would have $258,128.86 in cash at age sixty-five. If she chose the life-only option, her TSA would pay her $2,434.16 per month; if she chose the ten-years-certain option, her monthly income would be $2,250.80 for life, no matter how long she might live. Here are some projections of the total she might receive if she chose the ten-years-certain option, depending on the number of years she lived after age sixty-five:

If she received $2,250.80 per month	
In 10 years she would receive a total of	$ 270,096.00
In 20 years,	540,192.00
In 25 years,	675,240.00
In 30 years	810,316.80
In 35 years	945,369.60
In 40 years	1,080,422.40

The important point is that she cannot outlive her income. It must be paid to her as long as she lives. That's the purpose of an annuity. That's how annuities differ from almost any other investment. Accumulating a fund at age sixty-five is only part of the story. If the purpose of accumulating a fund at sixty-five is to provide a retirement income, an annuity serves the purpose for most people. A notable exception would be if anyone were able to accumulate enough to choose the interest-only option, the income would be available without depleting the principal. This, of course, is the ideal. Reality is such that most clergypersons cannot accumulate enough to produce an adequate monthly income from the interest-only option.

4-11 How to Set Up a Tax-Sheltered Annuity

A minister decides to purchase a tax-sheltered annuity. The church board must approve the action even though only the minister's money is involved. It is always possible for the church board to object, but it may well be unconstitutional for them to do so. The only thing the board must agree to do is to withhold the annuity deposit from the minister's salary and send it to the annuity company. The primary reason for obtaining the church board's approval is to make them accountable, both to the minister and to the federal government. A church official must verify the minister's date of employment and amount of income, which are needed to determine the maximum amount the minister can contribute to the TSA.

The following procedure may be used to establish a TSA for a minister employed by a church. In this example, only the minister's salary is involved:

1) The board must include an authorization in the official minutes, in compliance with the law, establishing a plan, making it available to all church employees. No funds can be deposited prior to the date of this authorization noted in the minutes of the church board.

2) The proper forms (an annuity application and a salary reduction agreement) are completed and signed by the minister and an officer of the church, usually the treasurer.

3) The completed forms and a church check made out to the annuity company are submitted to the annuity company. No evidence of insurability is required when an annuity is purchased unless life insurance is part of it.

4) The amount of the deposit is immediately excluded from all income tax including Social Security. (Public school teachers are in a different category when they purchase the tax-sheltered annuity and pay on a different basis.) The church takes that amount of money right off the top of the minister's income. It is not reported as income for any reason. That is the law.

4-12 How and When to Roll Over Your IRA or TSA to a Better Plan

From time to time, an annuity company will offer an incentive to people to roll over their annuity accounts to its plan. How can a company attract new money that way? First of all, competition is such that most companies have eliminated any going-in fees and annual service fees. Almost all companies have an early withdrawal penalty.

Obviously, the most enticing initial appeal is made by offering a higher annual interest rate. If Pastor John Smith has $10,000 in his TSA account that is paying 7 percent, he may be swayed into rolling his funds into a company offering 9 percent or higher for a limited time only. It is a strong appeal. Usually, the higher interest rate is offered only the first year or two. Companies are willing to do this in return for including an early withdrawal penalty clause in the contract. The annuitant, who is the buyer, could reasonably assume that making the change would be beneficial. But all is not gold that glitters. In addition to the variables mentioned—the going-in interest rate, the annual service fee, the early withdrawal clause—consider one other significant variable: the monthly retirement income.

If an inquirer wrote twenty different annuity companies and asked, "If I invest $200 per month from my present age to age sixty-five, what will the monthly retirement income be beginning at age sixty-five?" such an inquirer will receive twenty different answers with the possibility that the company with the highest monthly amount might pay twice that of the lowest of the twenty companies. It is shocking but true. A company might pay an annuitant a higher monthly income at retirement age from a lower amount of accumulation. The ranking of annuity companies to show these comparative retirement incomes is published every year in the *Annuity Shopper* by United States Annuities, Englishtown, New Jersey. You can look it up.

So, if you are considering the possibility of rolling over the funds in your annuity to another company, investigate these variables thoroughly. You may be fully justified in making the change. Keep in mind, however, that the primary purpose of an annuity is to provide a lifetime income at retirement age. Therefore, look carefully at the monthly income produced at retirement age by any annuity. Obviously, you should seek responses only from financially sound, reputable companies.

Under the law, you have sixty days to roll over such an account to another one. Usually, a rollover is accomplished company-to-company. However, you may withdraw all your funds, place them in your bank account, and keep them there fifty-nine days without any income tax liability. You *must complete* the rollover within that sixty-day period.

Keep copies of the paperwork to show your tax preparer. Occasionally, an annuity company will mistakenly report your rollover funds as an income distribution to you. Such a mistake is troublesome but easily rectified if you have the proper records. You must be able to prove that you rolled over your funds from one company to another within the allotted sixty days.

Second rollover. If you roll over a qualifying distribution to an IRA, you can, under certain conditions, later roll the distribution into another TSA. For more information, see IRS Publication 590, *Individual Retirement Arrangements*. There are limitations to the number of times you can roll over a TSA. Each situation is different, and I cannot generalize on this subject.

There are many rules. You must seek competent help with the purchase, maintenance, and withdrawal of funds from the TSA. Anyone who suggests to you that the TSA is simple probably doesn't really understand the subject.

4-13 Which Employees Are Eligible to Buy a TSA?

Church employees. All church employees, including ministers, secretaries, custodians, and other salaried employees, are eligible for the TSA. Once the plan is approved by the church board and noted in the official board minutes, any and all employees may buy up to the maximum amount allowable to each of them. We will discuss the maximum allowance later.

Any full-time or part-time employee of a qualified employer may buy a TSA. You are considered to be an employee "if you are subject to the will and control of an employer regarding what work you do and how you do it." If you are accountable to another only for the results of your work, and not the method you use, you are considered to be an independent contractor, not a qualified employee.

Employees of public schools. You are eligible to buy a TSA if you work, "directly or indirectly, for a public school." Included, generally, are principals, clerical employees, custodial employees, and teachers.

If you work in a public school program carried out away from the school itself, you are considered an employee performing indirect services for a public school.

In-home teachers. In-home teachers can buy a TSA. If it is organized by the public schools, it is merely "an extension of the activities carried on by public schools."

Department of Education employees appointed by a state commissioner of education. "Janitors, custodial persons, and general clerical employees" are eligible. Appointed executives or policy-making persons are eligible if they have "required training or experience in the field of education." All these persons are considered to be indirect employees and are eligible for the TSA.

Persons elected or appointed to office. Persons in these two categories are not usually considered to be employees who perform services for an educational organization *unless* the office "is one to which you can be elected or appointed only if you have training or experience in the field of education."

While "commissioners or superintendents of education are generally considered to be employees performing services for an educational organization," university regents, trustees, or board of education members are not considered to be eligible employees.

Employees of a state teachers' retirement system. Such persons are not eligible to participate in a TSA. Teachers in public schools are eligible.

4-14 Discrimination Is Allowed

Under the provisions of the TSA, a church may discriminate as to which persons and what amounts of contributions it wishes to include and pay for. The church may decide to pay the senior pastor's entire contribution into the TSA as part of the negotiated pay package. On the other hand, it may not wish to pay anything, for whatever reason, in behalf of any other employee. All other employees may still elect to participate by having contributions withheld from their salaries. Unlike a qualified pension plan, which has to treat all employees alike, the church may discriminate, so long as the TSA is available to all employees on a voluntary basis.

4-15 Which Organizations Are Considered to Be Qualified Employers?

Educational organizations. These organizations are qualified if their employees perform services "directly or indirectly." Thus, "a state or local government or any of its agencies or instrumentalities can be a qualified employer," including "an Indian tribal government."

To qualify as an *educational organization,* such an organization must maintain a regular faculty, curriculum, and regular student body meeting at a regular place known as a school.

Tax-exempt organizations. Organizations are tax-exempt if they are "organized and operated exclusively for religious, charitable, scientific, public safety testing, literary, or educational purposes." Also, certain national or international amateur sports organizations and those organized to prevent cruelty to animals and children are eligible: "The organization can be a corporation, community chest, fund, or foundation."

A cooperative hospital service organization. This organization may be a qualified employer. You would have to check with your local IRS office for the answer to this question in your region.

Government instrumentalities (other than public schools, described already) that are wholly owned state or municipal instrumentalities generally are not qualified employers. However, if the organization is a **separate entity** that is specifically tax exempt because it is organized and operated only for the charitable, etc., purposes already stated, it is a qualified employer.

Uniformed Services University of the Health Sciences. This is a federal organization authorized to train medical students for the uniformed services. The rules in this publication apply to annuities bought for civilian faculty and staff for work they performed after 1979.

4-16 Who Is Considered to Be an Employee of a Tax-Exempt Organization?

Most employees of tax-exempt organizations are eligible to purchase a TSA, including "those who perform services as social workers, members of the clergy, teachers, professors, clerks, and secretaries." Even some physicians who work in hospitals as employees may be eligible. See IRS Publication 571 for details.

4-17 The First Thing You Must Do to Establish a TSA

To establish a tax-sheltered annuity, before anything else is done, the church board must approve the establishment of the plan and insert an official notation in the minutes of the church board. This step is required by the federal government. Your church can use the following example:

Authorization by the Board
Establishing a Tax-Sheltered
Annuity Program

Name of
church_____
Date_____

As of this date, the board authorizes a tax-sheltered annuity program under the provisions of IRC Section 403(b) for all eligible employees who wish to participate in the program. The board authorizes the treasurer to sign all forms required to facilitate the enrollment of all participating eligible employees. The church agrees to withhold moneys from the salary of any eligible employee and send them to an annuity company, or if the church decides to increase an employee's pay in the form of an annuity payment, it will forward those funds to an annuity company in behalf of the annuitant. This is being done to comply with federal government requirements since the church is considered, by law, to be the applicant and employer.

Signed_____
(Treasurer)

This authorization makes the plan official in the eyes of the federal government. It does not obligate the church other than to withhold and forward money. It must be a church check. It cannot be the clergyperson's personal check.

There is absolutely no legal reason why a church should refuse to set up the necessary paperwork so that a pastor or other church employee can establish a tax-sheltered annuity.

4-18 How to Set Up a Salary
Reduction Agreement

Before your church (or any eligible employer) can withhold any money from your salary and deposit it into your TSA account, a salary reduction agreement (SRA) must be completed and recorded in the employer's official board of directors' minutes. You can either have the money taken out of your existing salary or receive the money in lieu of a raise from your employer. You must state an exact amount that you intend to contribute to your TSA during one year. The SRA must be "legally binding and irrevocable." You are allowed only one SRA per year with the same employer. You can always deposit less than the amount stated on the SRA but never more.

If you have an existing SRA from an earlier tax year, you can complete a new SRA anytime during the current tax year. You can make contributions based on a percentage of salary or a stated amount of dollars.

The mere change in the amount of your employer's contribution because of an increase or decrease in your salary during the year will not constitute a new agreement.

Similarly, changing insurers during a tax year in which a salary reduction agreement was made will not result in a new agreement for that year, even though the name of the first insurer was initially specified in the agreement.

You can have only one SRA per year unless you change employers or insurers. You could not, for example, have two or more SRAs during one year with the same employer. In the event that your employer has two or more TSAs to offer, you can buy from several of these companies, but you must have a redesigned SRA that combines choices from all the annuity companies on that one SRA.

4-19 What Tax Advantages Will an Exclusion Allowance Afford You?

Exclusion from gross income. Notice the difference between an exclusion and a deduction. IRA contributions are deducted, while TSA contributions are excluded from income. It is as if that amount of money never existed. For clergypersons, exclusion usually includes exclusion from local, state, federal, and Social Security income tax. We will go over this later in more detail.

Generally, if you are an eligible employee who works for a qualified employer, and you participate in a qualified tax-sheltered annuity program, you can exclude from gross income your employer's contributions toward the program equal to the lesser of:

The **exclusion allowance** for your tax year,

The **annual employer contribution limit** for the limitation year ending with or within your tax year, or

The **combined annual limit on elective deferrals.**

Rollovers from other TSAs or IRAs cannot be included as employer's contributions.

Limitation year. Usually, the limitation year is the calendar year for an employee for whom a tax-sheltered annuity is purchased.

However, you can elect to change to a different limitation year consisting of a period of 12 consecutive months by attaching a statement to your individual income tax return for the tax year a change is made. If you control an employer, your limitation year is the same as the limitation year of the employer. Control is defined in sections 414(b) and 414(c) (as modified by section 415(h)) of the Internal Revenue Code.

Ministers with no other employment outside qualified churches, fortunately, do not have to worry about this question of control and discrimination. Section 403(b)(1) spells out the details. If that isn't enough to clear up any questions you may have, you would be wise, as always, to seek clarification from the IRS or a competent tax adviser.

Annual employer contribution limits. In most cases, tax-sheltered annuity programs are treated as defined contribution plans [described in 4-24]. The general rule is that annual employer contributions for the limitation year cannot be more than the lesser of:

$30,000 (or, if greater, ¼ of the dollar limit for defined benefit plans), or

25% of the employee's compensation for the year. . . .

Contributions for a year beginning after January 24, 1980, made to a tax-sheltered annuity program for your benefit by your employer reduce the **exclusion allowance** for future tax years. The exclusion allowance is reduced by the amount that the employer's contributions are more than the annual employer contribution limit. This is because, in figuring the exclusion allowance for future tax years, the excess is treated as if it were an amount previously excludable.

4-20 What Is the Exclusion Allowance?

It is an amount of money that you can contribute to a TSA and does not have to be reported as income for the tax year. Here's how to figure it:

1) 20% 20%
2) **Includible compensation for most recent period of service** . . . . $_____
3) **Years of service** . . . .   _____
4) (1) × (2) × (3) . . . . $_____
5) Minus: **Amounts previously excludable** . . . .   _____
6) Exclusion allowance (before reduction for any excess contributions) . . . . $_____

The terms emphasized here are defined later in detail.

Reduction of the exclusion allowance. You must reduce your exclusion allowance by the amount that your employer's contributions for tax years beginning after January 24, 1980, were more than the limit on employer contributions for those years. [See "Contributions in excess of employer limit" in 4-24.] The excess is treated as though it were an amount previously excludable.

Example. At the end of 1991, you had completed 3 years of service with your employer. Your salary for 1991 was $20,000 after being reduced under a salary reduction agreement by $2,400 to finance your employer's contributions toward an insurance contract. Your employer's contributions for the year totaled $2,400. This was applied as a premium for the contract, $100 of which was for current term life insurance protection.

In previous years, your employer's contributions to the regular retirement plan totaled $7,200, all of which you properly excluded from gross income. You determine your exclusion allowance and the amount includible in gross income for 1991 as follows:

Step 1—Limit on Employer Contributions
1) Lesser of $30,000 or 25% of employee's
   compensation (25% × $20,000 = $5,000) . . . . $ 5,000

Step 2—Contributions in Excess of Employer Limit
2) 1991 employer contribution for purchase of tax-
   sheltered annuity. . . . . $ 2,400
3) Minus: Portion of line 2, if any, representing term
   cost of life insurance that is includible in gross
   income 100
4) Balance of contributions applied to purchase of
   tax-sheltered annuity contract . . . . $ 2,300
5) Minus: Limit on employer contributions (Line 1) 5,000
6) Excess (if any) . . . . $ -0-

Step 3—Exclusion Allowance
7) 20% 20%
8) Includible compensation for most recent period of
   service $20,000
9) Years of service 3
10) (7) × (8) × (9) $12,000
11) Minus: Amounts previously excludable 7,200
12) Balance . . . .$ 4,800
13) Minus: Prior year contributions in excess of
    employer limit. . . . . -0-
14) Exclusion allowance. . . . . $ 4,800

Step 4—Amount Excludable from Gross Income
15) a) Employer contribution [Line 4] $2,300
    b) Limit on employer contributions [Line 1] . $5,000
    c) Exclusion allowance [Line 14] $4,800
16) Amount excludable from gross income [least of 15(a),
    (b), or (c)] . . . . $ 2,300

Step 5—Amount Includible in Gross Income

17) Employer contribution [Line 4] . . . . $ 2,300
18) Minus: Amount excludable [Line 16] 2,300
19) Amount includible in gross income . . . . $ -0-

Refer to Worksheets 1 through 6 at the end of this chapter to figure the amount of employer contributions that are excludible from gross income and the amount that are includible in gross income.

Special election for certain employees. Certain employees can elect to figure the exclusion allowance under an alternate rule called the **Overall Limit** [explained in 4-25]. Only employees of educational organizations, hospitals, home health service agencies, health and welfare service agencies, churches, and certain church-related organizations can make the election.

Employer must remain qualified. The exclusion allowance applies only to those contributions made while your employer was a qualified employer. If, for example, your employer loses tax-exempt status and is no longer qualified, your exclusion allowance will not apply to the employer's contributions made after losing the exemption.

More than one qualified employer. You must figure a separate exclusion allowance for each qualified employer. Do not include amounts contributed, compensation, or years of service for one qualified employer in the computation for another qualified employer. Special rules apply to church employees, as discussed next.

Special rule for church employees. For figuring your exclusion allowance, treat all of your years of service with related church organizations as years of service with one employer. Therefore, if during your career with a church you transfer from one organization to another within that church, or from the church to an associated organization, treat all this service as service with a single employer. Contributions on your behalf to annuity contracts by these organizations are treated as made by the same employer. This is not true for independent churches. As noted earlier, when ministers change employment from one independent church to another, there is no carryover of years of service for purposes of determining the exclusion allowance.

A church employee includes anyone who is an employee of a church or a convention or association of churches. This includes an employee of a tax-exempt organization controlled by or associated with a church or a convention or association of churches.

Minimum exclusion allowance for church employees. If you are a church employee and your adjusted gross income (figured without regard to community property laws) is not more than $17,000, you are entitled to a minimum exclusion allowance. The minimum is your exclusion allowance figured as explained earlier, but not less than the smaller of:

$3,000, or

Your includible compensation [defined in 4-21].

If you are a foreign missionary during the tax year, your includible compensation includes contributions by the church during the year toward your tax-sheltered annuity.

You are a foreign missionary if your principal duties are spreading religious doctrine, or performing sacerdotal functions or humanitarian good works for the church outside the United States.

4-21 What Is Includible Compensation?

As a first step in figuring your exclusion allowance for a tax year, you must figure 20% of your includible compensation. Generally, your includible compensation is the salary from your employer (who made contributions to the tax-sheltered annuity) that is:

Earned during your **most recent period of service,** and

Includible in your gross income.

However, you should examine the following exceptions and definitions.

Special rules for determining includible compensation. Do not count compensation earned while your employer was not a qualified employer. On the other hand, your employer's status is immaterial in terms of the time you actually receive the compensation.

Contributions by your employer for a tax-sheltered annuity are not part of includible compensation. [However, see "If you are a foreign missionary" in 4-20.] Contributions that are more than your exclusion allowance are not part of compensation for figuring your exclusion allowance, but they must be included in your gross income.

Example. After taking a reduction in salary to pay for your employer's contribution for an annuity during your first year of employment, you received a salary of $12,000. According to your agreement, $2,800 ($400 more than your exclusion allowance) is contributed for your annuity. The includible compensation to be used in figuring the applicable exclusion allowance is $12,000, even though you must include $12,400 in gross income.

Contributions to two retirement plans. Your employer can make contributions for you toward both a tax-sheltered annuity contract and a **qualified** retirement plan (contributions to which are excludable from your gross income). The contribution to the qualified retirement plan is also not part of includible compensation for figuring your exclusion allowance.

The cost of incidental life insurance provided under a tax-sheltered annuity contract is not includible compensation even though this cost is taxable to you.

Compensation from other employers who either are not qualified or are not purchasing your tax-sheltered annuity contract or compensation from other sources is not includible compensation. Only the compensation earned from the qualified employer purchasing your tax-sheltered annuity contract can qualify as includible compensation. [However, see "Special rule for church employees" in 4-20.]

Foreign earned income exclusion. Excludable foreign earned income is part of includible compensation.

Most recent period of service. Your includible compensation is only the compensation earned during your most recent period of service that ends on or before the end of the tax year for which the exclusion allowance is being determined. The period must be a full year of service if the total time you worked for your employer equals at least one full year. Thus, your most recent period of service will include more than one tax year if you were a part-time employee or if you were a full-time employee who worked only part of a tax year and you worked for your employer at least one full year over a period of more than one tax year.

If you worked less than a full year for your employer by the end of a tax year for which you are figuring the exclusion allowance, the actual period of your employment is considered your most recent period of service for figuring your includible compensation.

For example, if you became employed on October 1, 1990, your most recent period of service for figuring your includible compensation for your 1992 exclusion allowance is the period from October 1 through December 31, 1992. If your annual salary is $20,000, your includible compensation would be $5,000 (one-fourth of $20,000).

Even if you worked the entire year but decided to enter into a TSA program late in the year, you could use only that amount of compensation still coming to you for the balance of the year to determine qualified compensation.

Example. Suppose you had been working for a qualified employer for many years and had only recently decided to participate in the TSA program offered by the employer. Your salary is $20,000 annually. If you decided prior to January 1 to begin having deposits withheld from your salary on January 1 and all your required forms were completed prior to January 1, you would be eligible to tax-shelter 20 percent of your salary. But suppose you decided to begin withholdings on October 1; then you would be eligible for only three-twelfths of your eligible amount for the current year. In addition, if you were not aware of the limitation rules of the TSA and decided at the end of December to deposit a full year's amount of withholdings for the current year, you cannot do it. You can tax-shelter only a percentage of the amount of salary you have left coming to you in the current year.

Earned in a prior tax year. Your includible compensation may include all or part of your compensation earned in a tax year before the one for which the exclusion allowance is being determined. What is important is when you perform the service, not when you actually receive the compensation or the tax year in which it is includible in your gross income.

For example, if you are figuring your exclusion allowance for your 1992 tax year, and you were employed half time by your employer for all of 1991 and 1992, your includible compensation will include the amount earned in 1991 and 1992. (A part-time employee or a full-time employee who works part of a year, discussed below, must combine earnings for fractional parts of a year until they equal a full year's earnings.)

In figuring your includible compensation, you must first take into account the service you performed during the tax year for which the exclusion allowance is being determined. Therefore, your most recent period of service may not be the same as your employer's most recent annual work period.

Example. You are employed as a professor at a university and you use the calendar year as your tax year. You are employed on a full-time basis during the university's 1991 and 1992 academic years (which run from October through May). In figuring your exclusion allowance for your 1992 tax year, your most recent period of service consists of the service performed from January through May 1992 (which is part of the 1991–92 academic year), and the service performed from October through December 1992 (which is a part of the 1991–92 academic year).

Note: Your most recent period of service for determining includible compensation may not be the same period as your limitation year for determining the limit on employer contributions. [See "Limitation year" in 4-19.]

Full-time employee for a full year. If you are a full-time employee for a full year, your most recent period of service generally will be your current tax year.

To determine whether you are employed full time, compare the amount of work you are required to do with that required of individuals holding the same position with the same employer, and who receive most of their compensation from that position. If your position with your employer is the only one of its kind with your employer, you cannot make this comparison. You should consider the same position with similar employers, or similar positions with your employer.

In measuring the amount of work required by a particular position, any method that reasonably and accurately reflects the amount of work can be used. For example, the fact that a full-time English professor at your school normally performs 16 hours of classroom teaching each week may be used as a measure of the amount of work required in the position.

A full year of service for a particular position means the usual annual work period of individuals employed full time in that general type of employment at the place of employment. For example, if you are a doctor employed by a hospital 12 months of the year, except for a one-month vacation, and the other doctors at the hospital work 11 months of the year with a one-month vacation, you will be considered employed for a full year. Similarly, if the usual annual work period at a university consists of the fall and spring semesters, and you teach at the university during these semesters, you will be considered as working a full year.

Part-time employee, or full-time employee working for part of a year. If you are a part-time employee, or a full-time employee who worked for part of a year, you are treated as having a fraction of a year of service for each year you were so employed. You must total these fractional periods of service to determine your most recent period of service that equals one year of service. You first take into account your service during the current tax year, then the next preceding tax year, and so forth, until your service equals one year of service.

Example. If you are figuring your exclusion allowance for your 1989 tax year (which also is a calendar year), and you have worked full time one-fourth of a year for the last 10 years, your most recent period of service includes the service you performed in the period 1989 through 1992, determined as follows:

```
1992 fractional period of service .....................  1/4
1991 fractional period of service .....................  1/4
1990 fractional period of service .....................  1/4
1989 fractional period of service ....................   1/4
1 year of service equals ..........................      4/4
```

Full-time employee for part of a year. If you were a full-time employee for part of a year, the numerator (top number) of the fraction that represents your fractional year of service is the number of weeks (or months) that you were a full-time employee during that year, and the denominator (bottom number) is the number of weeks (or months) considered to be the usual work period for your position.

Example. You are employed full time as an instructor by a university for the 1992 spring semester (which lasts from February through May). The academic year of the university is 8 months long, beginning in October and ending the following May. You are considered as having completed four-eighths (or $\frac{1}{2}$) of a year of service.

Part-time employee for a full year. If you are a part-time employee for a full year, the numerator of the fraction that represents your fractional year of service is the amount of work you are required to perform, and the denominator is the amount of work normally required of individuals who hold the same position.

Example. If you are a practicing physician teaching one course at a local medical school 3 hours a week for two semesters, and other faculty members at that medical school teach 9 hours a week for two semesters, then you are considered to have completed three-ninths (or $\frac{1}{3}$) of a year of service.

Part-time employee for part of a year. If you are a part-time employee for part of a year, you determine the fraction that represents your fractional year of service by:

1) Determining a fractional year as if you were a full-time employee for part of a year,
2) Determining a fractional year as if you were a part-time employee for a full year, and
3) Multiplying the fractions in (1) and (2).

Example. You are an attorney and a specialist in federal tax law. In addition to your private practice, you teach tax law for 3 hours a week for one semester (the 4-month spring semester) at a nearby law school. Full-time instructors at the law school teach 12 hours a week for two semesters (or an 8-month academic year).

A fractional year of service determined as if you were a full-time employee for part of a year is one-half (the numerator being the period you worked, or 4 months, and the denominator being the usual work period, or 8 months).

A fractional year of service determined as if you were a part-time employee for a full year is three-twelfths (the numerator being the number of hours you are employed, and the denominator being the usual number of hours required for that position).

Your fractional year of service is $\frac{3}{24}$ ($\frac{1}{2} \times \frac{3}{12}$).

4-22 How to Figure Your Years of Service

Your next step in figuring your exclusion allowance is to determine your years of service with the employer who contributes to your annuity. Your years of service are the total number of years you worked for your employer determined as of the end of the tax year for which you are figuring an exclusion allowance. Your years of service cannot be less than one year (if your "most recent period of service" is less than a year, your "years of service" is one year). The service need not be continuous. You cannot count service for any other employer. [However, see "Special rule for church employees" in 4-20.]

Status of employer. Your years of service will only include periods that your employer was a **qualified employer,** as defined earlier.

Full-time employee for a full year. Your years of service will be the actual number of years you have worked for the employer who pays the premiums. The concepts *full-time employee for a full year* and *a full year of service* were discussed earlier.

Part-time or full-time employee for part of a year. You must determine the fraction that represents your fractional year of service. The rules for this are the same as those for determining your *most recent period of service,* discussed earlier.

4-23 Amounts Previously Excludable

The next step in determining your exclusion allowance is to subtract the amounts previously excludable from the result of multiplying 20% of includible compensation by your years of service.

Amounts previously excludable refers to the total of all contributions for annuities made for you by your employer—but only contributions that were excludable from your gross income for the tax years before the one for which the current exclusion allowance is being determined. (After a few years, it may be possible that you will have no exclusion allowance, especially if large contributions were made by your employer.)

Amounts previously excludable are contributions in earlier years to:

- A tax-sheltered annuity,
- A qualified annuity plan or a qualified pension, profit-sharing, or stock bonus trust,
- An eligible deferred compensation plan of a state or local government or tax-exempt organization (under Code section 457),
- A qualified bond-purchase plan, or
- A retirement plan under which the contributions originally were excludable by you only because your rights to the contributions were forfeitable when made, and which also were excludable by you when your rights became nonforfeitable. (This does not apply to contributions made after 1957 to purchase an annuity contract if your employer was an exempt organization when the contributions were made.)

Contributions to a state teachers' retirement system made for you in earlier tax years must be treated as amounts previously excludable, up to the amount that was excludable from your gross income and must be used to reduce your exclusion allowance.

Employer contributions in earlier years (beginning after January 24, 1980) that were more than the limit on employer contributions are treated as if they were amounts previously excludable. [See 4-24.]

If the amount of your employer's contributions to a plan for you is not known, you can determine your part of your employer's contributions by any method using recognized actuarial principles that are consistent with your employer's plan and the method used by your employer for funding the plan. You may also use the following formula.

Formula. The contributions your employer made for you as of the end of any tax year are the result of multiplying the following four items:

1) The projected annual amount of your pension (as of the end of the tax year) to be provided at normal retirement age from employer contributions, based on your plan in effect at that time, and assuming your continued employment with that employer at your then current salary rate,
2) The value from Table I based on the normal retirement age as defined in the plan,
3) The amount from Table II for the sum of—
   a) The number of years remaining from the end of the tax year to normal retirement age, plus
   b) The lesser of the number of years of service credited through the end of the tax year or the number of years that the plan has been in existence at that time, and
4) The lesser of the number of years of service credited through the end of the tax year or the number of years that the plan has been in existence at that time.

Table I

[Value at normal retirement ages of annuity of $1 per year payable in equal monthly installments during the life of the employee.] [For tax years beginning after July 1, 1986.]

Normal retirement age	Value	Normal retirement age	Value
40	11.49	48	10.68
41	11.40	49	10.56
42	11.31	50	10.43
43	11.22	51	10.30
44	11.12	52	10.18
45	11.01	53	10.04
46	10.91	54	9.89
47	10.79	55	9.75

56	. . . . . . 9.60	69	. . . . . . 7.29
57	. . . . . . 9.44	70	. . . . . . 7.10
58	. . . . . . 9.28	71	. . . . . . 6.88
59	. . . . . . 9.13	72	. . . . . . 6.68
60	. . . . . . 8.96	73	. . . . . . 6.46
61	. . . . . . 8.79	74	. . . . . . 6.25
62	. . . . . . 8.62	75	. . . . . . 6.03
63	. . . . . . 8.44	76	. . . . . . 5.82
64	. . . . . . 8.25	77	. . . . . . 5.61
65	. . . . . . 8.08	78	. . . . . . 5.40
66	. . . . . . 7.88	79	. . . . . . 5.20
67	. . . . . . 7.70	80	. . . . . . 4.99
68	. . . . . . 7.50		

Note: If the normal form of retirement benefit under the plan is other than a straight-life annuity, the value from Table I should be divided by the appropriate figure as follows:

Annuity for 5 years certain and life thereafter	0.97
Annuity for 10 years certain and life thereafter	0.90
Annuity for 15 years certain and life thereafter	0.80
Annuity for 20 years certain and life thereafter	0.70
Life annuity with installment refund	0.80
Life annuity with cash refund	0.75

The term **cash refund** refers to a refund of accumulated employer contributions, not to a refund of employee contributions only, often referred to as **modified cash refund.**

TABLE II

[Level annual contribution which will accumulate to $1.00 at end of number of years.]
[For tax years beginning after July 1, 1986.]

Number of years	Amount	Number of years	Amount
1	$1.0000	10	$.0690
2	.4808	11	.0601
3	.3080	12	.0527
4	.2219	13	.0465
5	.1705	14	.0413
6	.1363	15	.0368
7	.1121	16	.0330
8	.0940	17	.0296
9	.0801	18	.0267

19	.0241	35	.0058
20	.0219	36	.0053
21	.0198	37	.0049
22	.0180	38	.0045
23	.0164	39	.0042
24	.0150	40	.0039
25	.0137	41	.0036
26	.0125	42	.0033
27	.0114	43	.0030
28	.0105	44	.0028
29	.0096	45	.0026
30	.0088	46	.0024
31	.0081	47	.0022
32	.0075	48	.0020
33	.0069	49	.0019
34	.0063	50	.0017

Example. Joe Blue, who was 28 at the end of 1992, has been employed by the Oak County school system since 1990. In 1990, Joe's employer contributed amounts to a tax-sheltered annuity program. Since 1987, Joe's employer has contributed to both the tax-sheltered annuity program and a statewide retirement system that provides a straight-life annuity upon retirement. Joe is covered by both plans.

For 1992, Joe wishes to figure the **amounts previously excludable** so that he can figure the exclusion allowance for that year. His employer's contributions to the statewide retirement system were not divided among the individual employees.

Joe's employer gives him the following information:
Employer contributions to tax-sheltered annuity:

1990	$2,000
1991	2,400
1992	2,800

Projected annual amount of Joe's retirement system pension (as of the end of 1992) is $12,000. The pension is to begin at age 65 from the employer's contributions, based on 1992 plan provisions and assuming that Joe works for the same employer until age 65 at his 1992 salary. Normal retirement age is 65.

Joe figures the **amounts previously excludable** as follows:

A. Projected annual amount of pension at normal
   retirement age (65) $12,000
B. Table I value at normal retirement age (65)   8.08

C. Table II amount for the sum of:
1) Number of years from end of the tax year
(1989) to normal retirement age (65 minus
28) 37
2) Plus: Lesser of years of plan existence or
years of service 3
40

Table II amount for total of 40 .... .0039
D. Lesser of years of plan existence or years of
service 3

Joe multiplies A times B times C times D.
$12,000 × 8.08 × .0039 × 3 = $1,134.43
Joe then adds the amounts contributed to the tax-sheltered annuity
($7,200) to determine the **amounts previously excludable** of $8,334.43.
Note: [See "Contributions in excess of employer limit" in 4-24.]

4-24 Limit on Employer Contributions

Limits are placed on the contributions that can be made by an employer to tax-sheltered annuity programs for each **limitation year.** Most
tax-sheltered annuity programs are **defined contribution plans.** Under
the general rule, an employer's contributions to an employee's account
under a defined contribution plan should not be more than the lesser of:

1) $30,000 (or, if greater, 1/4 of the dollar limit for defined benefit plans),
or
2) 25% of the employee's **compensation** for the year.

This limit applies instead of the exclusion allowance, discussed earlier,
if this limit is less than the exclusion allowance. [However, see 4-25.]

The dollar limit for defined benefit plans is $90,000 for years beginning
before 1988. Thereafter, it is subject to annual cost-of-living adjust-
ments. However, it will probably be some years before these adjust-
ments increase that amount to more than $120,000, in which case 1/4 of
the increased limit amount would exceed $30,000.

Limitation year. Your limitation year is the calendar year, unless you
choose to change the limitation year to another 12-month period.

Defined contribution plans. Generally, tax-sheltered annuities purchased for employees by educational organizations and tax-exempt organizations are treated as defined contribution plans. A defined contribution plan is one that provides for an individual account for each
participant and for benefits based only on the amount contributed to the
participant's account, and any income, expenses, gains, losses, and for-

feitures of other participants' accounts, which may be allocated to the participant's account.

Contributions in excess of employer limit. If in earlier years your employer made annual contributions to a program that were more than the annual maximum permitted under the preceding limit, your **exclusion allowance** is reduced by the excess.

If the limit is exceeded for a tax year beginning after January 24, 1980, then for figuring the exclusion allowance for future years, the excess is considered as if it were an amount that was excludable from your gross income in an earlier tax year. Thus, for future tax years, the exclusion allowance is reduced by this excess contribution even though it was not excludable from your gross income in the tax year when it was made.

If the limit was exceeded for a tax year beginning before January 25, 1980, the excess is used to reduce your exclusion allowance only for that year.

If you must combine a tax-sheltered annuity with a qualified plan, and, as a result, the limit is exceeded, the excess is includible in your gross income for the tax year the excess contribution was made, and reduces your exclusion allowance for any future years in which you are a participant in a tax-sheltered annuity program.

If you are a participant in both a tax-sheltered annuity program and a qualified plan, [see 4-32].

Worksheet 2 at the end of [this chapter] will help you figure the limit on employer contributions and the amount excludable from gross income.

Compensation. Generally, for the 25% limit (item (2) at the beginning of this discussion), compensation includes:

- Wages, salaries, and fees for personal services with the employer maintaining the plan, even if excludable as foreign earned income,
- Certain taxable accident and health insurance payments, and
- Moving expense payments or reimbursements for such payments that are not deductible.
- The value of nonqualified stock options granted by the employer that are includible in the employee's gross income in the year granted.

Generally, compensation does not include:

- Contributions toward a tax-sheltered annuity contract,
- Contributions toward a deferred compensation plan if, before applying the limit on employer contributions, the contributions are not taxable,
- Distributions from a deferred compensation plan,
- Proceeds from the disposition of stock acquired under a qualified stock option, and
- Certain other amounts that are excludable from an employee's in-

come, such as group term life insurance premiums that are not taxable to the employee.

More than one annuity contract. For each year you apply this limit, you must combine the contributions to tax-sheltered annuity contracts by your employer and any **related employer.** This is done without regard to whether you elect, or state an intention to elect, one of the alternative limits discussed [in 4-25]. This combining is in addition to the combining that may be required when you participate in both a tax-sheltered annuity and a qualified pension plan.

Related employer. Another employer is related to your employer if the other employer is a member of a controlled group of corporations or a group of trades or businesses (whether or not incorporated) under common control, in which your employer is a member.

4-25 Special Election for Certain Employees

If you are an employee of an educational organization, a hospital, a home health service agency, a health and welfare service agency, or a church or church-related organization, in determining the amount excludable from gross income, you may elect to have the limits on your employer's contributions figured by using one of three alternative limits. [See also 4-30.]

An **educational organization** and a **church employee** have been defined earlier. A **home health service agency** is a tax-exempt organization that has been determined by the Secretary of Health and Human Services to be a home health agency as defined in Section 1861(o) of the Social Security Act. A **church,** for this purpose, includes a church, convention or association of churches, or a tax-exempt organization controlled by or associated with a church or a convention or association of churches.

Employees of these organizations typically have a pattern of low employer contributions in the early stages of their careers and relatively high catch-up contributions later. Generally, the election to use one of the first two alternative limits listed below will permit you to exclude from gross income a larger amount of your employer's contributions than allowed under the general rule that limits the contributions to 25% of your compensation. If you elect to use the third alternative listed, you can disregard the **exclusion allowance** (discussed earlier) that would otherwise apply. The three alternative limits are as follows:

- Year of separation from service limit,
- Any year limit, and
- Overall limit.

You can make one of the three elections as explained later [in 4-31]. You cannot make more than one election and, once one is made, you cannot change it.

Aggregation rules—more than one annuity contract. [See "More than one annuity contract" in 4-24.]

4-26 Year of Separation from Service Limit

For the limitation year (defined earlier) that ends with or within the tax year you separate from the service of an educational organization, hospital, church, or other organization listed above, you can elect to substitute your exclusion allowance (defined earlier) in place of the 25% of your compensation limit on employer contributions under the general rule. The $30,000 limit on employer contributions still applies.

Figure your exclusion allowance as explained earlier. For your years of service, which end on the date of separation, do not use more than 10 years even if that is less than your actual number of years of service. Your amounts previously excludable are the amounts excludable during your years of service (limited to 10 years). All service for your employer performed within the period must be taken into account.

If your employer's annual contributions are more than the lesser of your exclusion allowance or $30,000, you must include the excess in gross income.

Example. Frank Green, who is president of a university, plans to retire on December 31, 1992, after 20 years of service. His compensation for 1992 is $50,000. During the 10-year period before the date of separation from service, Frank's employer contributed $20,000 to the tax-sheltered annuity program. The contributions were excludable from Frank's gross income. During all his years of service, his employer contributed a total of $30,000 that was excludable from Frank's gross income. He agrees to have his employer contribute the maximum amount permitted under law to be excluded from gross income. He figures the amount under the *Year of Separation from Service Limit* as follows:

Step 1—Exclusion Allowance

1) 20% 20%
2) Includible compensation . . . . $ 50,000
3) Years of service   20
4) Multiply (1) × (2) × (3) $200,000
5) Minus: Amounts previously excludable   30,000
6) Exclusion allowance $170,000

Step 2—Year of Separation from Service Limit

7) a) $30,000 . . . . $ 30,000
   b) Exclusion allowance (modified)

(i)	20%	20%
(ii)	Includible compensation	$ 50,000
(iii)	Years of service (Limited to 10 years)	10
(iv)	Multiply (i) × (ii) × (iii)	$100,000
(v)	Minus: Amounts previously excludable during 10-year period	20,000
(vi)	Exclusion allowance (modified)	$ 80,000
c)	Limit [Lesser of (a) or (b)(vi)]	$ 30,000

If Frank elects this alternative limit, his employer could contribute $30,000 toward an annuity contract during the year of separation from service without having a contribution in excess of the employer limit or Frank having to include any amount in gross income. In Step 1, Frank's exclusion allowance is $170,000; however, in Step 2, the maximum amount the employer may contribute for him is $30,000. If it were not for this election, the limit on employer contributions under the general rule would be $12,500 (24% × $50,000).

Worksheet 3 at the end of this chapter will help you figure the *Year of Separation from Service Limit* and the amount excludable from gross income.

4-27 Any Year Limit

For any limitation year (defined earlier), you can substitute for the 25% of employee's compensation limit, the **least** of the following:

1) $4,000, plus 25% of your includible compensation for the tax year in which the limitation year ends;
2) The exclusion allowance for the tax year in which the limitation year ends; or
3) $15,000.

Because of the $15,000 maximum limit, the $30,000 limit cannot apply if you elect this limit.

If your employer's annual contributions are more than the *Any Year Limit* amount, you must include the excess in your gross income. You must also reduce your exclusion allowance in future years [explained in 4-20].

Example. Bill Black is a principal with the Maple County school system. In 1992, his 17th year of service, Bill's salary is $29,000 without reduction for an amount under a salary reduction agreement. Bill's employer had contributed $34,000 to the tax-sheltered annuity program in earlier years, and all the contributions were excluded from Bill's income. Bill and his employer agree to a salary reduction of $9,000 that may be excluded from Bill's gross income. To find the maximum employer contribution allowed, Bill figured the *Any Year Limit* as follows:

Step 1—Exclusion Allowance

1) 20%	. . . .	20%
2) Includible compensation	. . . .	$20,000
3) Years of service	. . . .	17
4) Multiply (1) × (2) × (3)	. . . .	$68,000
5) Minus: Amounts previously excludable	. . . .	34,400
6) Exclusion allowance	. . . .	$33,600

Step 2—Any Year Limit

7) a) $4,000 plus 25% of includible compensation $4,000 + (25% × $20,000)	. . . .	$ 9,000
b) Exclusion allowance (from Line (6))	. . . .	$33,600
c) $15,000	. . . .	$15,000
d) Least of (a), (b), or (c)	. . . .	$ 9,000

Under this alternative limit, Bill's employer can contribute $9,000 to the annuity program and Bill can exclude that amount. In Step 1, the exclusion allowance is $33,600; in Step 2, the maximum amount the employer can contribute on Bill's behalf is $9,000. Since this is less than the amount in Step 1, $9,000 is the amount that may be excluded from gross income.

If not for this alternative limit, the maximum amount Bill's employer could contribute under the general rule is $5,000 (25% × $20,000).

Worksheet 4 at the end of this chapter will help you in figuring the *Any Year Limit* and the amount excludable from gross income.

4-28 Overall Limit

You can elect to have the limit on your employer's contributions and your exclusion allowance be equal to the lesser of $30,000 or 25% of compensation [see 4-21] for the limitation year ending in the tax year. You would disregard the computation of the exclusion allowance discussed [in 4-20].

Since the exclusion allowance and the limit are considered the same under this election, any contribution that is more than the lesser of $30,000 or 25% of compensation must be included in your gross income.

If you elect the *Overall Limit,* you must combine contributions to the tax-sheltered annuity program with your employer's contributions to a qualified plan to determine whether the limits on employer contributions have been exceeded. [See 4-32.]

Example. Mary White is employed as a nurse with Apple City General Hospital. In her 11th year of service, she agrees to have her employer contribute additional amounts to her tax-sheltered annuity program for catch-up contributions.

Her compensation for 1992 is $25,000, and she figures the limit on contributions (and the amount considered the exclusion allowance) to be $6,250 using the *Overall Limit* election as follows:

1) Maximum limit on employer contributions $30,000
2) 25% of compensation (25% × $25,000) . . . . $ 6,250
3) Limit on employer contributions and exclusion
   allowance—[lesser of (1) or (2)] . . . . $ 6,250

Worksheet 5 at the end of this chapter will help you in figuring the *Overall Limit* and the amount excludable from gross income.

4-29 Examples of Limit Elections

The following examples show how you can use the three alternative limits just discussed to maximize the amount of employer contributions to your annuity that you can exclude from income.

Example 1. Eli Green was an employee of Maple Hospital, a tax-exempt charitable organization, for the entire 1992 calendar year. Eli has includible compensation, and compensation for purposes of the limit, of $30,000 for the year. He has 4 years of service with his employer as of December 31, 1992. During Eli's prior service with Maple Hospital, his employer had contributed $12,000 on Eli's behalf for tax-sheltered annuity contracts, and Eli excluded the amount from gross income in earlier years. Thus, for 1992, Eli's exclusion allowance is $12,000, figured as follows:

1) 20% 20%
2) Includible compensation $30,000
3) Years of service 4
4) (1) × (2) × (3) $24,000
5) Minus: Amounts previously excludable 12,000
6) Exclusion allowance $12,000

The limit under the general rule for 1989 is the lesser of $30,000 or $7,500 (25% × $30,000).

Without the special elections provided for certain employees, $7,500 would be the maximum contribution Maple Hospital could make for annuity contracts on behalf of Eli for 1992 without increasing Eli's gross income for that year.

Since Eli is an employee of a hospital, he can elect one of the special limits. Eli can elect either the *Any Year Limit* or the *Overall Limit.* He cannot elect the *Year of Separation from Service Limit* since he does not separate from service in 1989.

If Eli elects the *Any Year Limit,* Maple Hospital could contribute

$11,500 on his behalf for 1989 for tax-sheltered annuity contracts, fig-
ured as follows:

1) $4,000, plus 25% of includible compensation $11,500
2) Exclusion allowance $12,000
3) $15,000 . . . . $15,000
4) Maximum contribution [least of (1), (2) or (3)] $11,500

If Eli elects the *Overall Limit,* Maple Hospital could contribute only a
maximum of $7,500 without increasing Eli's gross income for the year
figured as follows:

1) $30,000 . . . . $30,000
2) 25% of compensation . . . . $ 7,500
3) Maximum contributions [lesser of (1) or (2)] . . . . $ 7,500

Example 2. Assume the same facts as in Example 1, except that
Maple Hospital contributed $18,000 on Eli's behalf in earlier years for
tax-sheltered annuity contracts. The contributions were excludable from
his gross income. Thus, for 1992, Eli's exclusion allowance is $6,000
figured as follows:

1) 20% 20%
2) Includible compensation $30,000
3) Years of service 4
4) (1) × (2) × (3) $24,000
5) Minus: Amounts previously excludable 18,000
6) Exclusion allowance . . . . $ 6,000

The limit under the general rule for 1992 is the lesser of $30,000 or
$7,500 (25% × $30,000).

Without the special elections, $6,000 would be the maximum amount
Maple Hospital could contribute on Eli's behalf for tax-sheltered annuity
contracts without increasing Eli's gross income. However, if Eli elects the
Overall Limit, Maple Hospital could contribute up to $7,500 without in-
creasing Eli's gross income for 1992.

Example 3. Bob White, a teacher, is employed by Elm School, a tax-
exempt educational organization. Bob has includible compensation of
$24,000 for 1992.

Bob has 20 years of service as of May 30, 1989, the date he separates
from the service of Elm School. During Bob's service with Elm School
before tax year 1992, Elm School had contributed $68,000 toward the
purchase of tax-sheltered annuity contracts on behalf of Bob. The
amount was excludable from his gross income for the prior years. Of this
amount, $38,000 was contributed and excluded during the 10-year pe-
riod ending on May 30, 1992. For the tax year 1992, Bob's exclusion
allowance is $28,000 determined as follows:

1) 20% 20%
2) Includible compensation $24,000

3) Years of service 20
4) (1) × (2) × (3) $96,000
5) Minus: Amounts previously excludable 68,000
6) Exclusion allowance $28,000

Without the special elections, $6,000 [the lesser of the exclusion allowance ($28,000) or 25% of compensation ($6,000)] would be the maximum excludable contribution Elm School could make for tax-sheltered annuity contracts on Bob's behalf for 1992.

However, because Bob was an employee of an educational organization and has separated from service, he can elect any of the three special limits.

If Bob elects the *Year of Separation from Service Limit* for 1989, Elm School could contribute up to $10,000 for that year without increasing Bob's gross income, figured as follows:

1) 20% 20%
2) Includible compensation $24,000
3) Years of service (not to exceed 10) 10
4) (1) × (2) × (3) $48,000
5) Minus: Amounts previously excludable 38,000
6) Maximum contribution under *Year of Separation from Service Limit* $10,000

If Bob elects the *Any Year Limit,* for 1992, Elm School could contribute $10,000, which is the least of the following:

1) $4,000, plus 25% of includible compensation $10,000
2) Exclusion allowance $28,000
3) $15,000 .... $15,000

If Bob elects the *Overall Limit,* for 1992, Elm School could contribute $6,000, which is the lesser of the following:

1) $30,000 .... $30,000
2) 25% of compensation .... $ 6,000

4-30 Special Election for Church Employees

If you are a church employee and the *minimum exclusion allowance* [described in 4-20] applies, your employer can make contributions for the year up to the minimum exclusion allowance even though the contributions would otherwise be more than the limit on employer contributions to a defined contribution plan.

In addition to the "any year" or "overall" limit, you can make a special election that allows your employer to contribute up to $10,000 for the year, even if this is more than 25% of your compensation for the year. The total contributions over your lifetime under this election cannot be more than $40,000. In this situation, the exclusion allowance limit still applies, unless you also elect the *Overall Limit,* described earlier.

You cannot make this special election for a tax year in which you use the *Year of Separation from Service Limit,* described earlier.

4-31 Making the Election

You make the election for one of the alternative limits by figuring your tax using that limit. However, the election is treated as made only when **needed** to support the exclusion reflected on the return.

Election is irrevocable. If you elect to use an alternative limit, you cannot change the election. If you elect the *Any Year Limit* or the *Overall Limit,* you can use it for your later tax years.

If you elect one of the alternative limits, you cannot elect to have any of the others apply for any future year for any tax-sheltered annuity contract purchased for you by any employer.

If you elect the *Year of Separation from Service Limit,* you cannot elect any alternative limit in any later year for any tax-sheltered annuity. You can use this limit only once.

Failure to pay estimated income tax. If you amend an earlier year's return to elect an alternative limit, and that limit increases your tax for that year, the difference in tax due to the use of the alternative limit is not treated as an underpayment for the penalty for failure to pay estimated income tax.

4-32 Limit for Contributions to More Than One Program

Special rules apply in determining the limit on employer contributions for you to a tax-sheltered annuity program if you also are covered by a qualified plan.

Generally, contributions to tax-sheltered annuity programs must be combined with contributions to qualified plans of all corporations, partnerships, and sole proprietorships in which you have **more than 50% control** to determine whether the limits have been exceeded.

If you elect the *Overall Limit,* discussed earlier, you must combine contributions whether or not you have this control.

Example 1. You have an HR-10 plan (sometimes called a Keogh plan) for a sole proprietorship business, and you are also a participant in a tax-sheltered annuity program. You must combine the two plans since you have control over both plans.

Example 2. You are employed by an educational organization that provides a tax-sheltered annuity program and you are also a shareholder owning more than 50% of a professional corporation. You must combine any qualified plan of the professional corporation with the tax-sheltered annuity.

If you combine the tax-sheltered annuity contract and a qualified plan, the limit on employer contributions may be exceeded. The excess is includible in your gross income for the tax year that excess contribution was made, and it reduces your exclusion allowance for any future years.

4-33 Voluntary Employee Contributions

For tax years beginning after 1986, you cannot deduct voluntary employee contributions you make to your tax-sheltered annuity.

However, there may be amounts in your tax-sheltered annuity account that are attributable to deductible voluntary employee contributions you made in earlier years. If these amounts are distributed to you, you must include them in gross income unless you roll them over into an IRA or into another tax-sheltered annuity.

4-34 Tax on Excess Contributions to a Custodial Account

You are liable for a 6% excise tax on excess contributions made by your employer for you to purchase mutual fund shares through a custodial account. The tax **does not apply** to excess contributions made to pay premiums on an annuity contract.

You cannot deduct the tax. It is due each year until the year the excess contribution is returned to your employer or is corrected by your employer. The correction is made by contributing less than the amount that properly is excludable or is allowed to be contributed in future years. Simply, if there is an excess contribution in 1992 and no corrective action is taken for that year, you are liable for the tax for 1992 and later years (in addition to any tax due because of additional excess contributions in a later year).

How to figure tax. You figure the excess contributions tax for the current year as follows:

1) Total amount contributed for current year, minus rollovers . . . . _____
2) Lesser of exclusion allowance or annual limit on employer's contribution . . . . _____
3) Current year excess contributions (line 1 minus line 2, but not less than zero) . . . . _____
4) Preceding year excess contributions . . . . _____
5) Contribution credit (if line 2 is more than line 1, enter the excess, otherwise enter zero) . . . . _____
6) Total of all prior years' distributions out of the account included in your gross income (not including amounts received as an annuity) . . . . _____

7) Adjusted preceding year's excess contributions
(line 4 minus the total of lines 5 and 6) . . . . _____
8) Taxable excess contributions (line 3 plus line 7) . . . _____
9) Excess contributions tax—Enter the lesser of
6% of line 8 or 6% of the value of your account
as of the last day of the year . . . . _____

Reporting requirement. You must file Form 5330, *Return of Excise Taxes Related to Employee Benefit Plans,* if there has been an excess contribution to a **custodial account** and that excess has not been corrected in any year.

When to file. You must file Form 5330 on or before the last day of the 7th month after the end of your tax year. If you are a calendar year taxpayer, the due date is July 31 following the close of the calendar year. You may be granted an extension (not to exceed 6 months) by filing Form 5558, *Application for Extension of Time to File Certain Employee Plan Returns,* early enough to give IRS time to consider and act on it before the due date of Form 5330.

Where to file. You should file Form 5330 with the Internal Revenue Service Center where you normally file your income tax return.

4-35 What If I Have More Than One Contract?

If, during any of your tax years, the tax-sheltered treatment applies to two or more annuity contracts purchased for you by your employer, you must consider them as one contract.

4-36 Can I Deduct the Cost of Insurance Protection?

If your annuity contract provides you with incidental life insurance protection, you must include in your income each year the one-year term cost of the current protection. This cost is included with salaries and wages on Form W-2.

Your current life insurance protection under an ordinary retirement income life insurance policy is the amount payable upon your death minus the cash value of the contract at the end of the year.

For example, if your new contract provides that your beneficiary will receive $10,000 if you should die anytime before retirement, and if your cash value in the contract at the end of the first year is zero, your current life insurance protection for the first year is $10,000 ($10,000 minus 0).

The one-year term cost of the protection can be figured by using the [table in 4-37]. The premium rate is determined according to your age on your birthday nearest the beginning of the policy year.

If the current published premium rates per $1,000 of insurance protection charged by an insurer for individual 1-year term life insurance available to all standard risks are lower than those in the [table in 4-37], you can use the lower rates for figuring the cost of insurance in connection with individual policies issued by the same insurer.

4-37 Uniform One-Year Term Premiums for $1,000 Life Insurance Protection

(Based on Table 38, U.S. Life Table and Actuarial Table (U.S. Government Printing Office, Washington, D.C.—1946), and 2½% interest.)

Age	Premium	Age	Premium
15	$ 1.27	46	$ 6.78
16	1.38	47	7.32
17	1.48	48	7.89
18	1.52	49	8.53
19	1.56	50	9.22
20	1.61	51	9.97
21	1.67	52	10.79
22	1.73	53	11.69
23	1.79	54	12.67
24	1.86	55	13.74
25	1.93	56	14.91
26	2.02	57	16.18
27	2.11	58	17.56
28	2.20	59	19.08
29	2.31	60	20.73
30	2.43	61	22.53
31	2.57	62	24.50
32	2.70	63	26.63
33	2.86	64	28.98
34	3.02	65	31.51
35	3.21	66	34.28
36	3.41	67	37.31
37	3.63	68	40.59
38	3.87	69	44.17
39	4.14	70	48.06
40	4.42	71	52.29
41	4.73	72	56.89
42	5.07	73	61.89
43	5.44	74	67.33
44	5.85	75	73.25
45	6.30	76	79.23

77	86.57	80	111.04
78	94.09	81	120.57
79	102.23		

Example. Lynn Green and her employer enter into a tax-sheltered annuity purchase agreement that will provide her with a $500 a month annuity upon retirement at age 65. The agreement also provides that if she should die before retirement, her beneficiary will receive the greater of $20,000 or the cash surrender value in the retirement income life insurance contract.

Since the cash surrender value at the end of the first year is zero, her net insurance is $20,000 ($20,000 minus 0). Her age on the nearest birthday is 44. Using the preceding table she determines that her one-year term cost for $1,000 of insurance is $5.85. Thus, she must include in gross income $117 ($5.85 × 20) as the premium for her net insurance coverage of $20,000.

Lynn's cash value in the contract at the end of the 2nd year is $1,000. Thus, her life insurance coverage is $19,000 ($20,000 minus $1,000). The one-year term cost rate per $1,000 for age 45 in the 2nd year is $6.30, so the amount to be included in income is $119.70 ($6.30 × 19).

4-38 Federal Insurance Contributions Act (FICA)

The following two paragraphs do not apply to most clergypersons. I'm including them for those to whom they might apply because of their former employment.

The contributions toward the tax-sheltered annuity under a salary reduction agreement are considered wages for the FICA (social security) tax. The employer must take into account the entire amount of these contributions for FICA tax purposes, whether they are wholly or partially excludable for income tax purposes. Moreover, these wages may be credited to the employee's social security account for benefit purposes. If the employer makes a contribution to purchase an annuity, which is not under a salary reduction agreement, that amount is not considered wages for social security tax purposes.

A church or church-related organization may have chosen, for religious reasons, to have its employees be exempt from the FICA tax on all their earnings from that employment, including any tax-sheltered annuity contributions. However, if this choice is in effect, the wages from church employment are subject to social security self-employment tax (SECA) discussed next.

4-39 Self-Employment Contributions Act (SECA)

Generally, a person who renders services to a church as a minister is treated as a self-employed individual for the social security self-employment tax, even though the minister may be an employee for other purposes. For social security tax purposes (assuming the minister does not elect to be exempt from social security), some items of income excludable from the minister's gross income are not taken into account in determining the net earnings from self employment. Contributions for the minister toward a tax-sheltered annuity contract are not taken into account as net earnings from self employment to the extent the contributions are not more than the exclusion allowance or employer contribution limit.

If you are an employee of a church or church-related organization and you choose exemption from FICA tax, as mentioned above, you must include wages from that employment in net earnings from self employment. However, do not include tax-sheltered annuity contributions in figuring self-employment tax. The self-employment tax on wages from church employment is figured under special rules. See Schedule SE (Form 1040) and its instructions.

4-40 Income Tax Withholding by Employer

Your employer's contributions to your tax-sheltered annuity contract, to the extent excludable from your gross income, are not subject to income tax withholding. Any part of the premium used to purchase an annuity that is more than your exclusion allowance, or is used to purchase current life insurance protection, is subject to withholding.

4-41 Tax Liability of Employee for Employer Contributions

If your employer makes contributions to a tax-sheltered annuity contract for your benefit, the contributions are taxable to the extent they are more than the amount excludable from gross income [see "Exclusion from gross income" in 4-19], but only to the extent your rights under the contract are substantially vested. The amount excludable is the lesser of your exclusion allowance or the limit on employer contributions.

Your rights are **substantially vested** when they are transferable or are not subject to a substantial risk of forfeiture.

Your rights are **transferable** if you can transfer any interest in any property to any person other than the transferor, but only if your rights in the property are not subject to a substantial risk of forfeiture.

Property is transferable if you can sell, assign, or pledge your interest in it to anyone other than the transferor and if you do not have to give up the property or its value if the substantial risk of forfeiture materializes. Property is not transferable merely because you may designate a beneficiary to receive it in the event of your death.

A substantial risk of forfeiture exists where your rights in property that are transferred are directly or indirectly conditioned upon future performance (or refraining from performance) of substantial services by any person. A substantial risk of forfeiture also exists when rights in property depend on the occurrence of a condition related to the purpose of the transfer and the possibility of forfeiture is substantial if the condition is not satisfied.

Taxability of rights that change from nonvested to vested. The amount includible in your gross income when your rights change from nonvested to substantially vested is the value of the contract on that date of change

- is from contributions made by your employer before the date of change, and
- is more than the amount excludable from gross income.

The value of an annuity contract on the date your rights become substantially vested means the cash surrender value of the contract on that date.

Partial vesting. If, during your tax year, only part of the beneficial interest in an annuity contract becomes substantially vested, only a portion of the annuity contract value on the date of the change is includible in your gross income for the tax year.

The amount includible in your gross income is figured as follows:

1) Find the amount includible in gross income (regardless of the exclusion allowance or limit on employer contributions) if the **entire** beneficial interest in the annuity contract had changed to a substantially vested interest during the tax year.
2) Multiply the amount in (1) by the percent of your beneficial interest that became substantially vested during the tax year.

The resulting amount in (2) is taxable to the extent it is more than the amount excludable from gross income.

4-42 Gift Tax

"If, by choosing or not choosing an election or option, you provide an annuity for your beneficiary at or after your death, you may have made a taxable gift for gift tax purposes equal to the value of the annuity." Check with your income tax adviser for specific advice pertaining to your situation.

4-43 Joint and Survivor Annuity

If the gift is an interest in a joint and survivor annuity where **only** you and your spouse have the right to receive payments, the gift will generally be treated as qualifying for the unlimited marital deduction.

4-44 More Information

For information on the gift tax see Publication 448, *Federal Estate and Gift Taxes.*

4-45 Distributions and Rollovers

In most cases the payments you receive, or that are made available to you, under your tax-sheltered annuity contract are taxable in full as ordinary income. In general, the same tax rules apply to distributions from tax-sheltered annuities that apply to distributions from other retirement plans. These rules are explained in Publication 575, *Pension and Annuity Income (Including Simplified General Rule).*

4-46 Exchange of Annuity Contracts

If, under a binding agreement, you receive all the proceeds of an individual annuity [IRA] contract and immediately reinvest them in another annuity contract for you with a different insurer, you will not have to include the proceeds in gross income.

4-47 Tax-Free Rollovers

Special rules apply to certain distributions from tax-sheltered annuities that you roll over into another plan.

If you receive a distribution from a tax-sheltered annuity and you then roll over any portion of the distribution (transfer it) into another plan, you may not have to include the transferred portion in your income for the year.

The requirements for a tax-free rollover are:

- The rollover must be to another tax-sheltered annuity or to an individual retirement arrangement (IRA).
- The rollover must be made within 60 days of receipt of the distribution. However, [see 4-50] for extension of the 60-day period.
- The rollover must not be more than the amount you receive in the distribution, reduced by your contributions to the tax-sheltered annuity, other than certain voluntary employee contributions, if any. [See Voluntary deductible contributions, later.] If you receive noncash property in the distribution, figure the amount you receive at the property's fair market value. Generally, the property can be sold and the rollover made from the proceeds of the sale.

4-48 Qualifying Distributions

Only certain distributions qualify for this treatment. The distribution must be from a tax-sheltered annuity maintained by an employer for an employee, and it must be payable:

1) Because of the employee's death,
2) After the employee reaches age 59½ (in the case of total distributions),
3) Because of the employee leaving his or her job,
4) After the employee has become totally and permanently disabled, or
5) To an alternate payee under a **qualified domestic relations order** (in the case of a total distribution of the balance to the credit of the alternate payee within 1 tax year of the payee), if the alternate payee transfers the amount received to an IRA.

Total distributions. A total distribution that you receive from your tax-sheltered annuity qualifies for tax-free rollover treatment if both of the following apply:

- It is made under one of the above 5 conditions, and
- It consists of one or more payments within a single tax year (your tax year, not the plan's year), equal to the entire balance in your account.

For this purpose, your entire balance does not include accumulated deductible voluntary contributions and the net earnings on them. Distributions of accumulated deductible voluntary contributions can be rolled over separately.

Partial distributions. A partial distribution of at least 50% of your balance may also qualify for tax-free rollover treatment, if you so elect. For this purpose, your balance does not include accumulated deductible voluntary contributions. To qualify for rollover treatment, a partial distribution must be made because of your death, separation from service, or total and permanent disability. This rule for partial distributions does not apply to distributions made after March 30, 1988, if the distribution is one of a series of distributions. Partial distributions can be rolled over only to individual retirement arrangements (IRAs).

Required distributions. If a distribution is required to be made because you have reached age 70½, it is **not** eligible for tax-free rollover treatment.

Excess employer contributions. The portion of a distribution from a tax-sheltered annuity transferred to an individual retirement account that is from employer contributions that were not excluded from income because they were more than the exclusion allowance is not a rollover contribution.

Thus, the portion of the distribution that was previously included in the employee's income may not be rolled over into an IRA. The part of the amount transferred that is not a rollover contribution does not affect the rollover treatment of the eligible portion of the transferred amounts.

4-49 Spouses of Deceased Employees

If you are the spouse of a deceased employee, you can roll over the qualifying distribution attributable to the employee. You can make the rollover only to an IRA, not to another tax-sheltered annuity or qualified plan.

4-50 Frozen Deposits

The 60-day period for completing a rollover is extended for any time that the amount distributed is a **frozen deposit** in a financial institution. The 60-day period cannot end earlier than 10 days after the deposit ceases to be a frozen deposit.

A **frozen deposit** is any deposit that on any day during the 60-day period cannot be withdrawn because:

- The financial institution is bankrupt or insolvent, or
- The state where the institution is located has placed limits on withdrawals because one or more banks in the state are (or are about to be) bankrupt or insolvent.

Worksheet 1—Computation of Exclusion Allowance

Step 1—Exclusion Allowance
1) 20%   20%
2) Includible compensation for most recent period of service $ _____
3) Years of service   _____
4) (1) × (2) × (3) $ _____
5) Minus: Amounts previously excludable (including prior year excess contributions)   _____
6) Exclusion allowance $ _____

Step 2—Amount Includible in Gross Income
7) Current year employer contributions (excluding term cost of life insurance)¹ $ _____
8) Minus: Exclusion allowance (Line 6)   _____
9) Amount includible in gross income $ _____

Note
¹ Term cost of life insurance is includible in gross income.

Worksheet 2—Limit on Employer Contributions

Step 1—Limit on Employer Contributions
1) Maximum ($30,000) or, if greater, ½ of the dollar limit for defined benefit plans [See *Limit on Employer Contributions.*] $ _____
2) 25% of compensation $ _____
3) Limit on employer contributions [lesser of (1) or (2)] $ _____

Step 2—Contributions in Excess of Employer Limit
4) Current year contribution by employer (excluding term cost of life insurance)¹ $ _____
5) Minus: Limit on employer contributions (Line 3)   _____
6) Excess (if any) $ _____

Note
¹ Term cost of life insurance is includible in gross income.

Step 3—Amount Excludable from Gross Income
7) a) Employer contribution (Line 4) $ _____
   b) Limit on employer contributions (Line 3) $ _____
   c) Exclusion allowance (Worksheet 1, line 6) $ _____
8) Amount excludable from gross income [least of (a), (b), or (c)] $ _____

Step 4—Amount Includible in Gross Income
9) Employer contribution (Line 4) $ _____
10) Minus: Amount excludable (Line 8)   _____
11) Amount includible in gross income $ _____

Worksheet 3—Year of Separation from Service Limit Election ⁱ

Step 1—Limit on Employer Contributions
1) Maximum [See *Limit on Employer Contributions.*] $ 30,000
2) Exclusion allowance (modified)
   a) 20%   20%
   b) Includible compensation $ _____
   c) Years of service (limited to 10 years)   _____
   d) (a) × (b) × (c) $ _____
   e) Minus: Amounts previously excludable during 10 years (including prior year excess contributions)   _____
   f) Exclusion allowance (modified) $ _____
3) Limit on employer contributions [lesser of (1) or (2)(f)] $ _____

Step 2—Contributions in Excess of Employer Limit
4) Current year contribution by employer (excluding term cost of life insurance) ² $ _____
5) Minus: Limit on employer contributions (Line 3)   _____
6) Excess (if any) $ _____

Step 3—Amount Excludable from Gross Income
7) a) Employer contribution (Line 4) $ _____
   b) Limit on employer contributions (Line 3) $ _____
   c) Exclusion allowance (Worksheet 1, line 6) $ _____
8) Amount excludable from gross income [least of (a), (b) or (c)] $ _____

Step 4—Amount Includible in Gross Income
9) Employer contribution $ _____
10) Minus: Amount excludable (Line 8)   _____
11) Amount includible in gross income $ _____

Notes

ⁱ Election applies only to employees of certain organizations. See *Special Election for Certain Employees.*

² Term cost of life insurance is includible in gross income.

Worksheet 4—Any Year Limit Election ·

Step 1—Limit on Employer Contributions

1) $4,000 plus 25% of includible compensation $ ____

2) Exclusion allowance

  a) 20%   20%

  b) Includible compensation $ ____

  c) Years of service   ____

  d) (a) × (b) × (c) $ ____

  e) Minus: Amounts previously excludable (including prior year excess contributions)   ____

  f) Exclusion allowance $ ____

3) Maximum $ 15,000

4) Limit on employer contributions [least of (1), (2)(f), or (3)] $ ____

Step 2—Contributions in Excess of Employer Limit

5) Current year contribution by employer (excluding term cost of life insurance) ² $ ____

6) Minus: Limit on employer contributions (Line 4)   ____

7) Excess (if any) $ ____

Step 3—Amount Excludable from Gross Income

8) a) Employer contribution (Line 5) $ ____

  b) Limit on employer contributions (Line 4) $ ____

  c) Exclusion allowance (Worksheet 1, line 6) $ ____

9) Amount excludable from gross income [least of (a), (b), or (c)] $ ____

Step 4—Amount Includible in Gross Income

10) Employer contribution (Line 5) $ ____

11) Minus: Amount excludable (Line 9)   ____

12) Amount includible in gross income $ ____

Notes

· Election applies only to employees of certain organizations. See *Special Election for Certain Employees.*

² Term cost of life insurance is includible in gross income.

Worksheet 5—Overall Limit Election · · ·

Step 1—Limit on Employer Contributions

1) Maximum [See *Limit on Employer Contributions*] $ 30,000

2) 25% × includible compensation $ ____

3) Limit on employer contributions [lesser of (1) or (2)] $ ____

Step 2—Contributions in Excess of Employer Limitation

4) Current year contribution by employer (excluding term cost of life insurance)³ $ ____

5) Minus: Limit on employer contributions (Line 3) $ ____

6) Excess (if any) $ ____

Step 3—Amount Excludable from Gross Income

7) a) Employer contribution (Line 4) $ ____

  b) Limit on employer contributions (Line 3) $ ____

8) Amount excludable from gross income [lesser of (a) or (b)] $ ____

Step 4—Amount Includible in Gross Income

9) Employer contribution (Line 4) $ ____

10) Minus: Amount excludable (Line 8)   ____

11) Amount includible in gross income $ ____

Notes

¹ Election applies only to employees of certain organizations. See *Special Election for Certain Employees.*

² Limit on employer contributions is considered equal to the exclusion allowance.

³ Term cost of life insurance is includible in gross income.

Worksheet 6—Limit on Elective Deferrals

Step 1—Total Elective Deferrals

1) Contributions to tax-sheltered annuities $ ____

2) Contributions to cash or deferred arrangements (section 401(k) plans) or section 501(c)(18) plans   ____

3) Elective contributions to salary reduction simplified employee pension (SEP) plans   ____

4) Total deferrals for year (add lines (1), (2), and (3)) $ ____

Step 2—Increase in Limit for Long Service

Note: Skip this step if you do not have at least 15 years service with a qualifying organization (see *Special Election for Certain Employees*, earlier).

5) Number of years service with the qualifying organization   —

6) Multiply $5,000 by the number of years in (5) $ ____

7) Total elective deferrals for prior years made for you by the qualifying organization   ____

8) Subtract line (7) from line (6) $ ____

9) Enter all increases in the limit for long service (as figured in this Step 2) for prior years $ ____

10) Subtract line (9) from $15,000 $ ____

11) Enter the smaller of line (8) or line (10), but not more than $3,000 $ ____

Step 3—Limit on Elective Deferrals

12) Enter $9,500 plus the amount from line (11) $ ____

13) Basic allowable amount (enter $7,627 for 1989)   ____

14) Subtract line (13) from line (12) $ ____

15) Enter the smaller of line (1) or line (14)   ____

16) Add lines (13) and (15). This is your limit on elective deferrals for the year $ ____

17) Excess elective deferrals—Subtract line (16) from line (4). Do not enter less than zero. Include this amount in your income for the year the excess deferrals were made, unless you withdraw it by April 15 of the following year. $ ____

CHAPTER 5

The Individual Retirement Arrangement (IRA)

5-1 How the Individual Retirement Arrangement (IRA) Works

The Individual Retirement Arrangement has been available for several years to certain categories of persons. At first glance, the IRA seems to be a simple plan. Insofar as depositing money into the IRA, it is comparatively simple. Getting the money out, however, has many pitfalls, all discussed in great detail here.

The basic idea of the IRA is to put money aside for retirement, deduct it from income tax, let it grow in a tax-sheltered account, then draw it out at retirement when you should be in a lower tax bracket. It is fully taxable to you when you withdraw the funds at retirement. If you withdraw your funds prior to age 59½, with certain exceptions discussed later, you must pay income tax plus a 10 percent penalty.

I urge you to get advice from a competent tax counselor and/or an annuity specialist at the time you purchase an IRA, roll over funds from a pension plan into an IRA, or roll over funds from one IRA to another IRA. There are many specific rules to keep in mind —far too many and too complicated for the layperson to remember over a long period of time. You should have a well-thought-out plan in mind when you begin to make deposits into your various retirement vehicles. Take the time to make periodic reviews. Prevention is always better than cure.

I will list the primary points of interest and concern with special emphasis on how they affect clergypersons. The IRS instructions concerning the IRA vary little from year to year. I will include detailed instructions and examples, quoting from the 1991 edition of IRS Publication 590, *Individual Retirement Arrangements.* I will add comments aimed at simplifying and summarizing along the way.

5-2 Who Can Set Up an IRA?

Anyone under age 70½ who has taxable compensation, including salaries, commissions, wages, bonuses, separate maintenance accounts, taxable alimony, tips, or fees, can buy an IRA. In the case of married couples with individual incomes, each spouse is eligible to buy an IRA.

No matter how many other retirement plans you may participate in, you can buy an IRA. But if you or your spouse is participating in a retirement plan offered by your employer, "you may not be able to deduct all of your contributions." In short, many persons under age 70½, who have earned income, may be eligible to buy an IRA. (Limitations are explained in 5-8 and 5-9.)

5-3 What About an IRA for Your Spouse?

A spousal IRA of up to $250 is available for nonworking spouses. For eligible amounts, see Appendix A.

The joint ownership of one IRA by two spouses is not allowed. Each IRA contract must be issued separately. Neither can you roll the funds from one spouse's IRA into the other. Rollovers from one financial institution to another are possible (see 5-21). Of course, each spouse can be named as beneficiary for the other's IRA.

5-4 What Are the Eligibility Requirements for a Spousal IRA?

To contribute to a spousal IRA:

- You must be married at the end of the tax year,
- Your spouse must be under age 70½ at the end of the tax year,
- You must file a joint return for the tax year,
- You must have taxable compensation for the year, and
- Your spouse must either have no compensation, or choose to be treated as having no compensation for the tax year.

5-5 What Is the Definition of Compensation?

When you render personal service of any kind and receive income in the form of salary, wages, bonuses, commissions, or fees, such income is defined as *compensation.* Generally, net *earned* income from self-employment services rendered is considered to be compensation. "Compensation also includes earnings that are not subject to self-employment (Self-Employment Contributions Act) tax because of your religious beliefs." See IRS Publication 533, *Self-Employment Tax,* for more information. Losses from self-employment cannot be deducted in determining your net compensation.

Alimony and separate maintenance. All such funds are considered to be compensation.

5-6 What Income Is Not Considered to Be Compensation?

The term *compensation* does *not* include unearned or deferred income as a general rule. That would include pension and annuity income, deferred income payments delayed for one year or more, housing costs, money received when overseas, dividends, interest income, rental income, and any other income that has been excluded.

For most purposes, money has to be earned to be counted as compensation.

5-7 How to Set Up an IRA

Individual Retirement Account

An individual retirement account is a trust or custodial account set up in the United States for your exclusive benefit or for the benefit of your beneficiaries. The account is created by a written document. The document must show that the account meets all of the following requirements:

1) Any bank, savings and loan institution, or individual approved by the IRS can be the trustee of an IRA.
2) Not more than $2,000 of new money per person can be accepted by the trustee. But rollovers and simplified employee pension contributions by employers can exceed that amount.
3) All contributions, except rollover funds, must be in cash. While most rollovers are in cash, other property can be rolled over as well.
4) Your account is yours exclusively and must be available to you at any time.
5) You cannot buy a life insurance policy using funds from your IRA.

6) You cannot combine the assets in your account with other property unless you have a common trust or investment fund.
7) Payments to you from your account must be started by April 1 of the year following the year in which you reach age 70½.

Individual Retirement Annuity

IRAs can be purchased from a life insurance company. You must be listed as the owner. The funds must be exclusively available either to you or to your beneficiaries in the event of your death.

An annuity contract must meet the following requirements:

1) Your account must be nonforfeitable.
2) Your account cannot be transferred to another person.
3) The maximum you can contribute in any one year is $2,000. If you receive a premium refund, you must reinvest it in an IRA prior to the end of the year in which you received the refund.
4) Distributions from the account "must begin by April 1 of the year following the year in which you reach age 70½."
5) Contracts issued after November 6, 1978, "must have flexible premiums so that if your compensation changes, your payment may also change."

Simplified Employee Pension (SEP)

I will not go into detail here because, for the most part, employees of religious organizations have a more advantageous alternative method of producing retirement income: the tax-sheltered annuity (explained in detail in chapter 4).

Briefly, employers can use the SEP to provide all eligible employees a retirement plan. However, it *must* include all employees, and the employer who deposits money into the employees' accounts must use the same formula for each. In most cases, churches do not use the SEP; it is not nearly as favorable as the TSA and certainly not as simple despite its name.

Employer and Employee Association Trust Accounts

Your employer, labor union, or other employee association can set up a trust to provide individual retirement accounts for its employees or members. The rules for individual retirement accounts apply to these employer or union-established IRAs.

Obviously, there is little need for labor unions for pastors. There is also no real advantage for pastors to be involved in a trust inasmuch as each individual pastor can purchase an IRA.

5-8 How Much Can I Contribute to an IRA and Still Deduct It?

First, you must choose a life insurance company, a bank, a savings and loan institution, or some other qualified sponsor as trustee. There are advantages in choosing banks, life insurance companies, and savings and loan institutions. You can always choose a local bank or savings and loan and deal personally with people you know. But if you move away from the area and you choose to continue making yearly deposits with that bank or savings and loan, you will have to use the mail and telephones. A life insurance company usually has local offices throughout the country for your convenience. In addition, life insurance companies usually pay higher interest rates than banks or savings and loans. Most life companies do not charge fees; financial institutions usually do.

Once you have chosen a sponsor, you may deposit cash or money orders into your account. Property can be contributed only in the form of rollovers: "You may be able to transfer or roll over certain property from one account to another."

To qualify to deposit money into an IRA, you must be under age 70½ and have earned income. If you start your IRA one year, make a deposit into it, then have no income the following year, you cannot deposit anything into the IRA the following year "unless you receive alimony." Even if you don't work thereafter, your funds already deposited in your IRA may remain there until you reach age 70½. Any year after that in which you earn income, you can deposit up to $2,000 of those earnings, or $2,250 if you earn that much and have a nonworking spouse.

Most pastors will fall into the category that allows up to a $2,000 deduction or a $2,250 deduction if married to a nonworking spouse. A working spouse will also be allowed up to $2,000 if that amount is earned.

5-9 What Are the Limits I Can Contribute to an IRA?

Any amount you earn under $2,001 is eligible to be deposited into your IRA. Additional limited amounts are available to be deposited in behalf of your nonworking spouse. (Check with your local IRS office for specific amounts under $2,000.)

Example 1. John Doe earns $20,000. His spouse, Jane, does not work outside the home. John may deposit a maximum of $2,000 into his IRA; Jane, a maximum of $250.

Example 2. Jane Doe is a student working part time. She earns $2,000. She can deposit the full $2,000 into her IRA.

Example 3. Both John and Jane Doe work full time, earning $20,000 each. Each has an IRA, and each can deposit $2,000.

Example 4. John Doe earns $20,000; Jane earns $1,000. John can deposit $2,000 into his IRA; Jane can deposit $1,000.

Example 5. Jane Doe earns $20,000; John earns $100. Jane can deposit $2,000 into her IRA; John can deposit $250 into a spousal IRA, which would be more advantageous to him than having his own IRA, which would be limited to his earned income of $100.

If John Doe is 70½ years old or more, he cannot contribute to his IRA. However, if Jane Doe is under 59½, she can continue to make a deposit into a spousal IRA until the year she becomes 70½.

You can make steady deposits each year, subject to your eligibility, or you can skip any year or years you wish in your individual account or a spousal account.

If you did not deposit the total amount for which you were eligible during any year, you cannot make up any difference in future years. If you have more than one IRA, your combined contributions cannot exceed the total allowable yearly limits. Of course, rollovers would be in addition to that.

Filing status has no effect on the amount of the permitted contribution to an IRA. However, if you or your spouse is covered by a retirement plan at work, your **deduction** may be reduced or eliminated, depending on your filing status and income.

Example. Sam and Helen are married. They both work and each has an IRA. Sam earned $1,800 and Helen earned $28,000 in 1992. Sam can contribute to his IRA up to $1,800 for the year. Helen can contribute up to $2,000 to her IRA. Whether they file a joint return or separate returns, the amount they can contribute is the same.

IRA contributions under community property laws. Even in community property states, any deposits into your IRA must be based on your earned income unless you have a spousal IRA. Then the limitations already discussed will apply.

Annuity or endowment contracts. Usually, such contracts have a cost for life insurance in addition to the amount earmarked for investment in your IRA. In this case, you are still limited to a total of $2,000 or $2,250 for a spousal account each year. If you deposit more than that into an annuity or endowment contract, your IRA will be disqualified.

Inherited IRAs. If you have elected to take the IRA as your own, you may deduct contributions to an IRA that you inherited from your spouse. If, however, you inherited an IRA from someone who died after December 31, 1983, and you were not the decedent's spouse, you will not be allowed to contribute to that inherited IRA.

Broker's commissions. If there is a broker's commission attached to the purchase of your IRA, it is not deductible for income tax purposes.

Trustee's fees. Trustee's administrative fees can be deducted (on Schedule A, Form 1040) in most cases if they are billed to and separately paid by you so long as they are "ordinary and necessary." The 2 percent adjusted gross income limitation applies. Such fees do not count as part of your IRA limit.

Deductible contributions. Most pastors will probably be able to deduct their IRA deposits. But employer retirement plans can reduce or eliminate your eligibility to buy IRAs. Your filing status and your income will have to be considered to determine your total eligibility for an IRA and a spousal IRA.

The "Can You Take an IRA Deduction?" chart, Appendix A from IRS Publication 590, provides a quick reference for determining the answer to the question, How much can I deduct?
eve 9147.t3

5-10 How Does Social Security Income Affect My IRA Deduction?

If you receive social security benefits, have taxable compensation, contribute to your IRA, and are covered (or considered covered) by an employer retirement plan, complete the worksheets in Appendix B of [Publication 590]. Use these worksheets to figure your IRA deduction and the taxable portion, if any, of your social security benefits.

5-11 How Do I Figure My Maximum IRA Deduction?

Your deduction depends on your income, your filing status, and your or your spouse's employer retirement plan.

Full deduction. If you or your spouse is not participating in an employer retirement plan, each of you can deduct up to $2,000 or 100 percent of compensation if less than $2,000. But that amount would be less if you have contributed to a plan created prior to June 25, 1959, which was funded by employee contributions.

Reduced or no deduction. If either you or your spouse is covered by an employer retirement plan, you may be entitled to only a partial (re-

APPENDIX A

CAN YOU TAKE AN IRA DEDUCTION?
This chart sums up whether you can take a full deduction, a partial deduction, or no deduction.

If Your Modified AGI* is:		If You Are Covered by a Retirement Plan at Work and Your Filing Status is:			If You Are Not Covered by a Retirement Plan at Work and Your Filing Status is:			
At Least	But Less Than	•Single •Head of Household	• Married Filing Jointly (even if your spouse is not covered by a plan at work) • Qualifying Widow(er)	Married Filing Separately**	Married Filing Jointly (and your spouse is covered by a plan at work)	•Single •Head of Household	• Married Filing Jointly or Separately (and your spouse is not covered by a plan at work) • Qualifying Widow(er)	Married Filing Separately (even if your spouse is covered by a plan at work)***
		You Can Take	You Can Take	You Can Take	You Can Take	You Can Take	You Can Take	You Can Take
$-0-	$10,000	Full deduction	Full deduction	Partial deduction	Full deduction			
$10,000	$25,000	Full deduction	Full deduction	No deduction	Full deduction			
$25,000	$35,000	Partial deduction	Full deduction	No deduction	Full deduction	Full Deduction	Full Deduction	Full Deduction
$35,000	$40,000	No deduction	Full deduction	No deduction	Full deduction			
$40,000	$50,000	No deduction	Partial deduction	No deduction	Partial deduction			
$50,000 or over		No deduction	No deduction	No deduction	No deduction			

*Modified AGI (adjusted gross income) is: (1) for Form 1040A—the amount on line 14 increased by any excluded series EE bond interest shown on Form 8815, *Exclusion of Interest from Series EE U.S. Savings Bonds Issued after 1989,* or (2) for Form 1040—the amount on line 31, figured without taking into account any IRA deduction or any foreign earned income exclusion and foreign housing exclusion (deduction), or any series EE bond interest exclusion from Form 8815.

**If you did not live with your spouse at any time during the year, your filing status is considered, for this purpose, as Single (therefore your IRA deduction is determined under the "Single" column).
***You are entitled to the full deduction only if you did not live with your spouse at any time during the year. If you did live with your spouse during the year, you are, for this purpose, treated as though you are covered by a retirement plan at work (therefore, your IRA deduction is determined under the "Married Filing Separately" column in the "If You Are Covered by a Retirement Plan..." section of the chart).

duced) deduction or no deduction at all, depending on your income and your filing status. Your deduction begins to decrease (phase out) when your income rises above a certain amount and is eliminated altogether when it reaches a higher amount. The amounts vary depending on your filing status.

Adjusted Gross Income Limitation

The effect of income on your deduction, as just described, is sometimes called the adjusted gross income limitation (AGI limit). To compute your **reduced IRA deduction,** you must first determine your modified adjusted gross income and your filing status.

Modified adjusted gross income (**modified AGI**) is defined as follows:

If you file Form 1040—the amount on the page 1 "adjusted gross income" line, but modified by figuring it without taking any:

a) IRA deduction,

b) Foreign earned income exclusion,

c) Foreign housing exclusion or deduction, or

d) Exclusion of series EE bond interest shown on Form 8815, *Exclusion of Interest From Series EE U.S. Savings Bonds Issued After 1989.*

If you file Form 1040A—the amount on the page 1 "adjusted gross income" line, but modified by figuring it without any IRA deduction, or any exclusion of series EE bond interest shown on Form 8815.

APPENDIX B

WORKSHEETS FOR SOCIAL SECURITY RECIPIENTS WHO CONTRIBUTE TO AN IRA

If you receive social security benefits, have taxable compensation, contribute to your IRA, and are covered (or considered covered) by an employer retirement plan, complete the following worksheets.

Use Worksheet 1 to figure your modified adjusted gross income. This amount is needed in the computation of your IRA deduction, if any, which is figured using Worksheet 2.

The IRA deduction figured using Worksheet 2 is entered on your tax return.

You then use Worksheet 3 to figure the taxable portion, if any, of your social security benefits. (Do not use the worksheet contained in the instructions to Form 1040.) You will note that, in using Worksheet 3, you will need to know the IRA deduction entered on your tax return, which, as mentioned, is figured using Worksheet 2. Worksheet 3 is only for figuring the taxable portion of your social security benefits. Its result does not affect your IRA computation.

Worksheet 1
Computation of Modified AGI
(For use only by taxpayers who receive social security benefits)

1) Adjusted gross income (AGI) from Form 1040 or Form 1040A (not taking into account any social security benefits from Form SSA-1099 or RRB-1099, any deduction for an IRA, or any exclusion of interest from savings bonds to be reported on Form 8815) .... _____

2) Enter 1/2 of amount in Box 5 of all Forms SSA-1099 and Forms RRB-1099 .... _____

3) Enter the amount of any foreign earned income exclusion, foreign housing exclusion, U.S. possessions income exclusion, or exclusion of income from Puerto Rico you claimed as a bona fide resident of Puerto Rico.. _____

4) Enter the amount of any tax-exempt interest reported on line 8b of Form 1040 or 1040A............. _____

5) Add lines 1, 2, 3, and 4 .... _____

6) Enter the amount listed below for your filing status... _____

   • **$25,000** if you filed as single, head of household, qualifying widow(er) with dependent child, or married filing a separate return, and you did not live with your spouse at any time during the year, or

   • **$32,000** if you are married filing a joint return, or

   • **$–0–** if you are married filing a separate return, and you lived with your spouse at any time during the year

7) Subtract line 6 from line 5. If zero or less, enter 0 on this line and on lines 8 and 9....................... _____

8) Divide line 7 by 2 .... _____

9) Taxable social security benefits to be included in AGI for determining IRA deduction—compare lines 2 and 8 and enter the smaller .... _____

10) Enter the amount of any foreign earned income exclusion and foreign housing exclusion or deduction that you claimed .... _____

11) **Modified AGI** for determining your partial IRA deduction—add lines 1, 9, and 10. (Also enter this amount on line 2 of Worksheet 2, next.).. _____

APPENDIX B

Worksheet 2
Computation of IRA Deduction
(For use only by taxpayers who receive social security benefits)

If your filing status is:	And your modified AGI is over:	Enter on line 1 below:
Single, or Head of household	$25,000*	$35,000
Married-joint return, or qualifying widow(er)	$40,000*	$50,000
Married-separate return**	$ –0–*	$10,000

* If your modified AGI is <u>not</u> over this amount, you can take an IRA deduction for your contributions of up to the lesser of $2,000 or your taxable compensation. Skip this worksheet and proceed to Worksheet 3.

** If you did <u>not</u> live with your spouse <u>at any time</u> during the year, consider your filing status as single.

NOTE: If you were married and both you and your spouse worked and you both contributed to IRAs, figure the deduction for each of you separately.

1. Enter the applicable amount from above .... _____

2. Enter your **modified AGI** from Worksheet 1, line 11 .... _____

NOTE: If line 2 is equal to or more than the amount on line 1, **stop here**; your IRA contributions are <u>not</u> deductible. Proceed to Worksheet 3.

3. Subtract line 2 from line 1. .... _____

4. Multiply line 3 by 20% (.20). If the result is not a multiple of $10, round it to the next highest multiple of $10. (For example, $611.40 is rounded to $620.) However, if the result is less than $200, enter $200 .... _____

5. Enter your compensation. (Do not include your spouse's compensation.) .... _____

6. Enter contributions you made to your IRA for 1991, but do not enter more than $2,000 .... _____

7. **IRA deduction.** Compare lines 4, 5, and 6. Enter the smallest amount here (or a smaller amount if you choose). Enter this amount on the Form 1040 or 1040A line for your IRA. (If the amount on line 6 is more than the amount on line 7 and you want to make a nondeductible contribution, go to line 8.) .... _____

8. **Nondeductible contributions.** Subtract line 7 from line 5 or 6, whichever is smaller. Enter the result here and on line 2 of your Form 8606, *Nondeductible IRA Contributions, IRA Basis, and Nontaxable IRA Distributions* .... _____

Worksheet 3
Computation of Taxable Social Security Benefits
(For use only by taxpayers who receive social security benefits)

1) Adjusted gross income (AGI) from Form 1040 or Form 1040A (*taking into account* any IRA deduction, but *not taking into account* any social security benefits from Form SSA-1099 or RRB-1099, or any exclusion of interest from savings bonds to be reported on Form 8815) .... _____

2) Enter 1/2 of amount in Box 5 of all Forms SSA-1099 and Forms RRB-1099.. _____

3) Enter the amount of any foreign earned income exclusion, foreign housing exclusion, exclusion of income from U.S. possessions, or exclusion of income from Puerto Rico you claimed as a bona fide resident of Puerto Rico.. _____

4) Enter the amount of any tax-exempt interest reported on line 8b of Form 1040 or 1040A .... _____

5) Add lines 1, 2, 3, and 4... _____

6) Enter the amount listed below for your filing status .... _____

   • **$25,000** if you filed as single, head of household, qualifying widow(er) with dependent child, or married filing a separate return, and you *did not* live with your spouse at any time during the year,* or

   • **$32,000** if you are married filing a joint return, or

   • **$–0–** if you are married filing a separate return, and you lived with your spouse at any time during the year

7) Subtract line 6 from line 5. If zero or less, enter 0 on this line and on lines 8 and 9 .... _____

8) Divide line 7 by 2.. _____

9) **Taxable social security benefits.**

   • First, multiply the amount on line 2, above, by 2, and enter the result on Form 1040, line 21a (or Form 1040A, line 13a).

   • Then, compare the amounts on lines 2 and 8 above. Enter the smaller amount here and on Form 1040, line 21b (or Form 1040A, line 13b).. _____

---

* If your filing status was married filing a separate return, and you did not live with your spouse at any time during the year, write the letter "D" on the dotted line next to line 21a of Form 1040 (or in the space to the left of line 13a on Form 1040A).

Note: You will find that your modified AGI may include income in addition to your taxable compensation.

5-12 How to Determine Your Filing Status

Filing status. You must state whether you are filing as a single person, head of household, married filing jointly, qualifying widow(er), or married filing separately. IRS Publication 501, *Exemptions, Standard Deduction, and Filing Information,* has more detailed information if you require it.

Married filing separate exception. Your filing status is considered to be single if "you did not live with your spouse at any time during the year and you file a separate return."

Deduction phaseout. Your IRA deduction is reduced or eliminated entirely depending on your filing status and modified AGI as follows:

If your **filing status** is:	Your IRA deduction is reduced if your **modified AGI** is within the **phaseout range** of:	Your deduction is eliminated if your **modified AGI** is:
Single, or Head of household	$25,000–$35,000	$35,000 or more
Married—joint return, or Qualifying widow(er)	$40,000–$50,000	$50,000 or more
Married—separate return	$ -0- –$10,000	$10,000 or more

5-13 How to Figure Your Reduced IRA Deduction

If your modified AGI is within the phaseout range for your filing status [see table in 5-12], your IRA deduction must be reduced. You can figure your reduced IRA deduction for either Form 1040 or Form 1040A by using [the worksheet in 5-14]. Also, the instructions for these tax forms include an *IRA Worksheet 2* (see Appendix B), which you can use instead.

Note: If you were married and both you and your spouse worked and you both contributed to IRAs, figure the deduction for each of you separately.

If you are divorced or legally separated before the end of the year, you cannot deduct any contributions you make to your spouse's IRA. After a divorce or legal separation, you can deduct only the contributions you make to your own IRA and your deductions are subject to the adjusted gross income limitation under the rules for single individuals.

Deductible (and nondeductible) IRA contributions for an unmarried individual or a working spouse. Complete lines 1 through 8 [of the worksheet in 5-14] to figure your deductible and nondeductible IRA contributions for the year.

5-14 Worksheet for Reduced IRA Deduction

(Use only if you are covered, or considered covered, by an employer plan and your modified AGI is within phaseout range)

If your **filing status** is:	And your **modified AGI** is over:	**Enter** on line 1 below:
Single, or Head of household $25,000		$35,000
Married—joint return, or Qualifying widow(er) $40,000		$50,000
Married—separate return . . . . -0-		$10,000

1. Enter applicable amount from above . . . . ._____
2. Enter your **modified AGI** (combined, if married filing jointly) . . . . ._____
   Note: If line 2 is equal to or more than the amount on line 1, **stop here;** your IRA contributions are not deductible; [see 5-17].
3. Subtract line 2 from 1. (**If line 3 is $10,000 or more, stop here;** you can take a full IRA deduction for contributions of up to $2,000 or 100% of your compensation, whichever is less.) . . . . ._____
4. Multiply line 3 by 20% (.20). If the result is not a multiple of $10, round it to the next highest multiple of $10. (For example, $611.40 is rounded to $620.) However, if the result is less than $200, enter $200 . . ._____
5. Enter your compensation. (**Do not** include your spouse's compensation, and, if you file Form 1040, do not reduce your compensation by any losses from self-employment.) ._____
6. Enter contributions you made, or plan to make, to your IRA for 1992, but **do not** enter more than $2,000. (If contributions are more than $2,000, [see 5-41].) . . . . ._____

7. **IRA deduction.** Compare lines 4, 5 and 6. Enter the smallest amount here. Enter this amount on the Form 1040 or 1040A line for your IRA, whichever applies. (If line 6 is more than line 7 and you want to make a nondeductible contribution, go to line 8.) . . . _____

8. **Nondeductible contribution.** Subtract line 7 from line 5 or 6, whichever is smaller. Enter the result here and on line 2 of your Form 8606. [See 5-17.] . . . . . _____

As a general rule, you can deduct the full amount as a single person if your adjusted gross income is less than $25,000; and as a married person, you can take the full deduction if your combined adjusted gross income is less than $40,000. Don't forget to consult Appendix A to determine your deductible amount.

Even though there is much discussion regarding nondeductible IRAs, it is best to limit your IRA contributions to your deductible amounts. If you want to invest more than your deductible amount in an annuity, it is wise to buy a separate annuity contract so there is no commingling of deductible and nondeductible funds. It is, therefore, much easier to keep correct records if you will take the time to figure your precise amount of deductible IRA deposits each year.

5-15 How to Determine Deductible and Nondeductible IRA Contributions for a Spousal IRA

Spousal IRAs are subject to the same phaseout rules as yours: If you have a spousal IRA, are covered by an employer retirement plan, and your modified AGI is within the phaseout range, you can only take a reduced spousal IRA deduction.

Complete lines 9 through 17 to figure deductible and nondeductible contributions (discussed later) for the year to a spousal IRA. [Note that references to lines 1–8 apply to the worksheet in 5-14.]

9. Enter the smaller of (a) $2,250 or (b) the amount from line 5 . . . . _____

10. Add lines 7 and 8. Enter the total. (**If this amount is equal to or more than line 9, stop here;** you cannot make contributions to a spousal IRA.) [Also, see 5-41.] . . . . _____

11. Subtract line 10 from line 9 . . . . _____

12. Enter the smallest of (a) IRA contributions for 1992 to your spouse's IRA; (b) $2,000; or (c) the amount on line 11. (If contributions are more than $2,000, [see 5-41].) . . . . _____

13. Multiply line 3 by 22.5% (.225). If the result is not a multiple of $10, round it to the next highest multiple of $10. However, if the result is less than $200, enter $200 . . . . _____
14. Enter the amount from line 7 . . . . _____
15. Subtract line 14 from line 13. Enter the result but do not enter more than the amount on line 12 . . . . _____
16. **Spousal IRA deduction.** Compare lines 4, 5, and 15. Enter the smallest amount here and on your Form 1040A or 1040. If line 12 is more than line 16 and you want to make a nondeductible contribution to your spouse, go to line 17 . . . . _____
17. **Spousal IRA nondeductible contributions.** Subtract line 16 from line 12. Enter the result here and on your spouse's Form 8606, line 2 . . . . _____

A note of caution: if you begin making your IRA deposits and are eligible for the full amount for several years, you may forget the necessity of figuring your eligible amounts each year as your income grows. Then, one day your income may rise to the point that you will not be allowed the full deductible amount. The limits to remember are the $25,000 adjustable gross income ceiling for the single person and the $40,000 adjustable gross income ceiling for married couples. After you have reached those ceilings, be sure to use the formula to determine your eligible amount of IRA deduction. Visit your local IRS office and get a copy of Publication 590, updated every few years.

5-16 How to Report Deductible IRA Contributions

For Form 1040, your IRA contributions must be deducted on line 24a and your spouse's IRA contribution on line 24b if you file a joint return. If you use Form 1040A, deduct your contributions on line 15a and your spouse's on line 15b if you file a joint return. You can use either form in most instances.

You must use Form 1040 instead of Form 1040A if you owe tax on any early distributions from your IRA, any excess contributions made to your IRA, or any excess accumulations in your IRA account. [See 5-38.]

The self-employed. If you are self-employed (a sole proprietor or partner), use line 27, Form 1040, to indicate your deduction for a SEP-IRA.

Withholding allowances. Since any regular contributions from your employer are not included in your income, they cannot be deducted. However, your estimated deductible IRA contributions can. These contributions must be considered for the proper completion of your Form W-4, Employee's Withholding Allowance Certificate. IRS Publication 505, *Tax Withholding and Estimated Tax,* has more information.

Form 5498. Your plan sponsors have until May 31 to receive Form 5498, *Individual Retirement Arrangement Information,* or comparable information, detailing all contributions made to your IRA for the past year.

5-17 How to Determine Your Nondeductible IRA Contributions

Even if your income is high enough to eliminate any deductible contributions during a year, you can still make nondeductible contributions to your IRA. If your income is so high that you have no eligibility at all, you can still contribute $2,000 or $2,250 including a nonworking spouse to a nondeductible IRA. If your IRA eligibility is limited to $1,000 of deductible contributions, you are allowed an additional $2,000 of nondeductible contributions plus an additional amount for spouse contributions.

"The difference between your total permitted contributions and your total deductible contributions, if any, is your **nondeductible contribution.**" Keep your contributions within the allowable limits so that you will not be taxed until you withdraw your funds. Generally speaking, any withdrawal prior to age 59½, other than a proper rollover, is taxable as income during the year it was withdrawn.

As long as your contributions are within the contribution limits just discussed, none of the earnings on any contributions (deductible or nondeductible) will be taxed until they are distributed. (See 5-24.)

Both your deductible and nondeductible IRA contributions, if any, will have cost bases. "Your **basis** is the sum of the nondeductible amounts you have contributed to your IRA less any distributions of those amounts. When you withdraw (or receive distributions of) these amounts, you can do so tax-free." (See 5-33. To figure, use Form 8606, line 2.)

Note. Any withdrawals must generally include both taxable and nontaxable amounts.

Example. Sonny Jones is single. In 1992, he is covered by a retirement plan at work. His salary is $52,312. Sonny makes a $2,000 IRA contribution that year. Because he is covered by a retirement plan and his income is above $35,000, he cannot deduct his $2,000 IRA contribution on his 1992 tax return. However, he may choose to either:

1) Designate this contribution as a **nondeductible** contribution by reporting it on his tax return, as explained next, or,
2) Withdraw the contribution as explained later under Tax-Free Withdrawal of Contributions.

5-18 How to Report Nondeductible IRA Contributions

The deadline for reporting a nondeductible contribution is the date you file your tax return.

When you file, **you can designate otherwise deductible contributions as nondeductible.** To designate contributions as nondeductible, you must file Form 8606, *Nondeductible IRA Contributions, IRA Basis, and Nontaxable IRA Distributions.* . . . You must file Form 8606 to report nondeductible contributions even if you do not have to file a tax return for the year.

File Form 8606 if:

- You made nondeductible contributions to your IRA [for the current tax year], or
- You received IRA distributions in [the current tax year] and you have at any time made nondeductible contributions to any of your IRAs.

If you do not report nondeductible contributions to an IRA, **all** of your IRA contributions will be treated as deductible. Thus, when you make withdrawals from your IRA, the amounts you withdraw will be taxed unless you can show, with satisfactory evidence, that nondeductible contributions were made.

There is a recordkeeping worksheet, Appendix F, *Summary Record of IRA(s)* [for the current tax year], that you can use to keep records of your deductible and nondeductible IRA contributions.

Penalty for overstatement. If you overstate the amount of your nondeductible contributions on your Form 8606 for any tax year, you must pay a penalty of $100 for each overstatement, unless it was due to reasonable cause.

Penalty for failure to file Form 8606. You will have to pay a $50 penalty if you do not file a required Form 8606, unless you can prove that the failure was due to reasonable cause.

5-19 How to Avoid Penalty If You Overstate Your IRA Contribution

Suppose you make an IRA contribution during the current tax year, but for some reason you feel it was a mistake. You can back

Form **8606**	**Nondeductible IRA Contributions,**	OMB No. 1545-1007
	IRA Basis, and Nontaxable IRA Distributions	**1991**
Department of the Treasury Internal Revenue Service	▶ Please see Recordkeeping Requirements on page 2. ▶ Attach to Form 1040, Form 1040A, or Form 1040NR.	Attachment Sequence No. **47**

Name. (If married, file a separate Form 8606 for each spouse. See instructions.)	Your social security number

Fill In Your Address Only If You Are Filing This Form by Itself and Not With Your Tax Return ⟩

Home address (number and street, or P.O. box if mail is not delivered to your home) | Apt. no.

City, town or post office, state, and ZIP code

1	Enter the total value of **ALL** your IRAs as of 12/31/91. (See instructions.)	**1**
2	Enter your IRA contributions for 1991 that you choose to be nondeductible. Include those made during 1/1/92–4/15/92 that were for 1991: (See instructions.)	**2**
3	Enter your total IRA basis for 1990 and prior years. (See instructions.)	**3**
4	Add lines 2 and 3. If you did not receive any IRA distributions (withdrawals) in 1991, skip lines 5 through 13 and enter this amount on line 14	**4**
5	Enter only those contributions included on line 2 that were made during 1/1/92–4/15/92. (This amount will be the same as line 2 if all of your nondeductible contributions for 1991 were made in 1992 by 4/15/92.) (See instructions.)	**5**
6	Subtract line 5 from line 4	**6**
7	Enter the amount from line 1 plus any outstanding rollovers. (See instructions.)	**7**
8	Enter the total IRA distributions received during 1991. Do not include amounts rolled over before 1/1/92. (See instructions.)	**8**
9	Add lines 7 and 8	**9**
10	Divide line 6 by line 9 and enter the result as a decimal (to at least two places). Do not enter more than "1.00"	**10**
11	Multiply line 8 by line 10. This is the amount of your **nontaxable distributions for 1991.** (See instructions.) . . . . ▶	**11**
12	Subtract line 11 from line 6. This is the **basis in your IRA(s) as of 12/31/91**	**12**
13	Enter the amount, if any, from line 5	**13**
14	Add lines 12 and 13. This is your **total IRA basis for 1991 and prior years** . . . . . . ▶	**14**

Sign Here Only If You Are Filing This Form by Itself and Not With Your Tax Return

Under penalties of perjury, I declare that I have examined this form, including accompanying attachments, and to the best of my knowledge and belief, it is true, correct, and complete.

Your signature ▶ Date

Paperwork Reduction Act Notice.—We ask for the information on this form to carry out the Internal Revenue laws of the United States. You are required to give us the information. We need it to ensure that you are complying with these laws and to allow us to figure and collect the right amount of tax.

The time needed to complete and file this form will vary depending on individual circumstances. The estimated average time is: **Recordkeeping, 26 minutes; Learning about the law or the form, 7 minutes; Preparing the form, 22 minutes; and Copying, assembling, and sending the form to the IRS, 20 minutes.**

If you have comments concerning the accuracy of these time estimates or suggestions for making this form more simple, we would be happy to hear from you. You can write to both the **Internal Revenue Service,** Washington, DC 20224, Attention: IRS Reports Clearance Officer, T:FP; and the **Office of Management and Budget,** Paperwork Reduction Project (1545-1007), Washington, DC 20503. **DO**

NOT send this form to either of these offices. Instead, **see When and Where To File** on this page.

General Instructions

Purpose of Form.—You must use Form 8606 to report your IRA contributions that you choose to be nondeductible. You may wish to make nondeductible contributions, for example, if all or part of your contributions are not deductible because of the income limitations for IRAs. First, figure your deductible contributions using the instructions for Form 1040 or Form 1040A, whichever apply to you. Report the deductible contributions on Form 1040, Form 1040A, or Form 1040NR. Then, enter on line 2 of Form 8606 the amount you choose to be nondeductible.

The part of any distributions you receive attributable to nondeductible contributions will not be taxable. If you have at any time made nondeductible contributions, also use Form 8606 to figure the nontaxable part of any IRA distributions you received in 1991. Line 11 will show the amount that is not taxable.

Who Must File.—You must file Form 8606 for 1991 if either of the following applies:

- You made nondeductible contributions to your IRA for 1991, or

- You received IRA distributions in 1991 and you have at any time made nondeductible contributions to any of your IRAs.

When and Where To File.—Attach Form 8606 to your 1991 Form 1040, Form 1040A, or Form 1040NR.

If you are required to file Form 8606, but do not have to file an income tax return because you do not meet the requirements for filing a return, you still have to file a Form 8606 with the Internal Revenue Service at the time and place you would be required to file Form 1040, Form 1040A, or Form 1040NR.

Penalty for Not Filing Form 8606.—The law provides for a penalty if you make nondeductible IRA contributions and do not file Form 8606. You will have to pay a $50 penalty for each failure to file Form 8606, unless you can show that the failure to file was due to reasonable cause.

Cat.No. 63966F

Form **8606** (1991)

APPENDIX F

Summary Record of IRA(s) for 1991
(You May Keep This for Your Records)

Name _____

I was ☐ covered ☐ not covered by my employer's retirement plan during the year.

I became age 59½ on _____
                     (month) (day) (year)

I became age 70½ on _____
                     (month) (day) (year)

Contributions

Name of IRA	Date	Amount contributed for 1991	Check, if rollover contribution	Fair Market value of IRA as of December 31, 1991, from Form 5498
1.				
2.				
3.				
4.				
5.				
Total				

Total contributions deducted on tax return $_____

Total contributions treated as nondeductible on Form 8606 $_____

Distributions

Name of IRA	Date	Amount of distribution	Reason (e.g., for retirement, rollover, withdrawal of excess contributions, etc.)	Income earned on IRA	Taxable amount reported on income tax return	Nontaxable amount from Form 8606, line 11
1.						
2.						
3.						
4.						
Total						

Basis of all IRAs as of 12/31/91 (from Form 8606, line 12) $_____

Basis of all IRAs for 1991 (from Form 8606, line 14) $_____

Note: You should keep copies of your income tax return, and Forms W–2, 8606, and 5498.

WORKSHEET
FOR
DETERMINING REQUIRED ANNUAL DISTRIBUTIONS FROM YOUR IRA(s)

	70½	71½	72½	73½	74½	75½
1. Age						
2. Year age was reached						
3. Value of IRA at the close of business on December 31 of the year immediately prior to the year on line 2[1]						
4. Divisor from Life Expectancy Table I or Table II[2]						
5. Required distribution (divide line 3 by line 4)[3]						

[1] If you have more than one IRA, you must figure the required distribution separately for each IRA.

[2] Use the appropriate divisor for each year and for each IRA. You can either (a) use the appropriate divisor from the table each year, or (b) use the appropriate divisor from the table for your 70½ year and reduce it by 1 (one) for each subsequent year. To find the appropriate divisor, use your age (and that of your beneficiary, if applicable) as of your birthday(s) in the year shown on line 2. If your beneficiary is someone other than your spouse, see *Minimum Distribution Incidental Benefit Requirement* in Chapter 6.

[3] If you have more than one IRA, you must withdraw an amount equal to the total of the required distributions figured for each IRA. You can, however, withdraw the total from one IRA or from more than one IRA.

out if you withdraw your funds tax-free prior to April 15 of the following year "or a later date, if you have an extension to file your return." However, any earnings you make on the funds will be taxable. This is allowable if

- the withdrawn contributions were not deducted.
- you withdrew and reported as income "any interest or other income earned on the contributions."

My advice: Don't put both deductible and nondeductible funds in the same IRA. Establish a separate IRA for nondeductible deposits.

5-20 Can I Transfer (Roll Over) Retirement Plan Assets?

IRA rules permit you to transfer, tax-free, assets (money or property) from other retirement programs (including IRAs) to an IRA. The rules permit the following kinds of transfer:

- Transfers from one trustee to another,
- Rollovers, and
- Transfers incident to divorce.

Let's discuss each of these in detail.

What About Transferring Retirement Plan Assets from One Trustee to Another?

A transfer of funds in your IRA from one trustee directly to another, either at your request or at the trustee's request, is **not a rollover.** As such, it is not affected by the one-year waiting period that is required between rollovers, discussed next.

5-21 What Is a Rollover?

From time to time, you may wish to take funds out of an existing IRA and put them into another. Sometimes, the interest rate on your existing IRA seems too low, and other plans offer higher interest rates. Sometimes, you discover an IRA that has more favorable contractual provisions, such as no front-end load, no annual service fee, and a lower penalty percentage if you withdraw funds prematurely. In addition, you may discover an IRA that has a higher guaranteed lifetime monthly income at retirement age. One or several of these reasons may motivate you to change your financial institution.

The government allows a tax-free rollover without labeling it a "taxable event." Obviously, it will ultimately become taxable when you withdraw it without benefit of a rollover.

A rollover is used (1) when you roll your account from one carrier to another and (2) when you wish to roll over a qualified employer account into an IRA.

Rollover notice. All participating employees must be given a written explanation of the rollover procedure by the sponsoring carrier.

Inherited IRA. Beneficiaries who are spouses may elect to roll over funds they inherit at the death of an IRA owner. They would then own the IRA the same as if they had originally purchased it. Nonspouse beneficiaries cannot roll over an IRA or allow it to receive a rollover contribution if they do not elect to take the IRA as their own.

5-22 What Is the Time Limit for Making a Rollover Contribution?

You are allowed sixty days from the day you received your IRA distribution to roll over the funds to another IRA. There are, however, provisions for extension of the rollover period.

Rollovers Completed After the Sixty-Day Period

If you hold funds beyond the sixty-day limit and do not have an extension, those funds are treated as ordinary income, and you must pay taxes for that year. Furthermore, if you are under age 59½ when you hold your IRA rollover funds for more than sixty days, you will owe a 10 percent penalty on top of regular income taxes.

Treat a contribution after the 60-day period as a regular contribution to your IRA. Any part of the contribution that is more than the maximum amount you could contribute may be an excess contribution [see 5-41].

Extension of the Rollover Period

If you decide to roll over your IRA account and notify your current carrier of your intentions with proper legal procedure, or if you withdraw your funds and place them in your own savings account and then those funds become frozen, a special rule applies.

First of all, a *frozen deposit* is defined as

any deposit that cannot be withdrawn because:
1) The financial institution is bankrupt or insolvent, or 2) The state where the institution is located restricts withdrawals because one or more financial institutions in the state are (or are about to be) bankrupt or insolvent.

Waiting Period Between Rollovers

You may roll over your IRA funds from one IRA to another, in full or in part, only once each year. The date you receive the funds marks the beginning of your sixty-day period.

Each separate IRA you may own is subject to this rule. Although you may own several IRAs, each one is treated as a separate contract.

For example, if you have two IRAs, IRA-1 and IRA-2, and you roll over assets of IRA-1 into a new IRA-3, you may also make a rollover from IRA-2 into IRA-3, or into any other IRA within one year after the rollover distribution from IRA-1. These are both rollovers because you have not received more than one distribution from either IRA within one year.

If you roll over funds later in the same year, such a transaction is not a valid rollover and may be subject to a 10 percent tax for premature distribution.

Property

The same property must be rolled over. You must roll over into a new IRA the same property you received from your old IRA.

Partial Rollovers

You may decide to withdraw part of your IRA funds to keep and roll over another part of them. The part you keep is taxable as income plus a 10 percent penalty if withdrawn prior to age 59½. If you are over age 59½, you would have to pay ordinary income tax but not the 10 percent penalty tax. The amount rolled over will not be subject to tax at the time of the rollover.

Reporting

Report any rollover from one IRA to another IRA on lines 16a and 16b, Form 1040 or lines 10a and 10b, Form 1040A. Enter the total amount of the distribution on line 16a, Form 1040 or line 10a, Form 1040A. If the total amount on line 16a, Form 1040 or line 10a, Form 1040A was rolled over, enter zero on line 16b, Form 1040 or line 10b, Form 1040A. Otherwise, enter the taxable portion of the part that was not rolled over on line 16b, Form 1040 or line 10b, Form 1040A.

5-23 How to Roll Over Employer's Plan into an IRA

A company that goes out of business or stops its retirement plan must do something about the retirement accounts of its employees. Employees can then roll their funds into an IRA of their own. No deduction is allowed because those funds, less the interest earned, have already been deducted each year when they were first contributed. If you or your surviving spouse receives funds from a qualified pension, profit-sharing plan, stock bonus plan, annuity plan, or tax-sheltered plan (403(b) plan), you may be able to roll over all or part of it to an IRA.

Qualified Total Distribution

You can roll over into an IRA all or part of a **qualified total distribution.** A distribution from a plan is a qualified total distribution if

1) your employer ends your plan and you receive the funds within one tax year.
2) your employer stops contributing to your stock bonus or profit-sharing plan and you receive the funds within one year.
3) your employer distributes to you "all or part of your voluntary deductible employee contributions."
4) your employer gives you a *lump-sum distribution.*

The distribution in (1), (2), or (4) must be your complete share in the plan, other than voluntary deductible employee contributions. You can receive the distribution in more than one part.

If an employer plan is terminated, the U.S. government will not allow the rollover of a tax-sheltered annuity into an IRA.

When a plan administrator notifies the IRS that a plan is permanently stopped, no further contributions may be made.

Voluntary deductible employee contributions (DECs). If you made any deductible contributions to a qualified employer's plan prior to January 1, 1987, those funds can be rolled over.

A lump-sum distribution. This distribution of the total share of a participant's plan within one tax year is made

1) at the death of the participant.
2) at the participant's age 59½.
3) if the participant separates from service (this point does not apply to a self-employed individual).
4) if a self-employed person becomes disabled.

Partial distributions are discussed elsewhere in this section.

Complete share. If you receive a series of distributions from one or more employer plans within one tax year, that is generally considered to be a lump-sum distribution. Only if you have two or more plans of the same type are you required to take your full share from each plan. If you have different types of plans, play along with them; you do not have to take the full share of each plan.

Maximum rollover. The only portion of your assets that cannot be rolled over would be any nondeductible contributions you may have made. Fair market value is used to determine the value of your assets to be rolled over.

Time limit. You have sixty days to complete a rollover from a lump-sum distribution unless you have received an extension.

Tax treatment after the rollover. You cannot use the five- or ten-year long-term capital gain averaging method after once rolling over your assets into an IRA.

IRA as a holding account (conduit IRA). Once you receive your lump-sum distribution from an employer's plan with the intention of rolling it over to another employer's plan, you can place it in a conduit IRA during the interim. However, the funds in that conduit IRA must be exclusively those from your first employer's plan. You cannot mix funds from more than one plan, and *all* of the funds, including the earnings, must be included in the conduit IRA.

Required election. To qualify for your rollover, you must notify the trustee or issuer of the IRA in writing that you are requesting an irrevocable rollover when the contribution is made.

Partial Distributions

If you or your surviving spouse wishes to roll over what would otherwise be taxable from a qualified pension plan, an annuity plan, or a tax-sheltered annuity (403(b) plan), the following conditions are required.

Rollover requirements. The partial distribution:

1) Must equal at least 50% of the balance to the credit of the employee (attributable to both employee and employer contributions, but not including voluntary deductible employee contributions), and 2) Must **not** be one of a series of periodic payments.

Also, the distribution must be made:

1) Because the participant died,
2) Because the participant separated from service, or
3) After the participant has become permanently disabled.

Required election. To qualify for your rollover, you must notify the trustee or issuer of your IRA in writing that you are requesting an irrevocable rollover when the contribution is made.

Time limit. You have sixty days after the distribution date to roll over a partial distribution unless your assets are frozen.

Later rollovers. Once you elect a partial rollover distribution, your IRA may not be eligible for special averaging or capital gain treatment. You should seek counsel from a tax specialist or the IRS if you are in this situation. You should be sure of your position. It could cost you later.

Treatment of Amounts Not Rolled Over

Any amounts distributed to you from qualified plans that you do not roll over must include the deductible amount that you keep in your gross income for the year you receive it. These funds do not qualify for the five- or ten-year averaging and are not deductible.

Contributions You Made to Your Employer's Plan

Only the voluntary deductible employee contributions (DECs) you make to your employer's plan can be rolled over. If you do roll over nondeductible funds, they will be treated as regular contributions, and you may have to pay the excess contributions tax.

Note: Elective contributions from your pay to a 401(k) plan or a SEP are treated as employer contributions and can be rolled over.

Sale of Property Received in a Distribution from a Qualified Plan

Property or the cash from the sale of said property can be rolled over into an IRA.

Treatment of gain or loss. No gain or loss is recognized if you sell the distributed property and roll over all the proceeds into an IRA.

Rollover of part of the amount received from the sale of property. You are taxed on any part of a sale from property that you do not roll over. The difference between the fair market value on the date you received the property and the selling price will determine your capital gain or loss.

Property and Cash Received in a Distribution

You can roll over property or cash from the sale of that property or a combination of the two:

If your distribution includes your own employee contributions to the plan, property or cash that you do not roll over is considered to include the return of the amount you paid to the plan.

Identification of cash. If you receive cash from your employer's plan and also receive cash from a sale of the property, you must indicate whether the cash you roll over is from the cash you received in the distribution or the cash you received in the sale. You do not recognize any gain or loss on the sale to the extent that the cash you roll over is from the sale of property. Therefore, the identification you make will determine how much gain or loss you need to recognize from the sale. If you do not realize any gain or loss, no identification is needed.

The Internal Revenue Service requires you to file an election identifying the source of the cash you did not roll over. This election must be made by tax return filing time, including extensions. This election is irrevocable. If you fail to identify the amount you kept, the IRS will identify it for you on a pro rata basis.

For purposes of making a rollover, **you cannot substitute your own funds for property you receive** from your employer's retirement plan.

Life Insurance Contract

Life insurance contracts cannot be rolled over from a qualified plan into an IRA.

Distributions Received by a Surviving Spouse

If you die or your employer's qualified plan is terminated, your spouse can roll part or all of a lump-sum distribution from your employer's qualified plan into an IRA. For information regarding any estate or gift tax consequences, see IRS Publication 448, *Federal Estate and Gift Taxes.*

Death benefit exclusion. If you die, your spouse can exclude up to $5,000 from income from the distribution of your qualified plan or tax-sheltered annuity. No part of the $5,000 death benefit exclusion can be rolled over to an IRA. IRS Publication 575, *Pension and Annuity Income (Including Simplified General Rule)*, has more information.

No rollover into another employer qualified plan. If, at your death, your surviving spouse rolls over any part of a lump-sum distribution from your employer's qualified plan or tax-sheltered annuity into an IRA, those funds cannot later be rolled over into another qualified employer plan or annuity.

Distributions Under Divorce or Similar Proceedings

If you (as a spouse or former spouse of the employee) receive from a qualified employer plan a distribution that results from divorce or similar proceedings, you may be able to roll over all or part of it into an IRA if

1) It is the balance to **your** credit (not the employee's credit) in the plan,
2) It is made under a **qualified domestic relations order,**
3) You receive it within one tax year (your tax year, not the plan's year), and
4) In the case of a distribution of property other than money, you roll over the same property you received from the plan. Only an IRA can receive the rollover. A pension or annuity plan would not qualify.

Qualified domestic relations order. In the case of a divorce, a court may order a

judgment, decree, or order (including approval of a property settlement agreement) that is issued under the domestic relations law of a state. A "qualified domestic relations order" gives to a spouse, former spouse, child, or dependent of a participant in a retirement plan the right to receive all or part of the benefits that would be payable to the participant under the plan. The order requires certain specific information and it may not alter the amount or form of the benefits of the plan.

Tax treatment. If you roll over only part of the distribution, the amount you keep is taxable in the year you receive it. In figuring the taxable amount, however, you are allowed a prorated share of the participant's cost (investment in the contract). The special rules for lump-sum distributions (special 5 or 10-year averaging method or capital gain treatment) may apply. The 10% additional tax on premature distributions, as discussed later, does not apply.

Keogh Plans and Rollovers

You can roll over all or part of a qualified total distribution, including a lump-sum distribution (except your own nondeductible contributions as an employee), from a Keogh plan to an IRA.

If you are self-employed, under age 59½, and are not disabled, a distribution from your Keogh plan is not a lump-sum distribution and generally cannot be rolled over into an IRA. However, if you end your Keogh plan, you can take the complete distribution (other than your non-deductible contributions as an employee) and roll it over into an IRA tax free even though you are under age 59½ and not disabled.

Rollover from a Tax-Sheltered Annuity

Generally, you can roll over all or part of a lump-sum distribution (or any part of a distribution due to deductible employee contributions) from a tax-sheltered annuity to an IRA or another tax-sheltered annuity or custodial account if the lump-sum distribution was made on account of separation from service, or death, or you reached age 59½.

The proceeds from the sale of property cannot be rolled over into an IRA. You may roll over only the part that would normally be taxed. For example, amounts previously contributed by your employer have already been included in your income. You have sixty days after the asset distribution date to complete your rollover. Spouses of deceased employees may also take advantage of a rollover.

If your IRA contains only assets (including earnings and gains) that were rolled over from a tax-sheltered annuity, you may roll over these assets into another tax-sheltered annuity. Do not combine the assets in your IRA from the rollover with assets from another source if you plan another rollover into another tax-sheltered annuity. Do not roll over an amount from a tax-sheltered annuity into a qualified pension plan.

Partial distributions. The same rules regarding partial distributions apply to both the IRA and the TSA.

Chapter 4 of this book deals with the tax-sheltered annuity in detail.

Rollover from Bond Purchase Plan

You can roll over the tax-free portion of a qualified bond purchase plan to an IRA, and you can redeem these bonds prior to age 59½. You can also roll over the funds to a qualified employer plan without tax consequences, but you would not be eligible for the five- or ten-year averaging or capital gain treatment.

Maximum rollover. You cannot roll over your cost basis (i.e., the amount you have paid into the account). Any amount over that can be rolled over.

Reporting Rollovers from Employer Plans

Do not use lines 16a or 16b, Form 1040, or lines 10a or 10b, Form 1040A, to report a rollover from an employer retirement plan to an IRA; use lines 17a and 17b, Form 1040, or lines 11a or 11b, Form 1040A, instead.

Transfers Incident to Divorce

Starting from the date you receive a transferred IRA because of "divorce, a separate maintenance decree or a written document related to such a decree," the IRA is your property. (See "Distributions Under Divorce or Similar Proceedings" earlier in this section.)

5-24 When Can I Withdraw or Use the Assets in My IRA?

The primary purpose of the IRA is to save money in a tax-sheltered account until retirement and then draw an income for life. Funds should never be placed in an IRA for short-term purposes unless you are over age 59½. Except for a "properly handled rollover," most withdrawals from an IRA are subject to income tax in the year they are withdrawn. The exceptions will be discussed below.

5-25 What Is the Age 59½ Rule?

Any funds or property you withdraw from an IRA prior to age 59½, with the exception of the categories listed in 5-26, are fully taxable as income in the year withdrawn. Such early withdrawals are subject to an additional 10 percent penalty tax.

5-26 What Are the Exceptions to the Age 59½ Rule?

Disability exception. If you become disabled prior to age 59½, you may withdraw funds from your IRA without having to pay the additional 10 percent penalty tax. Of course, you still must report the withdrawn funds as regular income.

Disability is defined as being unable to "do any substantial gainful activity because of your physical or mental condition" as determined by a physician, who must declare that your condition has or will last for at least twelve months. Notice that the definition states that you must be unable to do *any* gainful activity. If you are a professionally trained person but could do some gainful activity, you are *not* considered to be disabled. For more information see IRS Publication 524, *Credit for the Elderly or the Disabled.*

Death exception. Your IRA fund can be distributed to your beneficiary or your estate, if you die prior to age 59½, without the imposition of the 10 percent penalty tax. But that would not be true if you had inherited an IRA from a spouse who died prior to age 59½. The 10 percent penalty would still be payable if you withdrew funds from the IRA prior to your age 59½.

Rollovers exception. A properly completed rollover is not subject to regular income tax or the 10 percent penalty tax.

Annuity exception. If you elect "substantially equal payments over your life (or your life expectancy), or over the lives of you and your beneficiary," you will not have to pay the 10 percent penalty tax. As always you must pay the regular income tax. A minimum of one distribution per year is required and must occur at least five years or until you reach age 59½, whichever is longer. However, if the owner of the IRA dies or is disabled, the five-year rule does not apply.

Timely contribution withdrawal. If, during a taxable year, you make a deposit into your IRA but decide to withdraw it before your income tax return is filed, you may do so. However, any interest you earned on the IRA must be reported as income for that year. Any such earnings must be withdrawn from the IRA before you file your income tax return.

Note. If you receive a distribution from an IRA that includes a return of **nondeductible contributions,** the additional tax does not apply to the portion of the distribution that is considered to be nontaxable. [See 5-34.]

5-27 What Are the Distribution Deadlines?

A time limit is imposed on your IRA after which you must begin to withdraw the funds. (See 5-43.) You must make one of the following choices:

- By withdrawing the entire balance in your IRA by the **required beginning date** (defined later), or
- By starting to withdraw periodic distributions of the balance in your IRA by the **required beginning date.**

Periodic distributions. If, when your required beginning date arrives, you have not withdrawn your entire balance, one or a combination of the following methods of distribution must be started:

1) Withdrawals over a period of the rest of your life.
2) Withdrawals over a period of your lifetime and your designated beneficiary's lifetime. (See the definition of a designated beneficiary below.)
3) Withdrawals over a period within your life expectancy.
4) Withdrawals over a period of time within the joint life and last survivor expectancy of you and your designated beneficiary.

(See 5-30 for more details.)

A **designated beneficiary** as used here means any individual who is named to receive your IRA upon your death. If you have more than one beneficiary, the beneficiary with the shortest life expectancy will be the designated beneficiary used to determine the period over which your withdrawals must be made.

Required beginning date (RBD). Distributions from your IRA must begin

by April 1 of the year following the year in which you reach age 70½.

You must receive a minimum amount for each year starting with the year you reach age 70½ (your 70½ year). If you did not receive distributions in your 70½ year, then you must receive the required **minimum distribution** by April 1 of the next year. That distribution is for your 70½ year.

Distributions after the RBD. After you are 70½, the required minimum distribution must be made by December 31 of that later year.

Example. You reach age 70½ on August 20, 1992. For 1992 (your 70½ year), you must receive the required minimum distribution from your IRA no later than April 1, 1993. You must receive the required minimum distribution for 1993 (the first year after your 70½ year) by December 31, 1993.

If the owner dies after the RBD. If periodic distributions begin by the RBD and the owner dies on or after that date, any undistributed amounts at the IRA owner's death must be distributed at least as rapidly as under the method being used at the owner's death.

If the owner dies before the RBD, the entire interest (the IRA account balance as of the close of business on December 31 of the preceding year) must be distributed under either:

Rule 1. By December 31 of the fifth year following the year of the owner's death, or

Rule 2. In annual amounts over the life or life expectancy of the designated beneficiary.

Either the owner or the beneficiary can choose rule 1 or 2 so long as the choice is "made by December 31 of the year following the year of the owner's death."

Rule 1 must be chosen for distribution "if the beneficiary is not the surviving spouse." Rule 2 must be chosen "if the beneficiary is the surviving spouse."

If rule 2 has been specified or chosen and the beneficiary is not the surviving spouse, distribution must begin by December 31 of the year following the year of the owner's death.

If rule 2 has been specified or chosen and the beneficiary is the spouse, distribution must begin by the later of:

- December 31 of the year the IRA owner would have reached age 70½, or
- December 31 of the year following the year of the owner's death.

If distributions are to be made to a spouse as designated beneficiary under rule 2,

a special rule applies **if the spouse dies before the date distributions to the spouse are required to begin.** In this case, distributions may be made to the spouse's beneficiary as if the spouse's beneficiary were the IRA owner's spouse and the owner died on the spouse's date of death.

These special rules would not apply to a new spouse if "the spouse has remarried since the owner's death."

5-28 What Is the Minimum Distribution Requirement?

The minimum distribution amount from your IRA must be determined each year if you are the owner of an IRA or the beneficiary of a deceased owner of an IRA.

The minimum amount is figured on the basis of your life expectancy or the joint life expectancy of the owner and last survivor of the owner and the designated beneficiary.

If the owner dies before the required beginning date, the designated beneficiary will receive the minimum amount based on the individual's life expectancy.

5-29 How to Figure the Minimum Distribution

Figure your required minimum distribution for each year by dividing the **IRA account balance** as of the close of business on December 31 of the preceding year by the applicable **life expectancy.** Or, if the distribution must satisfy the minimum distribution incidental benefit requirement, discussed [in 5-31], compare the **applicable divisor** and the applicable life expectancy and use the lower number. The applicable life expectancy is the owner's remaining life expectancy (or the remaining joint life expectancy of the owner and the owner's designated beneficiary, or the remaining life expectancy of the designated beneficiary, whichever applies).

To figure the required minimum distribution after the first distribution year (the owner's 70½ year), reduce the IRA account balance as of December 31 of that first year by any distribution made by April 1 of the following year.

The following example involves years 1990 and 1991. No doubt the numbers will change each year hereafter, but the example will help you understand. Each year you can obtain a current copy of IRS Publication 590, *Individual Retirement Arrangements* (IRAs).

Example 1. Joe, born October 1, 1921, reached 70½ in 1991. His wife (his beneficiary) turned 56 in September 1991. He must begin receiving distributions by April 1, 1992. Joe's IRA account balance as of December 31, 1990, is $29,000. Based on their ages at year end (December 31, 1991), the joint life expectancy for Joe (age 71) and his beneficiary (age 56) is 29 years (see Table II in Appendix E at the end of this chapter). The required minimum distribution for 1991, Joe's first distribution year (his 70½ year), is $1,000 ($29,000 divided by 29). This amount is distributed to Joe on April 1, 1992.

Joe's IRA account balance as of December 31, 1991, is $29,000. To figure the minimum amount required to be distributed for 1992, the IRA account balance (as of December 31, 1991) of $29,000 is reduced by the $1,000 minimum required distribution for 1991 that was made on April 1, 1992. Thus, the account balance for determining the required distribution for 1992 is $29,000.

5-30 How to Determine Life Expectancy

See Tables I and II in Appendix E at the end of this chapter to determine your life expectancy. For even more detailed information regarding life expectancy, see IRS Publication 939, *Pension General Rule (Nonsimplified Method)*.

To determine your annual minimum distribution, use the life expectancy in Table I, "Single Life Expectancy," if the periodic payments are for your life only. Use the life expectancy in Table II, "Joint Life and Last Survivor Expectancy," if the payments are for your life and that of your designated beneficiary.

(If your IRA is set up to provide payments that do not qualify as annuity payments to someone other than your spouse who is more than ten years younger than you, see 5-31.)

For distributions beginning by the required beginning date (RBD) (discussed earlier), determine life expectancies using the ages of the owner and the designated beneficiary as of their birthdays in the owner's 70½ year.

For distributions after the owner's death (if death occurred before the required beginning date), the life expectancy of the designated beneficiary is determined using the age as of the beneficiary's birthday in the year distributions must begin.

Refiguring life expectancy. If you own an IRA, your life expectancy (and that of your spouse, if applicable) must be **refigured annually** unless your IRA terms provide otherwise. [See "Further information" in 5-31 for special rules to refigure your life expectancy.]

If you or your spouse dies. If the joint life expectancy of you and your spouse is refigured annually and either of you dies, then only the survivor's life expectancy is used to figure distributions for the years after the year in which the death occurred.

If you and your spouse die. If the life expectancies of both you and your spouse are refigured and both of you die after the date distributions must start, the entire interest must be distributed before the last day of the year following the year of the second death.

Election to refigure life expectancy. Your IRA terms may permit you and your spouse to elect whether to refigure your life expectancies. You must make this election by the date of the first required minimum distribution. [See "Required beginning date (RBD)" in 5-27.]

If you do not use the tables to refigure your life expectancy, reduce your initial life expectancy by one for each year after your 70½ year to determine your remaining life expectancy.

5-31 What Is the Minimum Distribution Incidental Benefit (MDIB) Requirement?

The primary purpose of the IRA is to provide retirement benefits. The MDIB is set to ensure that the minimum amount is paid to the owner during his or her lifetime. But if the owner dies, residual benefits paid to the beneficiary are expected to be only "incidental."

If your spouse is your only beneficiary, you will satisfy the MDIB requirement if you satisfy the general minimum distribution requirements discussed above.

If someone other than your spouse is your beneficiary, there are additional steps to figure your required minimum distribution.

1) Find the applicable divisor for a person your age in Appendix E under *Table for Determining Applicable Divisor for MDIB.* Use your age as of your birthday in the year that you are figuring the minimum distribution.
2) Compare your applicable divisor and your applicable life expectancy . . . for the year, and determine which number is smaller.
3) To figure your required minimum distribution, divide the IRA account balance as of the close of business of the December 31 of the preceding year by the smaller number (your applicable divisor or your applicable life expectancy).

Example 2. Assume the same facts as in Example 1 [see 5-29], except that Joe's beneficiary is his brother. Because Joe's beneficiary is not his spouse, he must use the *Table for Determining Applicable Divisor for MDIB* (see Appendix E) and compare the applicable divisor from that table to the life expectancy determined using *Table II (Joint Life and Last Survivor Expectancy)* in Appendix E. Joe must use the smaller number from the tables. Thus, in this example, the required minimum distribution for 1991 is $1,146 ($29,000 divided by 25.3) instead of the $1,000 computed in Example 1. . . .

Effect of the IRA owner's death. The MDIB requirement does not apply to distributions in years after the death of the original IRA owner. Consequently, if you hold an IRA as the beneficiary of the IRA owner, minimum distributions from this IRA can be figured using the general rules for minimum distributions discussed earlier.

Further information. Required distribution rules are explained more fully in sections 1.401(a) (9)—1, 1.401(a) (9)—2, and 1.408 of the proposed income Tax Regulations. These regulations can be read in many libraries and IRS offices.

5-32 Miscellaneous Rules for Minimum Distributions

Here are the rules governing minimum distribution:

Installments allowed. You can choose monthly, quarterly, semiannual, or annual installments "as long as the total distributions for the year equal the minimum required amount."

If you have more than one IRA, you must receive the required minimum distribution from each IRA.

However, you can total these minimum amounts and take the total from any one or more of the IRAs.

Example. Mary, born August 1, 1920, became 70½ on February 1, 1991. She has two IRAs. She must begin receiving her IRA distributions by April 1, 1992. On December 31, 1990, Mary's account balance from IRA A was $10,000; her account balance from IRA B was $20,000. Mary's brother, age 64 as of his birthday in 1991, is the beneficiary of IRA A. Her husband, age 78 as of his birthday in 1991, is the beneficiary of IRA B.

Mary's required minimum distribution from IRA A is $427.35 ($10,000 divided by 23.4, the joint life and last survivor expectancy of Mary and her brother per Table II in Appendix E). The amount of the required minimum distribution from IRA B is $1,142.86 ($20,000 divided by 17.5, the joint life and last survivor expectancy of Mary and her husband per Table II in Appendix E). The required distribution that must be withdrawn by Mary from either one, or both, of her IRA accounts by April 1, 1992, is $1,570.21.

If you receive more, in any year, than the required minimum

amount for that year, you will not receive credit for the additional amount when determining the required minimum amounts for future years. However, any amount distributed in your 70½ year will be credited toward the amount that must be distributed by April 1 of the following year.

Annuity distributions from an insurance company. Special rules apply if you receive distributions from your IRA as an annuity purchased from an insurance company. [See "Further information" in 5-31.]

5-33 How Are Distributions Treated for Tax Purposes?

IRA distributions are considered to be income for the year in which you receive the funds unless your withdrawals are "timely withdrawals" or rollovers, discussed earlier.

You must report, as ordinary income, any IRA distribution you receive with the exceptions in the preceding paragraph. Furthermore, "you cannot use the special averaging or capital gain treatment that applies to lump-sum distributions from qualified employer plans" in figuring your income.

If You Made Deductible and/or Nondeductible Contributions

If all your IRA contributions were deductible, any future distribution is fully taxable when withdrawn because you have no cost basis. (See 5-37.)

If you made any nondeductible contributions to your IRA, the cost basis is not reported as income when you withdraw funds.

Form 8606. You must complete, and attach to your return, Form 8606, *Nondeductible IRA Contributions, IRA Basis, and Nontaxable IRA Distributions,* if you receive a distribution and, at any time, made nondeductible contributions. Using the form, you will figure the nontaxable distributions for 1990, and your total IRA basis for 1990 and prior years. See the illustrated Forms 8606.

5-34 How to Figure Nontaxable and Taxable Amounts

I would advise you to seek help from a qualified tax accountant or attorney in figuring the nontaxable and taxable amounts of your IRAs. It is complicated, and it must be done correctly. However, I include the following specific instructions from the IRS if you wish to do it yourself.

If you made no contributions, only fully deductible contributions, or only nondeductible IRA contributions for 1991, use Form 8606 to figure

Form **8606**	**Nondeductible IRA Contributions,**	OMB No. 1545-1007
	IRA Basis, and Nontaxable IRA Distributions	**1991**
Department of the Treasury Internal Revenue Service	▶ Please see Recordkeeping Requirements on page 2. ▶ Attach to Form 1040, Form 1040A, or Form 1040NR.	Attachment Sequence No. **47**

Name (If married, file a separate Form 8606 for each spouse. See instructions.)	Your social security number
Rose Green	001 00 0000

Fill in Your Address Only If You Are Filing This Form by Itself and Not With Your Tax Return ▷

Home address (number and street, or P.O. box if mail is not delivered to your home)   Apt. no.
1040 Any Street

City, town or post office, state, and ZIP code
Anytown, Virginia 22000

1	Enter the total value of ALL your IRAs as of 12/31/91. (See instructions.)	1	
2	Enter your IRA contributions for 1991 that you choose to be nondeductible. Include those made during 1/1/92–4/15/92 that were for 1991. (See instructions.)	2	
3	Enter your total IRA basis for 1990 and prior years. (See instructions.)	3	
4	Add lines 2 and 3. If you did not receive any IRA distributions (withdrawals) in 1991, skip lines 5 through 13 and enter this amount on line 14	4	
5	Enter only those contributions included on line 2 that were made during 1/1/92–4/15/92. (This amount will be the same as line 2 if all of your nondeductible contributions for 1991 were made in 1992 by 4/15/92.) (See instructions.)	5	
6	Subtract line 5 from line 4	6	
7	Enter the amount from line 1 plus any outstanding rollovers. (See instructions.)	7	
8	Enter the total IRA distributions received during 1991. Do not include amounts rolled over before 1/1/92. (See instructions.)	8	
9	Add lines 7 and 8	9	
10	Divide line 6 by line 9 and enter the result as a decimal (to at least two places). Do not enter more than "1.00"	10	
11	Multiply line 8 by line 10. This is the amount of your **nontaxable distributions for 1991**. (See instructions.) ▶	11	1,300 00 *
12	Subtract line 11 from line 8. This is the basis in your IRA(s) as of 12/31/91	12	
13	Enter the amount, if any, from line 5	13	
14	Add lines 12 and 13. This is your total IRA basis for 1991 and prior years ▶	14	

Sign Here Only If You Are Filing This Form by Itself and Not With Your Tax Return ▶

Under penalties of perjury, I declare that I have examined this form, including accompanying attachments, and to the best of my knowledge and belief, it is true, correct, and complete.

Your signature ▶ Rose Green   Date ▶ 1/15/92

Paperwork Reduction Act Notice.—We ask for the information on this form to carry out the Internal Revenue laws of the United States. You are required to give us the information. We need it to ensure that you are complying with these laws and to allow us to figure and collect the right amount of tax.

The time needed to complete and file this form will vary depending on individual circumstances. The estimated average time is: Recordkeeping, 26 minutes; Learning about the law or the form, 7 minutes; Preparing the form, 22 minutes; and Copying, assembling, and sending the form to the IRS, 20 minutes.

If you have comments concerning the accuracy of these time estimates or suggestions for making this form more simple, we would be happy to hear from you. You can write to both the Internal Revenue Service, Washington, DC 20224, Attention: IRS Reports Clearance Officer, T:FP; and the Office of Management and Budget, Paperwork Reduction Project (1545-1007), Washington, DC 20503. DO

NOT send this form to either of these offices. Instead, see **When and Where To File,** on this page.

General Instructions

Purpose of Form.—You must use Form 8606 to report your IRA contributions that you choose to be nondeductible. You may wish to make nondeductible contributions, for example, if all or part of your contributions to an IRA are not deductible because of the income limitations for IRAs. First, figure your deductible contributions using the instructions for Form 1040 or Form 1040A, whichever apply to you. Report the deductible contributions on Form 1040, Form 1040A, or Form 1040NR. Then, enter on line 2 of Form 8606 the amount you choose to be nondeductible.

The part of any distributions you receive attributable to nondeductible contributions will not be taxable. If you have at any time made nondeductible contributions, also use Form 8606 to figure the nontaxable part of any IRA distributions you received in 1991. Line 11 will show the amount that is not taxable.

Who Must File.—You must file Form 8606 for 1991 if either of the following applies:
• You made nondeductible contributions to your IRA for 1991, or
• You received IRA distributions in 1991 and you have at any time made nondeductible contributions to any of your IRAs.

When and Where To File.—Attach Form 8606 to your 1991 Form 1040, Form 1040A, or Form 1040NR.

If you are required to file Form 8606, but do not have to file an income tax return because you do not meet the requirements for filing a return, you still have to file a Form 8606 with the Internal Revenue Service at the time and place you would be required to file Form 1040, Form 1040A, or Form 1040NR.

Penalty for Not Filing Form 8606.—The law provides for a penalty if you make nondeductible IRA contributions and do not file Form 8606. You will have to pay a $50 penalty for each failure to file a Form 8606, unless you can show that the failure to file was due to reasonable cause.

Cat.No. 63966F

Form **8606** (1991)

* From Worksheet in IRS Publication 590

how much of your 1991 IRA contributions are tax-free (because the IRA includes nondeductible contributions). You can then determine how much you must include in taxable income (because the IRA includes contributions that you deducted and/or earnings and gains). If you have more than one IRA, you must consider them together, as if they were a single IRA.

If you made IRA contributions for 1991 that may be partly nondeductible, you can use the following worksheet to figure how much of your 1991 IRA distribution(s) is tax-free and how much is taxable.

1) Enter the basis in your IRA(s) as of 12/31/90 $_____
2) Enter all IRA contributions made for 1991, **whether or not deductible.** Include contributions made during 1/1/92–4/15/92 for the 1991 year, but exclude contributions rolled over from retirement plans . . . . . $_____
3) Add lines 1 and 2 . . . . $_____
4) Enter the value of ALL your IRA(s) as of 12/31/91 (including any outstanding rollovers) . . . . $_____
5) Enter the total IRA distributions received in 1991 (Do not include outstanding rollovers) . . . . $_____
6) Add lines 4 and 5 . . . . $_____
7) Divide line 3 by line 6. Enter the result as a decimal (to at least two places). Do not enter more than 1.00 $_____
8) **Nontaxable portion** of the distribution. Multiply line 5 by line 7. Enter the result here and on Form 8606, line 11 . . . . $_____
9) **Taxable portion** of the distribution. Subtract line 8 from line 5. Enter the result here and on Form 1040, line 16b or Form 1040A, line 10b . . . . $_____

Note: To figure the remaining basis in your IRA after distributions, you can:

1) Use the worksheet in the Form 1040 instructions to figure your deductible IRA contributions to report on lines 24a and 24b of Form 1040 or lines 15a and 15b of Form 1040A.
2) After you complete the worksheet in the Form 1040 or Form 1040A instructions, enter your nondeductible IRA contributions on line 2 of Form 8606.
3) Complete lines 1, 3–6, and 12–14 of Form 8606. Do not complete lines 7–10 of Form 8606.
4) Find the basis in your IRA(s) as of 12/31/91 on line 12 of Form 8606.
5) Find your total IRA basis for 1991 and prior years on line 14 of Form 8606.

Example. Rose Green has made the following contributions to her IRAs—

Year	Deductible	Nondeductible
1985	$2,000	-0-
1986	$2,000	-0-
1987	$2,000	-0-
1988	$1,000	$1,000
1989	$1,000	$1,000
1990	-0-	$2,000
Totals	$8,000	$4,000

In 1991, Rose makes a $2,000 contribution that may be partly nondeductible. She also withdraws $5,000. At the end of that year, the fair market value of her accounts, including earnings, totals $18,000. She did not have any tax-free withdrawals in earlier years. The amount she includes in income is figured as follows:

1) Enter the basis in your IRA(s) as of 12/31/90 . . . . $ 4,000
2) Enter all IRA contributions made for 1991, **whether or not deductible.** Include contributions made during 1/1/92–4/15/92, but exclude contributions rolled over from retirement plans . . . . $ 2,000
3) Add lines 1 and 2 . . . . $ 6,000
4) Enter the value of ALL your IRA(s) as of 12/31/91 (include any outstanding rollovers) $18,000
5) Enter the total IRA distributions received in 1991 (Do not include outstanding rollovers) . . . . $ 5,000
6) Add lines 4 and 5 . . . . $23,000
7) Divide line 3 by line 6. Enter the result as a decimal (to at least two places). Do not enter more than 1.00 26
8) **Nontaxable portion** of the distribution. Multiply line 5 by line 7. Enter the result here and on Form 8606, line 11 . . . . $ 1,300
9) **Taxable portion** of the distribution. Subtract line 8 from line 5. Enter the result here and on Form 1040, line 16b or Form 1040A, line 10b . . . . $ 3,700

See the illustrated Form 8606 for Rose.

5-35 How to Recognize Losses on IRA Investments

You must determine your cost basis, which is the total amount of contributions you made to your IRAs that you did *not* deduct. Once again, I strongly recommend that you keep deductible and nondeductible contributions in separate annuities, making only deductible contributions to your IRAs. But if you have commingled deductible and nondeductible contributions in your IRAs, you must determine your cost basis to ascertain whether you have any losses on your IRA investments.

Delegate this task to a qualified tax person. The primary problem is one of bookkeeping. You must keep track of the deductible and nondeductible contributions over a period of years. It is not easy. However, as in the example in 5-34, I include the following example from the IRS to guide you if you prefer to attempt this yourself.

Example. Bill King has made nondeductible contributions to an IRA totaling $2,000, giving him a basis at the end of 1990 of $2,000. By the end of 1991, his IRA earns $400 in interest income. In that year, Bill withdraws $600, reducing the value of his IRA to $1,800 at year's end. Bill figures the taxable part of the distribution and his remaining basis on Form 8606. . . .

In 1992, Bill's IRA has a **loss** of $500. At the end of that year, Bill's IRA balance is $1,300. Bill's remaining basis in his IRA is $1,500. Bill withdraws the $1,300 balance remaining in the IRA. He can claim a loss for 1992 of $200 (the $1,500 basis minus the $1,300 withdrawn IRA balance).

5-36 Other Special IRA Situations

Under the law, you may instruct the custodian or trustee of your IRA to purchase an annuity contract for you. There is no tax consequence until you withdraw payments from the annuity. As in the preceding cases, annuity payments are fully taxable if all the contributions were deducted. If your annuity has both deductible and nondeductible contributions, you must determine your cost basis. Then anything over and above that you receive is taxable as ordinary income.

Retirement Bonds

You must cash them in "before the end of the year in which you reach age 59½." If you don't cash them in prior to that time, "you will be taxed on the entire value of the bonds" as if "you had cashed in the bonds at that time. When the bonds are cashed later, you will not be taxed again."

Inherited IRAs

Any distributions to beneficiaries of your IRA must be included in their gross incomes.

Beneficiaries. You can name anyone, including your estate, as your beneficiary to receive your IRA funds at your death.

Form **8606**	Nondeductible IRA Contributions, IRA Basis, and Nontaxable IRA Distributions	OMB No. 1545-1007
Department of the Treasury Internal Revenue Service	▶ Please see Recordkeeping Requirements on page 2. ▶ Attach to Form 1040, Form 1040A, or Form 1040NR.	**1991** Attachment Sequence No. **47**

Name. (If married, file a separate Form 8606 for each spouse. See instructions.)

Bill King

Your social security number

002 00 0000

Fill in Your Address Only If You Are Filing This Form by Itself and Not With Your Tax Return

Home address (number and street, or P.O. box if mail is not delivered to your home)

8606 A Street

Apt. no.

City, town or post office, state, and ZIP code

Sometown, Virginia 22000

Sample Only

1	Enter the total value of **ALL** your IRAs as of 12/31/91. (See instructions.)	**1**	0 00
2	Enter your IRA contributions for 1991 that you choose to be nondeductible. Include those made durin~ 1/1/92–4/15/92 that were for 1991. (See instructions.)		0 00
3	Enter your total IRA basis for 1990 and prior years. (See instructions.)		1,500 00
4	Add lines 2 and 3. If you did not receive any IRA distributions (withdrawal~ through 13 and enter this amount on line 14	**4**	1,500 00
5	Enter only those contributions included on line 2 that were made ~s amount will be the same as line 2 if all of your nondeductible co~ ~ade in 1992 by 4/15/92.) (See instructions.)	**5**	0 00
6	Subtract line 5 from line 4	**6**	1,500 00
7	Enter the amount from line 1 plu~ ~s. (See instructions.)	**7**	0 00
8	Enter the total IRA dist~ ~1991. Do not include amounts rolled o~ ~uctions.)	**8**	1,300 00
9	Add lines 7	**9**	1,300 00
10	Div~ ~er the result as a decimal (to at least two ~re than "1.00"	**10**	1.00
	~y line 10. This is the amount of your **nontaxable distributions for 1991.** (See ~.) ▶	**11**	1,300 00
	~ract line 11 from line 6. This is the basis in your IRA(s) as of 12/31/91	**12**	200 00
	Enter the amount, if any, from line 5	**13**	0 00
14	Add lines 12 and 13. This is your total IRA basis for 1991 and prior years ▶	**14**	200 00

Sign Here Only If You Are Filing This Form by Itself and Not With Your Tax Return

Under penalties of perjury, I declare that I have examined this form, including accompanying attachments, and to the best of my knowledge and belief, it is true, correct, and complete.

▶ **Bill King** Your signature

▶ **4/15/93** Date

Paperwork Reduction Act Notice.—We ask for the information on this form to carry out the Internal Revenue laws of the United States. We need it to ensure that you are complying with these laws and to allow us to figure and collect the right amount of tax.

The time needed to complete and file this form will vary depending on individual circumstances. The estimated average time is: **Recordkeeping,** 26 minutes; **Learning about the law or the form,** 7 minutes; **Preparing the form,** 22 minutes; and **Copying, assembling, and sending the form to the IRS,** 20 minutes.

If you have comments concerning the accuracy of these time estimates or suggestions for making this form more simple, we would be happy to hear from you. You can write to both the **Internal Revenue Service,** Washington, DC 20224, Attention: IRS Reports Clearance Officer, T:FP; and the **Office of Management and Budget,** Paperwork Reduction Project (1545-1007), Washington, DC 20503. **DO**

NOT send this form to either of these offices. Instead, see **When and Where To File,** on this page.

General Instructions

Purpose of Form.—You must use Form 8606 to report your IRA contributions that you choose to be nondeductible. You may wish to make nondeductible contributions, for example, if all or part of your contributions are not deductible because of the income limitations for IRAs. First, figure your deductible contributions using the instructions for Form 1040 or Form 1040A, whichever apply to you. Report the deductible contributions on Form 1040, Form 1040A, or Form 1040NR. Then, enter on line 2 of Form 8606 the amount you choose to be nondeductible.

The part of any distributions you receive attributable to nondeductible contributions will not be taxable. If you have at any time made nondeductible contributions, also use Form 8606 to figure the nontaxable part of any IRA distributions you received in 1991. Line 11 will show the amount that is not taxable.

Who Must File.—You must file Form 8606 for 1991 if **either** of the following applies:

• You made nondeductible contributions to your IRA for 1991, or

• You received IRA distributions in 1991 and you have at any time made nondeductible contributions to any of your IRAs.

When and Where To File.—Attach Form 8606 to your 1991 Form 1040, Form 1040A, or Form 1040NR.

If you are required to file Form 8606, but do not have to file an income tax return because you do not meet the requirements for filing a return, you still have to file a Form 8606 with the Internal Revenue Service at the time and place you would be required to file Form 1040, Form 1040A, or Form 1040NR.

Penalty for Not Filing Form 8606.—The law provides for a penalty if you make nondeductible IRA contributions and do not file Form 8606. You will have to pay a $50 penalty for each failure to file Form 8606, unless you can show that the failure to file was due to reasonable cause.

Cat.No. 63966F

Form **8606** (1991)

Spouse. A spouse who inherits an interest in an IRA from his or her spouse "can elect to treat the entire inherited interest" as his or her own account. (See the discussion in 5-27 for the rules on when you must begin to make withdrawals from the IRA.)

Beneficiary other than spouse. The privileges in the preceding paragraph do not apply "if you inherit an IRA from someone other than your spouse." Rollovers are not allowed under these circumstances; neither are deductions. In addition, nondeductible contributions cannot be made to an inherited IRA.

IRA with basis. Any cost basis inherited in an IRA remains with that IRA. Only if you are the deceased's spouse can you combine his or her cost basis with your IRA. "If you take a distribution from an inherited IRA and your IRA, and each has basis, you must complete separate Forms 8606 to determine the taxable and nontaxable portions of those distributions."

5-37 Reporting and Withholding Requirements for Taxable Amounts

If you receive a total distribution from your IRA, you will receive **Form 1099-R,** *Statement for Recipients of Total Distributions from Profit-Sharing, Retirement Plans, Individual Retirement Arrangements, Insurance Contracts, Etc.,* or a similar statement. IRA distributions are shown in Boxes 1 and 2 of Form 1099-R. A number in Box 7 tells you what type of distribution you received from your IRA. The numbers mean the following:

1) Early (premature) distribution, no known exception.
2) Early (premature) distribution, exception applies.
3) Disability.
4) Death.
5) Prohibited transactions.
6) Section 1035 exchange.
7) Normal distribution.
8) Excess contributions plus earnings/excess deferrals (and/or earnings) taxable in 1991.
9) PS-58 costs; P—Excess contributions plus earnings/excess deferrals taxable in 1990;
   A—Qualifies for 5-year/10-year averaging;
   B—Qualifies for death benefit exclusion;
   C—Qualifies for A and B;
   D—Excess contributions plus earnings/excess deferrals taxable in 1989.

Form 8606

Nondeductible IRA Contributions, IRA Basis, and Nontaxable IRA Distributions

Department of the Treasury
Internal Revenue Service

► Please see Recordkeeping Requirements on page 2.
► Attach to Form 1040, Form 1040A, or Form 1040NR.

OMB No. 1545-1007

1991

Attachment
Sequence No. 47

Name. (If married, file a separate Form 8606 for each spouse. See instructions.)

Bill King

Your social security number

002 00 0000

Fill in Your Address Only If You Are Filing This Form by Itself and Not With Your Tax Return ▷	Home address (number and street, or P.O. box if mail is not delivered to your home) **8606 A Street**	Apt. no.
	City, town or post office, state, and ZIP code **Some town, Virginia 22000**	

1	Enter the total value of ALL your IRAs as of 12/31/91. (See instructions.)	**1**	1,800 00
2	Enter your IRA contributions for 1991 that you choose to be nondeductible. Include those made during 1/1/92–4/15/92 that were for 1991. (See instructions.)	**2**	0 00
3	Enter your total IRA basis for 1990 and prior years. (See instructions.)	**3**	2,000 00
4	Add lines 2 and 3. If you did not receive any IRA distributions (withdrawals) in 1991, skip lines 5 through 13 and enter this amount on line 14	**4**	2,000 00
5	Enter only those contributions included on line 2 that were made during 1991. (This amount will be the same as line 2 if all of your nondeductible contributions for 1991 were made in 1992 by 4/15/92.) (See instructions.)	**5**	0 00
6	Subtract line 5 from line 4	**6**	2,000 00
7	Enter the amount from line 1 plus any outstanding rollovers. (See instructions.)	**7**	1,800 00
8	Enter the total IRA distributions received during 1991. Do not include amounts rolled over before 1/1/92. (See instructions.)	**8**	600 00
9	Add lines 7 and 8	**9**	2,400 00
10	Divide line 6 by line 9 and enter the result as a decimal (to at least two places). Do not enter more than "1.00"	**10**	.83 33
11	Multiply line 8 by line 10. This is the amount of your **nontaxable distributions for 1991.** (See instructions.) ►	**11**	500 00
12	Subtract line 11 from line 6. This is the basis in your IRA(s) as of 12/31/91	**12**	1,500 00
13	Enter the amount, if any, from line 5	**13**	0 00
14	Add lines 12 and 13. This is your total IRA basis for 1991 and prior years ►	**14**	1,500 00

Sign Here Only If You Are Filing This Form by Itself and Not With Your Tax Return	Under penalties of perjury, I declare that I have examined this form, including accompanying attachments, and to the best of my knowledge and belief, it is true, correct, and complete. ▶ *Bill King* Your signature ▶ 4/15/92 Date

NOT send this form to either of these offices. Instead, see **When and Where To File,** on this page.

General Instructions

Purpose of Form.—You must use Form 8606 to report your IRA contributions that you choose to be nondeductible. You may wish to make nondeductible contributions, for example, if all or part of your contributions are not deductible because of the income limitations for IRAs. First, figure your deductible contributions using the instructions for Form 1040 or Form 1040A, whichever apply to you. Report the deductible contributions on Form 1040, Form 1040A, or Form 1040NR. Then, enter on line 2 of Form 8606 the amount you choose to be nondeductible.

The part of any distributions you receive attributable to nondeductible contributions will not be taxable. If you have at any time made nondeductible contributions, also use Form 8606 to figure the nontaxable part of any IRA distributions you received in 1991. Line 11 will show the amount that is not taxable.

Who Must File.—You must file Form 8606 for 1991 if **either** of the following applies:

• You made nondeductible contributions to your IRA for 1991, or

• You received IRA distributions in 1991 and you have at any time made nondeductible contributions to any of your IRAs.

When and Where To File.—Attach Form 8606 to your 1991 Form 1040, Form 1040A, or Form 1040NR.

If you are required to file Form 8606, but do not have to file an income tax return because you do not meet the requirements for filing a return, you still have to file a Form 8606 with the Internal Revenue Service at the time and place you would be required to file Form 1040, Form 1040A, or Form 1040NR.

Penalty for Not Filing Form 8606.—The law provides for a penalty if you make nondeductible IRA contributions and do not file Form 8606. You will have to pay a $50 penalty for each failure to file Form 8606, unless you can show that the failure to file was due to reasonable cause.

Cat.No. 63966F

Form **8606** (1991)

Form W-2P. If you receive an IRA payment that is not a total distribution, you will receive Form W-2P, Statement for Recipients of Annuities, Pensions, Retired Pay, or IRA Payments.

Withholding. Federal income tax is withheld from IRA distributions unless you choose not to have tax withheld.

When distributed, your annuity payments may have taxes withheld if you wish. The amount will depend on the number of allowances you claim on your Form W-4P. You automatically are treated as a "married individual claiming three withholding allowances" if you do not file a certificate, and "10% will be withheld on lump-sum distributions."

Withholding from IRA distributions outside the United States. Usually, you cannot choose exemptions from withholding on your IRA distribution if you are a U.S. citizen or resident alien whose address is outside the U.S. and its possessions.

But you can choose this exemption if

- you have given your IRA distributor your U.S. address.
- you are not a U.S. citizen, a resident alien of the U.S., or an expatriate attempting to avoid taxes.

In all other cases, taxes must be withheld.

IRS Publication 505, *Tax Withholding and Estimated Tax,* has more information in the section dealing with withholding on pensions and annuities. IRS Publication 515, *Withholding of Tax on Nonresident Aliens and Foreign Corporations,* has still more information.

Reporting taxable distributions on your return. Report fully taxable distributions, including premature distributions, on line 16b, Form 1040 (no entry is required on line 17a, or line 10b, Form 1040A). If only part of the distribution is taxable, enter the total amount on line 16a, Form 1040 (or line 10a), Form 1040A) and the taxable part on line 16b (or 10b). You cannot report distributions on Form 1040EZ.

Estate and gift tax. IRS Publication 448, *Federal Estate and Gift Taxes,* has more information regarding the impact of estate and gift laws on IRAs.

5-38 What Acts Result in Penalties?

Strict rules govern IRAs. Under the following circumstances you will be penalized:

- If you make excess contributions
- If you make early withdrawals (take premature distributions)

- If you allow excess amounts to accumulate without making the required withdrawals
- If you receive excess distributions
- If you overstate your nondeductible contributions or fail to file Form 8606, *Nondeductible IRA Contributions, IRA Basis, and Nontaxable IRA Distributions*

You could lose your IRA status by some of these acts.

5-39 What Are Prohibited Transactions?

Prohibited transactions occur when you or members of your family attempt to use your IRA by

1) Borrowing money from it,
2) Selling property to it,
3) Receiving unreasonable compensation for managing it, and
4) Using it as security for a loan.

Effect on an IRA account. If a prohibited transaction occurs, your IRA will lose its tax status as of the first of the following year.

Effect on you (or your beneficiary). If a prohibited transaction occurs, in most instances you or your beneficiary will then have to include the total value of your IRA in your gross income for that year. That could be extremely costly to you.

Suppose your IRA totals were $100,000 and you completed a prohibited transaction that year. You would then have to include that amount as additional, ordinary income that year and pay taxes accordingly. The government has made it plain that IRAs are not to be misused. Furthermore, if you are under age 59½, you will have to pay an additional 10 percent penalty. There is still more to worry about. You could also have to pay a 5 percent excise tax plus double that amount if you do not correct the transaction.

Trust account set up by an employer or an employee association. Your employer or employee association, not you, will be accountable if it engages in a prohibited transaction. However, if you participate in the prohibited transaction with your employer or association, your account will lose its IRA status. IRS Publication 560, *Retirement Plans for the Self-Employed,* has more on this issue.

5-40 What Other Acts Should Be Avoided?

The following acts are also prohibited:

Investment in collectibles. If your IRA invests in collectibles, the amount invested after 1981 is considered distributed to you in the year invested. You may also have to pay the 10% tax on premature distributions.

Collectibles include art works, rugs, antiques, metals, gems, stamps, stamps, coins, alcoholic beverages, and certain other tangible personal property.

Exception. Your IRA can invest in one, one-half, one-quarter, or one-tenth ounce U.S. gold coins, or one-ounce silver coins minted by the Treasury Department beginning October 1, 1986.

Acceptance of certain cash, property or services. If you accept certain cash, property, or services offered by any financial institution because the institution maintains an IRA for you, it may be considered a prohibited transaction. However, until the Department of Labor makes a final decision regarding a request for exemption from the prohibited transaction rules for the above items, the IRS will not raise issues concerning such transactions.

For more information, call the IRS at (202) 566-6783/6784 (not a toll-free number). Call between the hours of 1:30 and 4:00 p.m. Eastern time, Monday through Thursday.

5-41 How to Handle Excess Contributions

You cannot contribute to an IRA in one year more than your compensation or $2,000, or $2,250 if you have a spousal IRA, no matter if your contributions are deductible or nondeductible or if you had an improper rollover.

Tax on excess contributions. It is never a good idea to owe the government money because you will eventually have to pay either interest or penalties on the amount. If you overpay your allowable amount into an IRA and the time for your tax return to be filed has passed, you will be taxed 6 percent on the overage each year until you correct the overpayment. "The tax cannot be more than 6% of the value of your IRA as of the end of your tax year."

See Form 5329, *Return for Additional Taxes Attributable to Qualified Retirement Plans (Including IRAs), Annuities, and Modified Endowment Contracts.* (For more information on filing Form 5329, see 5-45.)

If you withdraw excess contributions, either before your current tax form is due or attributable to a previous year, you will receive Form W-2P, *Statement for Recipients of Annuities, Pensions, Retired Pay, or IRA Payments,* or Form 1099-R, *Statement for Recipients of Total Distribution from Profit-Sharing, Retirement Plans, In-*

Form **5329**

Department of the Treasury
Internal Revenue Service

Return for Additional Taxes Attributable to Qualified Retirement Plans (Including IRAs), Annuities, and Modified Endowment Contracts

(Under Sections 72, 4973, 4974 and 4980A of the Internal Revenue Code)
▶ Attach to Form 1040. See separate instructions.

OMB No. 1545-0203

1991

Attachment
Sequence No. **29**

Name of individual subject to additional tax. (Enter the name of one individual only. See the instructions for "Joint Returns.")

Your social security number

Address (number and street). (Enter P.O. box no. if mail is not delivered to street address.)

Apt. No.

City, town, or post office, state, and ZIP code

If this is an Amended Return, check here ▶ ☐

Part I Excess Contributions Tax for Individual Retirement Arrangements (Section 4973)

Complete this part if, either in this year or in earlier years, you contributed more to your IRA than is or was allowable and you have an excess contribution subject to tax.

1 Excess contributions for 1991 (see instructions). Do not include this amount on Form 1040, line 24a or 24b	**1**	
2 Earlier year excess contributions not previously eliminated (see instructions)	**2**	
3 Contribution credit. (If your actual contribution for 1991 is less than your maximum allowable contribution, see instructions for line 3; otherwise, enter -0-.)	**3**	
4a 1991 distributions from your IRA account that are includible in taxable income	**4a**	
b 1990 tax year excess contributions (if any) withdrawn after the due date (including extensions) of your 1990 income tax return, and 1989 and earlier tax year excess contributions withdrawn in 1991.	**4b**	
c Add lines 3, 4a, and 4b	**4c**	
5 Adjusted earlier year excess contributions. (Subtract line 4c from line 2. Enter the result, but not less than zero.)	**5**	
6 Total excess contributions (add lines 1 and 5).	**6**	
7 Tax due. (Enter the **smaller** of 6% of line 6 or 6% of the value of your IRA on the last day of 1991.) Also enter this amount on Form 1040, line 51	**7**	

Part II Tax on Early Distributions (Section 72)

Complete this part if a taxable distribution was made from your qualified retirement plan (including an IRA), modified endowment contract, or annuity contract before you reached age 59½. **Note:** *You must enter the amount of the distribution on the appropriate line (or lines) of Form 1040 or Form 4972.*

8 Early distributions included in gross income attributable to:		
a Qualified retirement plans (including IRAs)	**8a**	
b Annuity contracts	**8b**	
c Modified endowment contracts	**8c**	
d Prohibited transactions	**8d**	
e Pledging of accounts as security	**8e**	
f Cost of collectibles	**8f**	
g Total distributions (add lines 8a through 8f)	**8g**	
Note: *Include this amount on line 16b or 17b of Form 1040 or on the appropriate line of Form 4972*		
9 Exceptions to distributions subject to additional taxes (see instructions):		
a Due to death (does not apply to modified endowment contracts) . . .	**9a**	
b Due to total and permanent disability	**9b**	
c As part of a series of substantially equal lifetime periodic payments . .	**9c**	
Lines 9d through 9f DO NOT apply to distributions from IRAs, annuities, or modified endowment contracts.		
d Due to separation from service in or after the year of reaching age 55 .	**9d**	
e Distributions to the extent of deductible medical expenses	**9e**	
f Made to an alternate payee under a qualified domestic relations order .	**9f**	
g Other (specify)	**9g**	
h Total amount excluded from additional tax (add lines 9a through 9g)	**9h**	
10 Amount subject to additional tax (subtract line 9h from 8g)	**10**	
11 Total section 72 tax (multiply line 10 by 10% (.10)). Enter here and on Form 1040, line 51	**11**	

For Paperwork Reduction Act Notice, see page 1 of separate instructions.   Cat. No. 13329Q   Form **5329** (1991)

Part III Tax on Excess Accumulation in Qualified Retirement Plans (Including IRAs) (Section 4974)

12	Minimum required distribution (see instructions)	12	
13	Amount actually distributed to you	13	
14	Subtract line 13 from line 12. If line 13 is more than line 12, enter -0-	14	
15	Tax due (multiply line 14 by 50% (.50)). Enter here and on Form 1040, line 51	15	

Part IV Tax on Excess Distributions From Qualified Retirement Plans (Including IRAs) (Section 4980A)

Complete lines 16 through 19c for regular distributions ONLY.

16	Enter the total amount of regular retirement distributions		16	
17a	Enter the applicable threshold amount ($136,204 or $150,000) (see instructions)	17a		
b	1991 recovery of grandfather amount (from Worksheet 1 or 2)	17b		
c	Enter the **greater** of line 17a or 17b		17c	
18	Excess distributions (subtract line 17c from line 16). (If less than zero, enter -0-.)		18	
19a	Tentative tax (multiply line 18 by 15% (.15))		19a	
b	Section 72(t) tax offset (see instructions)		19b	
c	Tax due (subtract line 19b from line 19a). Enter here and on Form 1040, line 51		19c	

Complete lines 20 through 23c for lump-sum distributions ONLY.

20	Enter the total amount of your lump-sum distributions		20	
21a	Enter the applicable threshold amount ($681,020 or $750,000) (see instructions)	21a		
b	1991 recovery of grandfather amount (from Worksheet 1 or 2)	21b		
c	Enter the **greater** of line 21a or 21b		21c	
22	Excess distributions (subtract line 21c from line 20). (If less than zero, enter -0-.)		22	
23a	Tentative tax (multiply line 22 by 15% (.15))		23a	
b	Section 72(t) tax offset (see instructions)		23b	
c	Tax due (subtract line 23b from line 23a). Enter here and on Form 1040, line 51		23c	

Acceleration Elections (see the instructions for Part IV, Worksheet 1)

1 If you elected the discretionary method in 1987 or 1988 and wish to make an acceleration election beginning in 1991 under Temp. Regs. section 54.4981A-1T b-12, check here ▶ ☐

2 If you previously made an acceleration election and wish to revoke that election, check here ▶ ☐
Note: *If you checked 2 above, see the instructions for filing amended returns on page 2.*

Please Sign Here	Under penalties of perjury, I declare that I have examined this return, including accompanying schedules and statements, and to the best of my knowledge and belief, it is true, correct, and complete. Declaration of preparer (other than taxpayer) is based on all information of which preparer has any knowledge.		
	Your signature (Sign and date only if not attached to your income tax return.)	▶ Date	

Paid Preparer's Use Only	Preparer's signature ▶	Date	Check if self-employed ▶ ☐	Preparer's social security no. (see instructions)
	Firm's name (or yours, if self-employed) and address ▶		E.I. No. ▶	
			ZIP code ▶	

dividual Retirement Arrangements, Insurance Contracts, Etc., indicating the amount of the withdrawal. If the excess contribution was made in a previous tax year, these forms will indicate the year in which the earnings are taxable.

Excess contributions you withdraw after your return is due. You can withdraw any excess contribution after your tax return filing date—if the total contributions were $2,250 or less, other than rollovers, and your employer made no contributions that year—and not include the amount withdrawn in your gross income *only* if you did not deduct the excess.

Excess contribution deducted in an earlier year. You can remove the excess from your IRA and not include it in your gross income by filing Form 1040X, *Amended U.S. Individual Income Tax Return,* for that year without deducting the excess contribution on the amended return. You are allowed three years after you filed your return to do this, or two years from the time the tax was paid, whichever is later.

Excess due to incorrect rollover information. If a mistake resulting from a rollover in your IRA causes excess contributions to occur, you can withdraw the excess contribution. "The $2,250 limit, mentioned above, is increased by the amount of the excess that is due to the incorrect information. You will have to amend your return for the year in which the excess occurred. Do not include the excess contribution in your gross income in the year you withdraw it."

Taking a deduction in a later year for an excess contribution. You can apply excess contributions to a later year (but not to an earlier year) if the contributions for that later year are less than the maximum allowable amount. You can deduct excess contributions in your IRA from preceding years "up to the difference between the maximum amount that is deductible in the year and the amount actually contributed during the year." By doing that, you can avoid making a withdrawal, but you will still have to pay the 6 percent tax "on any excess contributions remaining at the end of a tax year."

Closed tax year. A special rule applies if you incorrectly deducted part of the excess contribution in a closed tax year (one for which the period to assess a tax deficiency has expired). The amount allowable as an IRA deduction for a later correction year (the year you contribute less than the allowable amount) must be reduced by the amount of the excess contribution deducted in the closed year.

5-42 How to Handle Premature Distributions (Early Withdrawals)

All premature distributions from an IRA are taxable as ordinary income in the year received. Any funds withdrawn prior to age 59$\frac{1}{2}$, except for those discussed earlier in this chapter, are subject to an additional 10 percent penalty.

Use Form 5329 to figure the tax. (See the discussion of Form 5329 in 5-45 for information on filing the form.)

5-43 How to Handle Excess Accumulations (Insufficient Distributions)

You must begin receiving required minimum distributions from your IRA by April 1 of the year after you became 70$\frac{1}{2}$. Otherwise, you may owe a 50 percent excise tax on the amount not distributed. Use Form 5329, *Return for Additional Taxes Attributable to Qualified Retirement Plans (Including IRAs), Annuities, and Modified Endowment Contracts,* to report the tax on excess accumulations. (For more information, see 5-45.)

Request to excuse the tax. You can request that the tax be excused if you can show that a reasonable mistake has been made and that you are in the process of correcting it.

How to file the request. When you file your Form 1040, include Form 5329 along with it, pay your excess accumulations tax, and provide an explanation for the excess and a statement that you are in the process of correcting the situation.

5-44 How to Handle Excess Distributions

You may have to pay a 15 percent excise tax if you receive more than $150,000 of retirement distributions during the year "from any plan, contract, or account that at any time has been treated as a qualified employer plan or IRA. Use Form 5329 to figure the tax." (See the discussion of Form 5329 in 5-45.)

Excluded distributions. The excess distribution tax does not apply if distributions occur because of

1) the employee's death.
2) a rollover.
3) their status as nondeductible contributions.

Combining distributions. All distributions in behalf of one person must be combined to figure the amount of excess distributions for the year.

Special limitation on tax. On a return filed for a tax year ended before January 1, 1989, you could have chosen not to pay the 15% tax on the part of any distribution that is related to your accrued benefits on August 1, 1986. This rule **applies only if** the accrued benefit as of August 1, 1986, exceeded $562,500.

However, if you made this choice to exclude from the tax on excess distributions a distribution amount allocable to your August 1, 1986, benefit accruals, your other retirement distributions are subject to the tax to the extent they are more than $128,228 for 1991 (instead of $150,000). Furthermore, this $128,228 amount is reduced (but not below zero) by any distributions received during the year that are allocable to the August 1, 1986, benefit accruals.

If you did not elect to apply this rule, then the 15% tax will apply to the part of the distribution that exceeds $150,000.

Increase in estate tax. For decedents dying after December 31, 1986, the estate tax will be increased by 15% of the excess retirement accumulation. A person's excess retirement accumulation, if any, is the value of the decedent's interest in all qualified employee plans, tax-sheltered annuities, qualified annuity plans, individual retirement accounts, and any other plans that the Internal Revenue Service may include over the "present value" of a single life annuity with payments equal to the annual ceiling ($150,000), and payable for a period equal to the decedent's life expectancy immediately before death. The tax may not be offset by any credits against the estate tax, such as the unified credit.

5-45 How to Report Additional Taxes

To report the tax on excess contributions, premature distributions, excess distributions, and excess accumulations, use Form 5329, *Return for Additional Taxes Attributable to Qualified Retirement Plans (Including IRAs), Annuities, and Modified Endowment Contracts.*

You also must file Form 5329 if you

- meet an exception to the 10% additional tax on early (premature) distributions, but only if the exception is **not** shown on the **Form 1099 or Form W-2P** that you received for the distribution, or
- receive excess distributions from a qualified retirement plan, whether or not you owe tax on them.

If you file Form 1040, complete Form 5329 and attach it to your Form 1040. Enter the total amount of IRA tax due on line 52, Form 1040.

If you do not have to file a Form 1040 but do have to pay one of the IRA taxes mentioned earlier, file the completed Form 5329 with IRS at the time and place you would have filed Form 1040. Include a check or money order payable to IRS for the tax you owe, as shown on Form 5329. Write your social security number, tax form number, and tax year on your check or money order.

5-46 Summary of IRA for Clergypersons

Most clergypersons are eligible to purchase an IRA. You write a check from your personal account and then deduct it for federal income tax purposes, *not* Social Security purposes. You can purchase an IRA up to April 15 of the year following the year you wish to report it as a deduction. For example, if you wish to show an IRA deduction for 1992, you have until April 15, 1993, to purchase and report it.

Although the IRA has some tax advantages, the tax-sheltered annuity has even more for clergypersons. If you have only enough money for one retirement program, you should choose the tax-sheltered annuity first before making deposits into an IRA. If you deposit all your allowable exclusion into a TSA, only then should you deposit money into the IRA—if you are an eligible clergyperson employed by a tax-exempt employer.

I caution you to take the IRA program and its strict rules seriously. If it's done correctly, the IRA will do its job and help you at retirement. If the IRA is done incorrectly, the penalties could ruin your investment.

APPENDIX E

Life Expectancy Tables

TABLE I
(Single Life Expectancy)*

AGE	DIVISOR	AGE	DIVISOR
35	47.3	71	15.3
36	46.4	72	14.6
37	45.4	73	13.9
38	44.4	74	13.2
39	43.5	75	12.5
40	42.5	76	11.9
41	41.5	77	11.2
42	40.6	78	10.6
43	39.6	79	10.0
44	38.7	80	9.5
45	37.7	81	8.9
46	36.8	82	8.4
47	35.9	83	7.9
48	34.9	84	7.4
49	34.0	85	6.9
50	33.1	86	6.5
51	32.2	87	6.1
52	31.3	88	5.7
53	30.4	89	5.3
54	29.5	90	5.0
55	28.6	91	4.7
56	27.7	92	4.4
57	26.8	93	4.1
58	25.9	94	3.9
59	25.0	95	3.7
60	24.2	96	3.4
61	23.3	97	3.2
62	22.5	98	3.0
63	21.6	99	2.8
64	20.8	100	2.7
65	20.0	101	2.5
66	19.2	102	2.3
67	18.4	103	2.1
68	17.6	104	1.9
69	16.8	105	1.8
70	16.0	106	1.6

AGE	DIVISOR	AGE	DIVISOR
107	1.4	112	.8
108	1.3	113	.7
109	1.1	114	.6
110	1.0	115	.5
111	.9		

* Table I does not provide for IRA owners younger than 35 years of age. For additional life expectancy tables, see Publication 939.

APPENDIX E
Life Expectancy Tables (continued)

TABLE II
(Joint Life and Last Survivor Expectancy)*

AGES	35	36	37	38	39	40	41	42	43	44
35	54.0	53.5	53.0	52.6	52.2	51.8	51.4	51.1	50.8	50.5
36	53.5	53.0	52.5	52.0	51.6	51.2	50.8	50.4	50.1	49.8
37	53.0	52.5	52.0	51.5	51.0	50.6	50.2	49.8	49.5	49.1
38	52.6	52.0	51.5	51.0	50.5	50.0	49.6	49.2	48.8	48.5
39	52.2	51.6	51.0	50.5	50.0	49.5	49.1	48.6	48.2	47.8
40	51.8	51.2	50.6	50.0	49.5	49.0	48.5	48.1	47.6	47.2
41	51.4	50.8	50.2	49.6	49.1	48.5	48.0	47.5	47.1	46.7
42	51.1	50.4	49.8	49.2	48.6	48.1	47.5	47.0	46.6	46.1
43	50.8	50.1	49.5	48.8	48.2	47.6	47.1	46.6	46.0	45.6
44	50.5	49.8	49.1	48.5	47.8	47.2	46.7	46.1	45.6	45.1
45	50.2	49.5	48.8	48.1	47.5	46.9	46.3	45.7	45.1	44.6
46	50.0	49.2	48.5	47.8	47.2	46.5	45.9	45.3	44.7	44.1
47	49.7	49.0	48.3	47.5	46.8	46.2	45.5	44.9	44.3	43.7
48	49.5	48.8	48.0	47.3	46.6	45.9	45.2	44.5	43.9	43.3
49	49.3	48.5	47.8	47.0	46.3	45.6	44.9	44.2	43.6	42.9
50	49.2	48.4	47.6	46.8	46.0	45.3	44.6	43.9	43.2	42.6
51	49.0	48.2	47.4	46.6	45.8	45.1	44.3	43.6	42.9	42.2

AGES	35	36	37	38	39	40	41	42	43	44
52	48.8	48.0	47.2	46.4	45.6	44.8	44.1	43.3	42.6	41.9
53	48.7	47.9	47.0	46.2	45.4	44.6	43.9	43.1	42.4	41.7
54	48.6	47.7	46.9	46.0	45.2	44.4	43.6	42.9	42.1	41.4
55	48.5	47.6	46.7	45.9	45.1	44.2	43.4	42.7	41.9	41.2
56	48.3	47.5	46.6	45.8	44.9	44.1	43.3	42.5	41.7	40.9
57	48.3	47.4	46.5	45.6	44.8	43.9	43.1	42.3	41.5	40.7
58	48.2	47.3	46.4	45.5	44.7	43.8	43.0	42.1	41.3	40.5
59	48.1	47.2	46.3	45.4	44.5	43.7	42.8	42.0	41.2	40.4
60	48.0	47.1	46.2	45.3	44.4	43.6	42.7	41.9	41.0	40.2
61	47.9	47.0	46.1	45.2	44.3	43.5	42.6	41.7	40.9	40.0
62	47.9	47.0	46.0	45.1	44.2	43.4	42.5	41.6	40.8	39.9
63	47.8	46.9	46.0	45.1	44.2	43.3	42.4	41.5	40.6	39.8
64	47.8	46.8	45.9	45.0	44.1	43.2	42.3	41.4	40.5	39.7
65	47.7	46.8	45.9	44.9	44.0	43.1	42.2	41.3	40.4	39.6
66	47.7	46.7	45.8	44.9	44.0	43.1	42.2	41.3	40.4	39.5
67	47.6	46.7	45.8	44.8	43.9	43.0	42.1	41.2	40.3	39.4
68	47.6	46.7	45.7	44.8	43.9	42.9	42.0	41.1	40.2	39.3
69	47.6	46.6	45.7	44.8	43.8	42.9	42.0	41.1	40.2	39.3
70	47.5	46.6	45.7	44.7	43.8	42.9	41.9	41.0	40.1	39.2
71	47.5	46.6	45.6	44.7	43.8	42.8	41.9	41.0	40.1	39.1
72	47.5	46.6	45.6	44.7	43.7	42.8	41.9	40.9	40.0	39.1
73	47.5	46.5	45.6	44.6	43.7	42.8	41.8	40.9	40.0	39.0
74	47.5	46.5	45.6	44.6	43.7	42.7	41.8	40.9	39.9	39.0
75	47.4	46.5	45.5	44.6	43.6	42.7	41.8	40.8	39.9	39.0
76	47.4	46.5	45.5	44.6	43.6	42.7	41.7	40.8	39.9	38.9

AGES	35	36	37	38	39	40	41	42	43	44
77	47.4	46.5	45.5	44.6	43.6	42.7	41.7	40.8	39.8	38.9
78	47.4	46.4	45.5	44.5	43.6	42.6	41.7	40.7	39.8	38.9
79	47.4	46.4	45.5	44.5	43.6	42.6	41.7	40.7	39.8	38.9
80	47.4	46.4	45.5	44.5	43.6	42.6	41.7	40.7	39.8	38.8
81	47.4	46.4	45.5	44.5	43.5	42.6	41.6	40.7	39.8	38.8
82	47.4	46.4	45.4	44.5	43.5	42.6	41.6	40.7	39.7	38.8
83	47.4	46.4	45.4	44.5	43.5	42.6	41.6	40.7	39.7	38.8
84	47.4	46.4	45.4	44.5	43.5	42.6	41.6	40.7	39.7	38.8
85	47.4	46.4	45.4	44.5	43.5	42.6	41.6	40.7	39.7	38.8
86	47.3	46.4	45.4	44.5	43.5	42.5	41.6	40.6	39.7	38.8
87	47.3	46.4	45.4	44.5	43.5	42.5	41.6	40.6	39.7	38.8
88	47.3	46.4	45.4	44.5	43.5	42.5	41.6	40.6	39.7	38.7
89	47.3	46.4	45.4	44.4	43.5	42.5	41.6	40.6	39.7	38.7
90	47.3	46.4	45.4	44.4	43.5	42.5	41.6	40.6	39.7	38.7
91	47.3	46.4	45.4	44.4	43.5	42.5	41.6	40.6	39.7	38.7
92	47.3	46.4	45.4	44.4	43.5	42.5	41.6	40.6	39.7	38.7

*Table II does not provide for IRA owners or survivors younger than 55 years of age. For additional life expectancy tables, see IRS Publication 939.

APPENDIX E

Life Expectancy Tables (continued)

TABLE II (continued)
(Joint Life and Last Survivor Expectancy)

AGES	45	46	47	48	49	50	51	52	53	54
45	44.1	43.6	43.2	42.7	42.3	42.0	41.6	41.3	41.0	40.7
46	43.6	43.1	42.6	42.2	41.8	41.4	41.0	40.6	40.3	40.0
47	43.2	42.6	42.1	41.7	41.2	40.8	40.4	40.0	39.7	39.3
48	42.7	42.2	41.7	41.2	40.7	40.2	39.8	39.4	39.0	38.7
49	42.3	41.8	41.2	40.7	40.2	39.7	39.3	38.8	38.4	38.1
50	42.0	41.4	40.8	40.2	39.7	39.2	38.7	38.3	37.9	37.5
51	41.6	41.0	40.4	39.8	39.3	38.7	38.2	37.8	37.3	36.9
52	41.3	40.6	40.0	39.4	38.8	38.3	37.8	37.3	36.8	36.4
53	41.0	40.3	39.7	39.0	38.4	37.9	37.3	36.8	36.3	35.8
54	40.7	40.0	39.3	38.7	38.1	37.5	36.9	36.4	35.8	35.3
55	40.4	39.7	39.0	38.4	37.7	37.1	36.5	35.9	35.4	34.9
56	40.2	39.5	38.7	38.1	37.4	36.8	36.1	35.6	35.0	34.4
57	40.0	39.2	38.5	37.8	37.1	36.4	35.8	35.2	34.6	34.0
58	39.7	39.0	38.2	37.5	36.8	36.1	35.5	34.8	34.2	33.6
59	39.6	38.8	38.0	37.3	36.6	35.9	35.2	34.5	33.9	33.3
60	39.4	38.6	37.8	37.1	36.3	35.6	34.9	34.2	33.6	32.9
61	39.2	38.4	37.6	36.9	36.1	35.4	34.6	33.9	33.3	32.6

AGES	45	46	47	48	49	50	51	52	53	54
62	39.1	38.3	37.5	36.7	35.9	35.1	34.4	33.7	33.0	32.3
63	38.9	38.1	37.3	36.5	35.7	34.9	34.2	33.5	32.7	32.0
64	38.8	38.0	37.2	36.3	35.5	34.8	34.0	33.2	32.5	31.8
65	38.7	37.9	37.0	36.2	35.4	34.6	33.8	33.0	32.3	31.6
66	38.6	37.8	36.9	36.1	35.2	34.4	33.6	32.9	32.1	31.4
67	38.5	37.7	36.8	36.0	35.1	34.3	33.5	32.7	31.9	31.2
68	38.4	37.6	36.7	35.8	35.0	34.2	33.4	32.5	31.8	31.0
69	38.4	37.5	36.6	35.7	34.9	34.1	33.2	32.4	31.6	30.8
70	38.3	37.4	36.5	35.7	34.8	34.0	33.1	32.3	31.5	30.7
71	38.2	37.3	36.5	35.6	34.7	33.9	33.0	32.2	31.4	30.5
72	38.2	37.3	36.4	35.5	34.6	33.8	32.9	32.1	31.2	30.4
73	38.1	37.2	36.3	35.4	34.6	33.7	32.8	32.0	31.1	30.3
74	38.1	37.2	36.3	35.4	34.5	33.6	32.8	31.9	31.1	30.2
75	38.1	37.1	36.2	35.3	34.5	33.6	32.7	31.8	31.0	30.1
76	38.0	37.1	36.2	35.3	34.4	33.5	32.6	31.8	30.9	30.1
77	38.0	37.1	36.2	35.3	34.4	33.5	32.6	31.7	30.8	30.0
78	38.0	37.0	36.1	35.2	34.3	33.4	32.5	31.7	30.8	29.9
79	37.9	37.0	36.1	35.2	34.3	33.4	32.5	31.6	30.7	29.9
80	37.9	37.0	36.1	35.2	34.2	33.4	32.5	31.6	30.7	29.8
81	37.9	37.0	36.0	35.1	34.2	33.3	32.4	31.5	30.7	29.8
82	37.9	36.9	36.0	35.1	34.2	33.3	32.4	31.5	30.6	29.7
83	37.9	36.9	36.0	35.1	34.2	33.3	32.4	31.5	30.6	29.7
84	37.8	36.9	36.0	35.1	34.2	33.2	32.3	31.4	30.6	29.7
85	37.8	36.9	36.0	35.1	34.1	33.2	32.3	31.4	30.5	29.6
86	37.8	36.9	36.0	35.0	34.1	33.2	32.3	31.4	30.5	29.6

AGES	45	46	47	48	49	50	51	52	53	54
87	37.8	36.9	35.9	35.0	34.1	33.2	32.3	31.4	30.5	29.6
88	37.8	36.9	35.9	35.0	34.1	33.2	32.3	31.4	30.5	29.6
89	37.8	36.9	35.9	35.0	34.1	33.2	32.3	31.4	30.5	29.6
90	37.8	36.9	35.9	35.0	34.1	33.2	32.3	31.3	30.5	29.6
91	37.8	36.8	35.9	35.0	34.1	33.2	32.2	31.3	30.4	29.5
92	37.8	36.8	35.9	35.0	34.1	33.2	32.2	31.3	30.4	29.5

APPENDIX E

Life Expectancy Tables (continued)

TABLE II (continued)
(Joint Life and Last Survivor Expectancy)

AGES	55	56	57	58	59	60	61	62	63	64	65	66	67	68	69	70	71	72	73	74
55	34.4	33.9	33.5	33.1	32.7	32.3	32.0	31.7	31.4	31.1										
56	33.9	33.4	33.0	32.5	32.1	31.7	31.4	31.0	30.7	30.4										
57	33.5	33.0	32.5	32.0	31.6	31.2	30.8	30.4	30.1	29.8										
58	33.1	32.5	32.0	31.5	31.1	30.6	30.2	29.9	29.5	29.2										
59	32.7	32.1	31.6	31.1	30.6	30.1	29.7	29.3	28.9	28.6										
60	32.3	31.7	31.2	30.6	30.1	29.7	29.2	28.8	28.4	28.0										
61	32.0	31.4	30.8	30.2	29.7	29.2	28.7	28.3	27.8	27.4										
62	31.7	31.0	30.4	29.9	29.3	28.8	28.3	27.8	27.3	26.9										
63	31.4	30.7	30.1	29.5	28.9	28.4	27.8	27.3	26.9	26.4										
64	31.1	30.4	29.8	29.2	28.6	28.0	27.4	26.9	26.4	25.9										
65	30.9	30.2	29.5	28.9	28.2	27.6	27.1	26.5	26.0	25.5	25.0	24.6	24.2	23.8	23.4	23.1	22.8	22.5	22.2	22.0
66	30.6	29.9	29.2	28.6	27.9	27.3	26.7	26.1	25.6	25.1	24.6	24.1	23.7	23.3	22.9	22.5	22.2	21.9	21.6	21.4
67	30.4	29.7	29.0	28.3	27.6	27.0	26.4	25.8	25.2	24.7	24.2	23.7	23.2	22.8	22.4	22.0	21.7	21.3	21.0	20.8
68	30.2	29.5	28.8	28.1	27.4	26.7	26.1	25.5	24.9	24.3	23.8	23.3	22.8	22.3	21.9	21.5	21.2	20.8	20.5	20.2
69	30.1	29.3	28.6	27.8	27.1	26.5	25.8	25.2	24.6	24.0	23.4	22.9	22.4	21.9	21.5	21.1	20.7	20.3	20.0	19.6
70	29.9	29.1	28.4	27.6	26.9	26.2	25.6	24.9	24.3	23.7	23.1	22.5	22.0	21.5	21.1	20.6	20.2	19.8	19.4	19.1
71	29.7	29.0	28.2	27.5	26.7	26.0	25.3	24.7	24.0	23.4	22.8	22.2	21.7	21.2	20.7	20.2	19.8	19.4	19.0	18.6

AGES	55	56	57	58	59	60	61	62	63	64	65	66	67	68	69	70	71	72	73	74
72	29.6	28.8	28.1	27.3	26.5	25.8	25.1	24.4	23.8	23.1	22.5	21.9	21.3	20.8	20.3	19.8	19.4	18.9	18.5	18.2
73	29.5	28.7	27.9	27.1	26.4	25.6	24.9	24.2	23.5	22.9	22.2	21.6	21.0	20.5	20.0	19.4	19.0	18.5	18.1	17.7
74	29.4	28.6	27.8	27.0	26.2	25.5	24.7	24.0	23.3	22.7	22.0	21.4	20.8	20.2	19.6	19.1	18.6	18.2	17.7	17.3
75	29.3	28.5	27.7	26.9	26.1	25.3	24.6	23.8	23.1	22.4	21.8	21.1	20.5	19.9	19.3	18.8	18.3	17.8	17.3	16.9
76	29.2	28.4	27.6	26.8	26.0	25.2	24.4	23.7	23.0	22.3	21.6	20.9	20.3	19.7	19.1	18.5	18.0	17.5	17.0	16.5
77	29.1	28.3	27.5	26.7	25.9	25.1	24.3	23.6	22.8	22.1	21.4	20.7	20.1	19.4	18.8	18.3	17.7	17.2	16.7	16.2
78	29.1	28.2	27.4	26.6	25.8	25.0	24.2	23.4	22.7	21.9	21.2	20.5	19.9	19.2	18.6	18.0	17.5	16.9	16.4	15.9
79	29.0	28.2	27.3	26.5	25.7	24.9	24.1	23.3	22.6	21.8	21.1	20.4	19.7	19.0	18.4	17.8	17.2	16.7	16.1	15.6
80	29.0	28.1	27.3	26.4	25.6	24.8	24.0	23.2	22.4	21.7	21.0	20.2	19.5	18.9	18.2	17.6	17.0	16.4	15.9	15.4
81	28.9	28.1	27.2	26.4	25.5	24.7	23.9	23.1	22.3	21.6	20.8	20.1	19.4	18.7	18.1	17.4	16.8	16.2	15.7	15.1
82	28.9	28.0	27.2	26.3	25.5	24.6	23.8	23.0	22.3	21.5	20.7	20.0	19.3	18.6	17.9	17.3	16.6	16.0	15.5	14.9
83	28.8	28.0	27.1	26.3	25.4	24.6	23.8	23.0	22.2	21.4	20.6	19.9	19.2	18.5	17.8	17.1	16.5	15.9	15.3	14.7
84	28.8	27.9	27.1	26.2	25.4	24.5	23.7	22.9	22.1	21.3	20.5	19.8	19.1	18.4	17.7	17.0	16.3	15.7	15.1	14.5
85	28.8	27.9	27.0	26.2	25.3	24.5	23.7	22.8	22.0	21.3	20.5	19.7	19.0	18.3	17.6	16.9	16.2	15.6	15.0	14.4
86	28.7	27.9	27.0	26.1	25.3	24.5	23.6	22.8	22.0	21.2	20.4	19.6	18.9	18.2	17.5	16.8	16.1	15.5	14.8	14.2
87	28.7	27.8	27.0	26.1	25.3	24.4	23.6	22.8	21.9	21.1	20.4	19.6	18.8	18.1	17.4	16.7	16.0	15.4	14.7	14.1
88	28.7	27.8	27.0	26.1	25.2	24.4	23.5	22.7	21.9	21.1	20.3	19.5	18.8	18.0	17.3	16.6	15.9	15.3	14.6	14.0
89	28.7	27.8	26.9	26.1	25.2	24.4	23.5	22.7	21.9	21.1	20.3	19.5	18.7	18.0	17.2	16.5	15.8	15.2	14.5	13.9
90	28.7	27.8	26.9	26.1	25.2	24.3	23.5	22.7	21.8	21.0	20.2	19.4	18.7	17.9	17.2	16.5	15.8	15.1	14.5	13.8
91	28.7	27.8	26.9	26.0	25.2	24.3	23.5	22.6	21.8	21.0	20.2	19.4	18.6	17.9	17.1	16.4	15.7	15.0	14.4	13.7
92	28.6	27.8	26.9	26.0	25.2	24.3	23.5	22.6	21.8	21.0	20.2	19.4	18.6	17.8	17.1	16.4	15.7	15.0	14.3	13.7
93	28.6	27.8	26.9	26.0	25.1	24.3	23.4	22.6	21.8	20.9	20.1	19.3	18.6	17.8	17.1	16.3	15.6	14.9	14.3	13.6
94	28.6	27.7	26.9	26.0	25.1	24.3	23.4	22.6	21.7	20.9	20.1	19.3	18.5	17.8	17.0	16.3	15.6	14.9	14.2	13.6
95	28.6	27.7	26.9	26.0	25.1	24.3	23.4	22.6	21.7	20.9	20.1	19.3	18.5	17.8	17.0	16.3	15.6	14.9	14.2	13.5
96	28.6	27.7	26.9	26.0	25.1	24.2	23.4	22.6	21.7	20.9	20.1	19.3	18.5	17.7	17.0	16.2	15.5	14.8	14.2	13.5

AGES	55	56	57	58	59	60	61	62	63	64	65	66	67	68	69	70	71	72	73	74
97	28.6	27.7	26.8	26.0	25.1	24.2	23.4	22.5	21.7	20.9	20.1	19.3	18.5	17.7	17.0	16.2	15.5	14.8	14.1	13.5
98	28.6	27.7	26.8	26.0	25.1	24.2	23.4	22.5	21.7	20.9	20.1	19.3	18.5	17.7	16.9	16.2	15.5	14.8	14.1	13.4
99	28.6	27.7	26.8	26.0	25.1	24.2	23.4	22.5	21.7	20.9	20.0	19.2	18.5	17.7	16.9	16.2	15.5	14.7	14.1	13.4
100	28.6	27.7	26.8	26.0	25.1	24.2	23.4	22.5	21.7	20.8	20.0	19.2	18.4	17.7	16.9	16.2	15.4	14.7	14.0	13.4
101	28.6	27.7	26.8	25.9	25.1	24.2	23.4	22.5	21.7	20.8	20.0	19.2	18.4	17.7	16.9	16.1	15.4	14.7	14.0	13.3
102	28.6	27.7	26.8	25.9	25.1	24.2	23.3	22.5	21.7	20.8	20.0	19.2	18.4	17.6	16.9	16.1	15.4	14.7	14.0	13.3
103	28.6	27.7	26.8	25.9	25.1	24.2	23.3	22.5	21.7	20.8	20.0	19.2	18.4	17.6	16.9	16.1	15.4	14.7	14.0	13.3
104	28.6	27.7	26.8	25.9	25.1	24.2	23.3	22.5	21.6	20.8	20.0	19.2	18.4	17.6	16.9	16.1	15.4	14.7	14.0	13.3
105	28.6	27.7	26.8	25.9	25.1	24.2	23.3	22.5	21.6	20.8	20.0	19.2	18.4	17.6	16.8	16.1	15.4	14.6	13.9	13.3
106	28.6	27.7	26.8	25.9	25.1	24.2	23.3	22.5	21.6	20.8	20.0	19.2	18.4	17.6	16.8	16.1	15.3	14.6	13.9	13.3
107	28.6	27.7	26.8	25.9	25.1	24.2	23.3	22.5	21.6	20.8	20.0	19.2	18.4	17.6	16.8	16.1	15.3	14.6	13.9	13.2
108	28.6	27.7	26.8	25.9	25.1	24.2	23.3	22.5	21.6	20.8	20.0	19.2	18.4	17.6	16.8	16.1	15.3	14.6	13.9	13.2
109	28.6	27.7	26.8	25.9	25.1	24.2	23.3	22.5	21.6	20.8	20.0	19.2	18.4	17.6	16.8	16.1	15.3	14.6	13.9	13.2
110	28.6	27.7	26.8	25.9	25.1	24.2	23.3	22.5	21.6	20.8	20.0	19.2	18.4	17.6	16.8	16.1	15.3	14.6	13.9	13.2
111	28.6	27.7	26.8	25.9	25.1	24.2	23.3	22.5	21.6	20.8	20.0	19.2	18.4	17.6	16.8	16.0	15.3	14.6	13.9	13.2
112	28.6	27.7	26.8	25.9	25.0	24.2	23.3	22.5	21.6	20.8	20.0	19.2	18.4	17.6	16.8	16.0	15.3	14.6	13.9	13.2
113	28.6	27.7	26.8	25.9	25.0	24.2	23.3	22.5	21.6	20.8	20.0	19.2	18.4	17.6	16.8	16.0	15.3	14.6	13.9	13.2
114	28.6	27.7	26.8	25.9	25.0	24.2	23.3	22.5	21.6	20.8	20.0	19.2	18.4	17.6	16.8	16.0	15.3	14.6	13.9	13.2
115	28.6	27.7	26.8	25.9	25.0	24.2	23.3	22.5	21.6	20.8	20.0	19.2	18.4	17.6	16.8	16.0	15.3	14.6	13.9	13.2

TABLE II (continued)
(Joint Life and Last Survivor Expectancy)

Ages	75	76	77	78	79	80	81	82	83	84	85	86	87	88	89	90	91	92	93	94
75	16.5	16.1	15.8	15.4	15.1	14.9	14.6	14.4	14.2	14.0										
76	16.1	15.7	15.4	15.0	14.7	14.4	14.1	13.9	13.7	13.5										
77	15.8	15.4	15.0	14.6	14.3	14.0	13.7	13.4	13.2	13.0										
78	15.4	15.0	14.6	14.2	13.9	13.5	13.2	13.0	12.7	12.5										
79	15.1	14.7	14.3	13.9	13.5	13.2	12.8	12.5	12.3	12.0										
80	14.9	14.4	14.0	13.5	13.2	12.8	12.5	12.2	11.9	11.6										
81	14.6	14.1	13.7	13.2	12.8	12.5	12.1	11.8	11.5	11.2										
82	14.4	13.9	13.4	13.0	12.5	12.2	11.8	11.5	11.1	10.9										
83	14.2	13.7	13.2	12.7	12.3	11.9	11.5	11.1	10.8	10.5										
84	14.0	13.5	13.0	12.5	12.0	11.6	11.2	10.9	10.5	10.2										
85	13.8	13.3	12.8	12.3	11.8	11.4	11.0	10.6	10.2	9.9	9.6	9.3	9.1	8.9	8.7	8.5	8.3	8.2	8.0	7.9
86	13.7	13.1	12.6	12.1	11.6	11.2	10.8	10.4	10.0	9.7	9.3	9.1	8.8	8.6	8.3	8.2	8.0	7.8	7.7	7.6
87	13.5	13.0	12.4	11.9	11.4	11.0	10.6	10.1	9.8	9.4	9.1	8.8	8.5	8.3	8.1	7.9	7.7	7.5	7.4	7.2
88	13.4	12.8	12.3	11.8	11.3	10.8	10.4	10.0	9.6	9.2	8.9	8.6	8.3	8.0	7.8	7.6	7.4	7.2	7.1	6.9
89	13.3	12.7	12.2	11.6	11.1	10.7	10.2	9.8	9.4	9.0	8.7	8.3	8.1	7.8	7.5	7.3	7.1	6.9	6.8	6.6
90	13.2	12.6	12.1	11.5	11.0	10.5	10.1	9.6	9.2	8.8	8.5	8.2	7.9	7.6	7.3	7.1	6.9	6.7	6.5	6.4
91	13.1	12.5	12.0	11.4	10.9	10.4	9.9	9.5	9.1	8.7	8.3	8.0	7.7	7.4	7.1	6.9	6.7	6.5	6.3	6.2

Ages	75	76	77	78	79	80	81	82	83	84	85	86	87	88	89	90	91	92	93	94
92	13.1	12.5	11.9	11.3	10.8	10.3	9.8	9.4	8.9	8.5	8.2	7.8	7.5	7.2	6.9	6.7	6.5	6.3	6.1	5.9
93	13.0	12.4	11.8	11.3	10.7	10.2	9.7	9.3	8.8	8.4	8.0	7.7	7.4	7.1	6.8	6.5	6.3	6.1	5.9	5.8
94	12.9	12.3	11.7	11.2	10.6	10.1	9.6	9.2	8.7	8.3	7.9	7.6	7.2	6.9	6.6	6.4	6.2	5.9	5.8	5.6
95	12.9	12.3	11.7	11.1	10.6	10.1	9.6	9.1	8.6	8.2	7.8	7.5	7.1	6.8	6.5	6.3	6.0	5.8	5.6	5.4
96	12.9	12.2	11.6	11.1	10.5	10.0	9.5	9.0	8.5	8.1	7.7	7.3	7.0	6.7	6.4	6.1	5.9	5.7	5.5	5.3
97	12.8	12.2	11.6	11.0	10.5	9.9	9.4	8.9	8.5	8.0	7.6	7.3	6.9	6.6	6.3	6.0	5.8	5.5	5.3	5.1
98	12.8	12.2	11.5	11.0	10.4	9.9	9.4	8.9	8.4	8.0	7.6	7.2	6.8	6.5	6.2	5.9	5.6	5.4	5.2	5.0
99	12.7	12.1	11.5	10.9	10.4	9.8	9.3	8.8	8.3	7.9	7.5	7.1	6.7	6.4	6.1	5.8	5.5	5.3	5.1	4.9
100	12.7	12.1	11.5	10.9	10.3	9.8	9.2	8.7	8.3	7.8	7.4	7.0	6.6	6.3	6.0	5.7	5.4	5.2	5.0	4.8
101	12.7	12.1	11.4	10.8	10.3	9.7	9.2	8.7	8.2	7.8	7.3	6.9	6.6	6.2	5.9	5.6	5.3	5.1	4.9	4.7
102	12.7	12.0	11.4	10.8	10.2	9.7	9.2	8.7	8.2	7.7	7.3	6.9	6.5	6.2	5.8	5.5	5.3	5.0	4.8	4.6
103	12.6	12.0	11.4	10.8	10.2	9.7	9.1	8.6	8.1	7.7	7.2	6.8	6.4	6.1	5.8	5.5	5.2	4.9	4.7	4.5
104	12.6	12.0	11.4	10.8	10.2	9.6	9.1	8.6	8.1	7.6	7.2	6.8	6.4	6.0	5.7	5.4	5.1	4.8	4.6	4.4
105	12.6	12.0	11.3	10.7	10.2	9.6	9.1	8.5	8.0	7.6	7.1	6.7	6.3	6.0	5.6	5.3	5.0	4.8	4.6	4.4
106	12.6	11.9	11.3	10.7	10.1	9.6	9.0	8.5	8.0	7.5	7.1	6.7	6.3	5.9	5.6	5.3	5.0	4.8	4.5	4.3
107	12.6	11.9	11.3	10.7	10.1	9.6	9.0	8.5	8.0	7.5	7.1	6.6	6.2	5.9	5.5	5.2	4.9	4.7	4.5	4.2
108	12.6	11.9	11.3	10.7	10.1	9.5	9.0	8.5	7.9	7.5	7.0	6.6	6.2	5.8	5.5	5.2	4.9	4.6	4.4	4.2
109	12.6	11.9	11.3	10.7	10.1	9.5	9.0	8.4	7.9	7.5	7.0	6.6	6.2	5.8	5.5	5.1	4.8	4.6	4.3	4.1
110	12.6	11.9	11.3	10.7	10.1	9.5	9.0	8.4	7.9	7.4	7.0	6.6	6.2	5.8	5.4	5.1	4.8	4.5	4.3	4.1
111	12.5	11.9	11.3	10.7	10.1	9.5	8.9	8.4	7.9	7.4	7.0	6.5	6.1	5.7	5.4	5.1	4.8	4.5	4.3	4.0
112	12.5	11.9	11.3	10.7	10.1	9.5	8.9	8.4	7.9	7.4	7.0	6.5	6.1	5.7	5.4	5.1	4.7	4.5	4.2	4.0
113	12.5	11.9	11.3	10.6	10.1	9.5	8.9	8.4	7.9	7.4	7.0	6.5	6.1	5.7	5.4	5.0	4.7	4.4	4.2	3.9
114	12.5	11.9	11.2	10.6	10.0	9.5	8.9	8.4	7.9	7.4	6.9	6.5	6.1	5.7	5.3	5.0	4.7	4.4	4.2	3.9
115	12.5	11.9	11.2	10.6	10.0	9.5	8.9	8.4	7.9	7.4	6.9	6.5	6.1	5.7	5.3	5.0	4.7	4.4	4.1	3.9

APPENDIX E

TABLE for Determining Applicable Divisor for MDIB*
(Minimum Distribution Incidental Benefit)

Age	Applicable Divisor	Age	Applicable Divisor
70	26.2	93	8.8
71	25.3	94	8.3
72	24.4	95	7.8
73	23.5	96	7.3
74	22.7	97	6.9
75	21.8	98	6.5
76	20.9	99	6.1
77	20.1	100	5.7
78	19.2	101	5.3
79	18.4	102	5.0
80	17.6	103	4.7
81	16.8	104	4.4
82	16.0	105	4.1
83	15.3	106	3.8
84	14.5	107	3.6
85	13.8	108	3.3
86	13.1	109	3.1
87	12.4	110	2.8
88	11.8	111	2.6
89	11.1	112	2.4
90	10.5	113	2.2
91	9.9	114	2.0
92	9.4	115 and older	1.8

*Use this table if your beneficiary is someone other than your spouse. For additional instructions, see *Minimum Distribution Incidental Benefit Requirement* in Chapter 6.

APPENDIX F

Summary Record of IRA(s) for 1991
(You May Keep This for Your Records)

Name _____

I was ☐ covered ☐ not covered by my employer's retirement plan during the year.

I became age 59½ on _____.
                  (month) (day) (year)

I became age 70½ on _____.
                  (month) (day) (year)

Contributions

Name of IRA	Date	Amount contributed for 1991	Check, if rollover contribution	Fair Market value of IRA as of December 31, 1991, from Form 5498
1.				
2.				
3.				
4.				
5.				
Total				

Total contributions deducted on tax return $_____

Total contributions treated as nondeductible on Form 8606 $_____

Distributions

Name of IRA	Date	Amount of distribution	Reason (e.g., for retirement, rollover, withdrawal of excess contributions, etc.)	Income earned on IRA	Taxable amount reported on income tax return	Nontaxable amount from Form 8606, line 11
1.						
2.						
3.						
4.						
Total						

Basis of all IRAs as of 12/31/91 (from Form 8606, line 12) $_____

Basis of all IRAs for 1991 (from Form 8606, line 14) $_____

Note: You should keep copies of your income tax return, and Forms W-2, 8606, and 5498.

WORKSHEET
FOR
DETERMINING REQUIRED ANNUAL DISTRIBUTIONS FROM YOUR IRA(s)

1. Age	70½	71½	72½	73½	74½	75½
2. Year age was reached						
3. Value of IRA at the close of business on December 31 of the year immediately prior to the year on line 2[1]						
4. Divisor from Life Expectancy Table I or Table II[2]						
5. Required distribution (divide line 3 by line 4)[3]						

[1]If you have more than one IRA, you must figure the required distribution separately for each IRA.

[2]Use the appropriate divisor for each year and for each IRA. You can either (a) use the appropriate divisor from the table each year, or (b) use the appropriate divisor from the table for your 70½ year and reduce it by 1 (one) for each subsequent year. To find the appropriate divisor, use your age (and that of your beneficiary, if applicable) as of your birthday(s) in the year shown on line 2. If your beneficiary is someone other than your spouse, see *Minimum Distribution Incidental Benefit Requirement* in Chapter 6.

[3]If you have more than one IRA, you must withdraw an amount equal to the total of the required distributions figured for each IRA. You can, however, withdraw the total from one IRA or from more than one IRA.

CHAPTER 6

Other Retirement Vehicles

6-1 Deferred Compensation Plans

Why defer compensation? While the primary advantage of deferring income is to keep the current year income tax rate low—to postpone the payment of income tax until a later date or until retirement age—there is another significant advantage to a small segment of the population, clergy and nonclergy alike.

After retiring and beginning to draw Social Security payments, a person is allowed to earn, under present law, a little over $10,000 if age sixty-five or over, and a little over $7,000 if age sixty-two or over, and still draw full Social Security benefits. This amount usually increases yearly. Furthermore, you are allowed to earn more than those maximums, but $1 for each $3 over the maximum is disallowed. There is sentiment in Congress to liberalize this limitation, but nothing concrete has come of it at this writing.

Any *deferred* income from a prior year received by the retiree does not have to be reported as income for Social Security purposes because it is not earned income in that tax year. Yes, it must be reported for income tax purposes but not for Social Security purposes. Check with your local Social Security office to learn the latest amount you would be allowed to earn and still draw full Social Security benefits.

6-2 The Keogh Plan

The Keogh plan, also known as the HR-10 plan, is a retirement vehicle for self-employed persons. A participant may put aside 15 percent of income with a maximum of $30,000 for a tax-sheltered retirement plan.

Ministers, by definition, are employees in most instances, and therefore, the income they receive as salary from an employer would not be eligible for tax shelter in the Keogh plan. However, if they receive any self-employment income from honoraria such as from speaking, writing, or performing weddings and funerals, that stream of income will usually qualify for the Keogh plan. Evangelists can use this vehicle as well. A qualified clergyperson can own, simultaneously, a TSA, an IRA, and a Keogh plan, with certain limitations discussed in chapters 4 and 5.

An additional requirement that sometimes prevents the selection of the Keogh plan would rarely apply to clergypersons. I must include this warning, however, because in certain denominations in America, the pastor is the president of the church as a corporation, and the pastor owns the building. In those cases, if the pastors choose to buy a Keogh plan, they would have to include each and every eligible employee in the plan, paying the same percentage rate of participation into each employee's Keogh account. Just as for a qualified pension plan, every eligible employee would have to be included in the plan. Discrimination is illegal in Keogh plans.

For most clergypersons, however, the only stream of income eligible for the Keogh plan would be their self-employed income as mentioned above.

6-3 The 401(k) Plan

The 401(k) allows employees to elect to have employer contributions made to them in cash or for deferred compensation purposes. However, tax-exempt employers, including churches, cannot do this in behalf of their employees, including ministers. Remember, once again, ministers are considered to be employees for income tax purposes but self-employed for Social Security purposes. This limitation was imposed by the Tax Reform Act of 1986. But the government "grandfathered" those plans in existence prior to July 2, 1986. They are allowed to continue.

6-4 The Nonqualified Retirement Plan

The nonqualified retirement plan is widely used in industry to reward faithful employees "for past services rendered."

Suppose Pastor Sam Jones has already purchased the maximum allowable TSA *and* the maximum allowable IRA. Perhaps he started in the ministry late in life and hasn't had an opportunity to build an adequate retirement plan. Here is a way for a church to help a deserving pastor and hold on to the person *if that is what the church wants* and if that is what the pastor wants.

In industry the loss of a key employee is guarded against by a very simple method. The key person is paid adequately and given proper recognition. One way a church can show regard for a pastor is through the use of the nonqualified retirement plan. Here's how it works.

6-5 How to Create the Nonqualified Retirement Plan

To create the plan, the church enters into a deferred compensation agreement with the pastor as a key person. The church buys a life insurance policy on the life of the pastor, is the owner and beneficiary, and pays the premium. The amount of the premium is not counted as income to the pastor. The cash value belongs to the church.

Suppose, for example, your church enters into a written contract with you as a key person. (Churches often do that, especially if there is a large mortgage.) There is no mention of the life insurance policy in the contract. It's a straightforward policy that pays the church tax-free dollars when the pastor dies. In the written contract, the church agrees to pay Pastor Sam Jones some "deferred compensation" at retirement age for "past services rendered." The insurance policy will fund the agreement, guaranteed, whether the pastor lives or dies.

If the minister becomes disabled, the premiums would be waived by virtue of the waiver-of-premium benefit in the policy. The church would not have to pay premiums so long as the minister was disabled, but the cash value would continue to grow as if the premiums were being paid. If a minister was totally and permanently disabled, the premiums would be waived until retirement age, yet the money necessary for the minister to retire on would be there anyway. This method is well established. A court case, *Casale v. Comm.,* 247 F.2d 440 (2d Cir. 1957), Revenue Ruling 59-184, 1959-1 CB 65, allows the employer to own a policy on a key employee and exempts the employee from income tax on that amount. Further references are Revenue Ruling 59-184, *U.S. v. Leuschner,* Sr. (DC, Calif.), 11 AFTR 2d 782; *Edward D. Lacey,* 41 TC 329, Acq. 1964-2 CB 6.

So, whether the minister lives to retirement, becomes disabled and lives to retirement as a person with a disability, dies prematurely, or resigns, the funds are available to the church. In turn, the church can fund the deferred key person retirement contract it has with the minister, or it can pay the minister's survivor(s) if the minister dies prematurely.

6-6 The Nonqualified Retirement Plan Could Be the Perfect Solution

For the right situation, the nonqualified retirement plan is the perfect solution, and it is *guaranteed*. But it has a very special function most people don't know about. It fills a gap in a person's retirement program in a unique way. Please recall reading about the pension trap in chapter 3. I showed that most retirees do not choose the life-only option because if the retiree dies, the beneficiary receives nothing further.

By using the nonqualified retirement plan, the retiree can choose the life-only option, hence the highest monthly retirement income, and by virtue of the written agreement, also receive additional funds from the church, which will have access to the accumulated cash values. The church can use those funds to pay the minister's retirement income in addition to whatever pension is paid. Or the church can continue paying on the life insurance policy until the minister dies, even after retirement, and receive the funds from the policy tax-free at the death of the minister. Or the church can borrow from the cash values anytime along the way. Of course, if the church spends all the cash value, there won't be funds for retirement purposes—only death benefit purposes.

The nonqualified retirement plan can be just the right financial tool for a church to use to keep a favorite pastor and meet the individual's needs for the future. This method can compensate for the growth of inflation and the resulting decrease in the buying power of the pastor's pension income at retirement age. The written agreement binds the church to pay the pastor at retirement or the beneficiary at the pastor's death. If the past is any predictor of the future, most retirees' needs will continue to increase.

It is, therefore, possible for a pastor to receive monthly retirement income from *all* the following sources (in addition to whatever Social Security income the person is eligible for):

- A TSA
- An IRA
- A Keogh plan
- A nonqualified plan
- A deferred income contract with the church

All of these sources have one thing in common: they offer tax-deferred accounts in which the funds grow sheltered from annual taxation until withdrawn.

CHAPTER 7

How to Be Ready If
Disability Occurs

7-1 A Widely-Held False Assumption

Most people live with the assumption that they will never have a
disability. They postpone planning for disability in much the same
way that they postpone getting a will. Only three out of ten Americans have wills. The percentage of people who own disability coverage is even less. There are two types of disability insurance: long-
term disability and short-term disability.

7-2 Do You Have Adequate Disability
Income Coverage?

It is probably safe to say that most ministers have inadequate
long-term disability (LTD) coverage; many have none. Sometimes
there is a token amount as part of a hospitalization plan. But the
future of hospitalization plans is in serious doubt, at this writing, as
hospital and medical costs skyrocket. So, any LTD riders attached
to hospitalization plans may not be available as we apparently move
closer to government hospitalization and medical plans. Most ministers of independent churches have no coverage at all.

7-3 If You Are Disabled, Will Social
Security Pay You?

Some ministers are counting on Social Security to pay them if
they become sick or injured. They should know about the waiting
period of one year before any benefits will come from that source
*unless a doctor will sign a form indicating that an illness or injury will
last a year.* In that case, the disability income from Social Security

will start after five months of disability. Very few churches can or will continue paying a minister with a disability that long.

According to the Social Security Administration, seven out of every ten applications for Social Security disability income are rejected. Most applicants are not disabled seriously enough or disabled long enough to qualify. Furthermore, an applicant must be unable to perform *any* gainful occupation. That means that ministers, who may have three or four educational degrees, must accept *any* menial job that they are capable of performing—age, experience, or location notwithstanding. (See Section 223D of the Social Security Act.) At best, those who do qualify for benefits receive inadequate income on which to live.

According to *Transactions*, Society of Actuaries, 1973, every year one out of eight persons is disabled for at least eight days.

7-4 What May Happen When You Are Disabled without Coverage

You face loss of income from your employer. In addition, you may experience the following:

- Even if you qualify for Social Security, there is a five- to twelve-month wait for benefits to begin to arrive.
- Your spouse (if not already working) might be forced to seek employment.
- Your debt will probably increase, and you probably will not be able to make payments on debt already incurred.
- Your savings, if any, may be drained.
- You may be forced to sell your home or other possessions.
- You may be forced to move in with relatives.
- You may be forced to accept charity from several sources.

Adding to the magnitude of this potential problem is the fact that large numbers of young pastors have decided to opt out of Social Security. More and more pastors decide that they cannot pay such a high percentage from their salaries on top of income tax. It seems to be an easy decision for young people who enjoy good health and may have difficulty envisioning themselves as older people. Opting out of Social Security may prove to be one of the worst decisions young pastors ever make. It may be a case of short-range expediency traded for long-time regret.

To those who might be thinking that way, I urge you to think about this: if you had no choice and had to pay into Social Security, you would find a way to do it. You would have no choice. Too many of us have to have money automatically withheld from us before we can save for a goal. In the case of opting out of Social Security, the price may be too high to pay in lost death benefits to your spouse and children, in retirement income to the older person you will be someday, and last, in lost benefits that Medicare and Medicaid would otherwise provide. My advice to anyone contemplating opting out of Social Security is to count the cost as well as what appears to be savings.

As of this writing, the Social Security tax rate paid by ministers is 15.3 percent of compensation. It is rising every year. The definition of *compensation* for most ministers is the total of salary, housing allowance and, in some cases, the utilities. Remember, even though you are considered to be an employee for income tax purposes, you are considered to be self-employed for Social Security purposes.

7-5 A Solution to Disability

Fortunately, there is a solution to the problem of the minister with a disability. It is not a full solution, for that is not possible in most cases. But it can make the difference for the minister's family and for the congregation as well.

The church can buy a disability policy, and the premium is not counted as income to the minister (subject to maximums; check with tax counsel). It is treated the same as hospitalization premiums. It is a way to minimize the possible burden to a congregation if the minister becomes disabled, and it is a legal way to reduce the minister's taxable income (Revenue Ruling 73-347, 1973-2 CB 25). It can also preserve the minister's dignity.

7-6 If the Church Pays for the Disability Policy, Who Owns It?

Even though the church pays the premium on the disability policy, the minister owns it and takes it from church to church throughout the ministerial career. The coverage, like the retirement plan, becomes a very important part of negotiations. That is the time for you to discuss such coverage. If you do not own such coverage, I suggest that you encourage your church board to buy it for you as part of your pay package.

7-7 What Kind of Disability Income Insurance Should You Buy?

There are several types of disability policies to consider. Many companies sell level premium, noncancelable, guaranteed renewable disability policies that pay to age sixty-five or beyond if you cannot perform the specific duties of the ministerial profession. That is the most expensive and the most difficult kind to buy. If you have any health problems (preexisting conditions), an underwriting decision will have to be made to determine your insurability. A policy issued on a noncancelable, guaranteed renewable basis means exactly what it says. Once a company issues such a policy, it becomes a unilateral contract: only you can cancel it.

For about half the cost of the noncancelable, guaranteed renewable coverage, you can buy a guaranteed renewable but not noncancelable policy, which pays benefits to age sixty-five. Once a claim is being paid in either type of policy, it cannot be canceled during disability. However, the owner of a guaranteed renewable, cancelable policy could be expected to return to work in other than his or her own occupation if able. Also, it could be canceled after recovery from an illness or accident. The noncancelable, guaranteed renewable policy pays for almost *any* disability if you are unable to perform your occupation. You would not be expected to work outside your profession. As a clergyperson, if you could not perform the duties of that profession, you would generally be considered disabled.

7-8 Just How Much Can a Disability Policy Mean to You?

Let's consider what the potential payments would be if you were disabled. Assume you are age forty and your disability coverage was set up to pay you $1,500 per month after a ninety-day waiting period (i.e., there will be no disability payments to you during the first ninety days of your disability).

Further assume that you are totally and permanently disabled. If you receive $1,500 per month for one year, that amounts to $18,000. If you draw disability all the way to age sixty-five, you would receive a total of $450,000. The good news is that you would not have to pay premiums during that time. The bad news is that your disability income would cease at age sixty-five. But the alternative of having no disability income is much worse.

CHAPTER 8

◆————————————————————————◆

Why You Should Own Professional Liability Insurance

8-1 Counseling: A Potential
Clergy Trap

In former, more innocent days, people did not sue each other as quickly and as often as they do today. Lawsuits have driven up the cost of professional liability insurance for all professions. Consequently, in a time when professionals need professional liability insurance more than ever, some of them feel they cannot afford it. It is safe to say that the majority of professional clergypersons are without professional liability insurance coverage. And sometimes this is for reasons other than prohibitive costs.

Ministers as a group tend to feel there is little chance that someone will sue them. The very essence of their training is couched in mercy, forgiveness, joy, peace, and love for their fellow humans. They live, for the most part, thinking of reconciliation, not revenge; grace, not legality. Society is changing to such an extent, however, that ministers would be wise to take the possibility of being sued more seriously.

Ministers are very vulnerable to lawsuits. Most ministers counsel parishioners on a one-to-one basis. They are usually alone in their offices with one counselee. A parishioner who seeks the advice and encouragement of a professional clergyperson usually finds a caring, sensitive, sympathetic person with whom to share woes. It is an old, old story. The counselee is drawn to such a person and temptations abound. Then there sometimes follow perceived rejection, anger, desire for revenge, and a possible "he said/she said" lawsuit. Many a minister has left the ministry because of this vulnerability.

8-2 How to Avoid a Lawsuit

There is probably no total guarantee against being sued. However, a simple preventive method should stop most lawsuits before they begin. Many ministers are now requiring all counselees to bring another person with them to be in attendance during the entire counseling session.

If that can't be arranged, the next best thing is for the minister to leave the office door open during counseling sessions and/or be sure a secretary is close by. Some male ministers tell their counselees that their wives help them in counseling situations and they will be in attendance. Of course, that arrangement is costly to the ministers' wives in terms of expended time. But many wives of male ministers say that they feel it is necessary in some cases.

The parishioner could be a male calling a female minister to come to his home. Either way, prevention is always better and cheaper than cure. But just in case, be sure to buy a professional liability insurance policy.

8-3 Where Can You Buy Affordable Professional Liability Insurance?

Usually, the best source of such coverage is a company that specializes in insuring churches against fire and casualty losses. The company will include professional liability coverage as a rider on the fire and casualty policy.

Buying professional liability coverage as a single policy usually costs much more than one attached as a rider.

8-4 Who Pays the Premiums for Professional Liability Coverage?

Most ministers pay the premiums for their coverage. Professional liability coverage for ministers is relatively new in our society. But increasingly, the payment of these premiums is becoming a negotiable item between church and minister.

CHAPTER 9

How to Understand Your Social Security Benefits

9-1 The Basic Benefits of Social Security

Benefits are available for covered workers and their families: a lump-sum death benefit, monthly income to the surviving family members within certain ages and categories, retirement income benefits, disability income benefits, and Medicare coverage. We will discuss each benefit in detail. Of particular interest to ministers should be the discussion of the pros and cons of opting out of Social Security.

Periodically in this chapter, I will quote from IRS Publication 517, *Social Security for Members of the Clergy and Religious Workers.* All quotes will be from this publication unless otherwise indicated. For more details of survivors' benefits, refer to U.S. Department of Health and Human Services, Social Security Administration, SSA Pub. No. 05-10034, *Benefits for Survivors.*

9-2 Ministers Are Self-Employed for Social Security Purposes

This statement will be repeated often. Some church treasurers still erroneously insist that ministers are employees and proceed to withhold FICA taxes. That causes great confusion and inconvenience for the ministers. Generally, any church that withholds FICA taxes from the minister's salary is making a mistake. The Internal Revenue Service makes it clear that ministers are self-employed for Social Security purposes in Internal Revenue Code 3121(b) (8) (A). Ministers are supposed to make quarterly estimates. For more details about self-employment, refer to the U.S. Department of Health and Human Services, Social Security Administration, SSA Pub. No. 05-10022, *If You're Self-Employed.*

9-3 What About the Eligibility of Ministers for Social Security Benefits?

Any duly ordained, commissioned, or licensed minister of a church, who receives earnings for performing ministerial duties, must report such income as self-employed earnings. However, if a minister has received an exemption from self-employment tax (discussed in 9-5), no tax is paid.

To qualify as ministers, they must be duly ordained, commissioned, or licensed by a religious body that is a church or denomination. Such ministers must have the authority to conduct religious worship, perform sacerdotal duties, and administer ordinances and sacraments according to the customs of the particular church or denomination.

Generally, members of religious orders who have taken a vow of poverty are exempt from paying self-employment tax on earnings received for performing services for their church.

Christian Science practitioners and readers are considered to be the same as ordained, commissioned, or licensed ministers.

9-4 Religious Workers

Religious workers are generally considered to be employees and are subject to Social Security withholding rather than the self-employment tax. Of course, tax-exempt churches and churches that are controlled by religious organizations may elect not to have their employees covered by FICA. Such employees would then be covered under the SECA and would have to pay self-employment taxes. The expenses of doing business could not then be deducted in computing self-employment income.

Any employee (except a minister or member of a religious order) who received $100 or more in wages from any electing church or church-controlled organization must complete Schedule SE (Form 1040), *Social Security Self-Employment Tax.* The church or organization can revoke this election, but if once done, it is irrevocable. In addition, the IRS can revoke the election if certain requirements for information returns are not met.

9-5 Exemption from Self-Employment Tax for Religious Workers

Exemption from self-employment tax may be requested by ministers, members of religious orders who have taken a vow of poverty, and Christian Science practitioners. This exemption applies only to the earnings from qualified services.

To claim the exemption from self-employment tax, you must:

1) File Form 4361,
2) Be conscientiously opposed to public, not private, insurance because of your individual religious considerations (not because of your general conscience), or be opposed because of the principles of your religious denomination,
3) File for other than economic reasons,
4) Inform the ordaining, commissioning, or licensing body of your church or order that you are opposed to public insurance if you are a minister or a member of a religious order (other than a vow-of-poverty member),
5) Establish that the organization that ordained, commissioned, or licensed you, or your religious order, is a tax-exempt religious organization,
6) Establish that the organization is a church or a convention or association of churches, and
7) Sign and return the statement the IRS mails to you to verify that you are requesting an exemption based on the grounds listed on the statement.

Form 4361. If you did not previously elect to be covered under social security and wish to be exempt from self-employment tax, file Form 4361, *Application for Exemption from Self-Employment Tax for Use by Ministers, Members of Religious Orders and Christian Science Practitioners,* in triplicate, to request exemption.

You must show in writing, in Form 4361, that you oppose public (government) insurance "for death, disability, old age, or retirement because of your conscience or religious principles." Your written statement must include that you are opposed to "insurance that helps pay for or provide services for medical care, and includes benefits from a system established by the Social Security Act." A copy of your filed Form 4361 will then be returned to you with or without an approval.

When to file. If you earn $400 in self-employment earnings for two consecutive years, "any part of which came from your services as a minister, a member of a religious order, or a Christian Science practitioner," you must file a Form 4361 in time for reporting your income tax for the second year.

Example 1. Pastor Richard Johnson, ordained in 1991, has net earnings of $400 in 1991 and $500 in 1992. He must file his application for exemption by April 15, 1993. He must receive his exemption by April 15, 1992, or he will have to pay his self-employment tax for 1991 anyway.

Example 2. Pastor George Tatum earned $300 in 1991 but earned $400 in both 1990 and 1992. He must file his exemption application by April 15, 1993. But he must pay his 1990 self-employment tax by April 15, 1990, if exemption is not granted by April 15, 1991.

Example 3. Pastor Michael Davis was ordained in 1989 and earned $700 as a minister. He earned $1,000 in 1990 in ministry, but his ministerial expenses exceeded $1,000, resulting in zero net earnings in 1990 from ministry. In addition, he opened a bookstore in 1990, resulting in net self-employment earnings of $8,000. He earned $1,500 in ministry in 1991 and $10,000 net self-employment earnings from his bookstore.

Davis must file for both 1989 and 1991 because his net earnings exceeded $400 each year, part of which came from his ministerial services. Therefore, his exemption application must be filed by the income tax due date, including extensions, in 1991.

Death of individual. No one can file an exemption application for a deceased clergyperson.

Effective date of exemption. An approved exemption is effective for all tax years after 1967 in which you have $400 or more of net earnings from self-employment, part of which is for services as a member of the clergy.

Example. Pastor Ben Collins was ordained in 1990 and earned $450 in ministry for 1990 and 1991. If he files his exemption application on February 15, 1992, and it is granted, his effective date is 1990 and all subsequent years.

Refunds of self-employment tax paid. Generally speaking, you have three years after a return is filed, or two years from the date you paid your tax, to request a refund for overpayment of your taxes. Use Form 1040X, *Amended U.S. Individual Income Tax Return,* to file your claim before the statutory period ends, or within two years from the date you paid the tax, whichever is later.

A return you filed before the due date is considered to have been filed on the due date.

If you file a claim after the 3-year period but within 2 years from the time you paid the tax, the credit or refund will not be more than the tax you paid within the 2 years immediately before you file the claim.

9-6 Members of Recognized Religious Sects

Such members can apply for exemption from self-employment tax on all self-employment income. You cannot apply for this exemption if

you received social security benefits or payments, or anyone else received these benefits or payments based on your wages or self-employment income.

Eligibility requirements. To claim this exemption from self-employment tax, **all** the following requirements must be met:

1) File Form 4029.
2) As a follower of the established teachings of the sect or division, you must be conscientiously opposed to accepting benefits of any **private or public** insurance that makes payments for death, disability, old age, retirement, or medical care, or provides services for medical care.
3) You must waive all rights to receive any social security payment or benefit and agree that no benefits or payments will be made based on your wages and self-employment income to anyone else.
4) The Secretary of Health and Human Services must determine that:
   a) Your sect or division has such established teachings,
   b) It is the practice, and has been for a substantial period of time, for members of the sect or division to provide for their dependent members in a manner that is reasonable in view of the members' general level of living, and
   c) The sect or division has existed at all times since December 31, 1950.

You do not have to apply for this exemption if you have already received approval.

Form 4029. You must file Form 4029, *Application for Exemption from Social Security and Medicare Taxes and Waiver of Benefits,* in triplicate, with the Social Security Administration to file for this exemption. The sect or division must complete its part of the form, also.

Effective date of exemption. Form 4029 can be filed at any time, and when approved, it "generally is effective for all tax years beginning after 1950" but "does not apply to any tax year beginning before you meet the requirements, or the Secretary of Health and Human Services makes the determinations discussed earlier."

Exemption from FICA. Eligible applicants can apply for exemption from the employer's share of FICA taxes. "An employee meeting the requirements can apply to be exempt from his or her share of these taxes on the wages paid by an employer whose exemption has been approved. A partnership in which each partner holds a religious exemption from social security is an employer under this provision." This exemption applies to wages paid after 1988.

Information for employers. If you are an employer qualifying for this exemption, you are not required to report the wages of employees who also meet this exemption. A partnership in which each partner holds a religious exemption from social security is an employer for this purpose.

Do not include these wages on Form 941, *Employer's Quarterly Federal Tax Return,* or on Form 943, *Employer's Annual Tax Return for Agricultural Employees.* If you have received an approved Form 4029, write 'Form 4029' on Form 941 on the line for 'Taxable social security wages paid' to the left of the wage entry space. If you have received an approved Form 4029, and you are a Form 943 filer, write 'Form 4029' on the line for 'Taxable cash wages paid during the year' to the left of the wage entry space. When preparing a Form W-2 for a qualifying employee, write 'Form 4029' in the box marked 'Other.'

Effective date. An approved exemption from FICA becomes effective on the first day of the first calendar quarter after the quarter in which Form 4029 is filed. The exemption will end in the calendar quarter before the quarter in which the employer, employee, sect, or division fails to meet the requirements.

9-7 Advantages and Disadvantages of Opting Out of Social Security

More and more young ministers are deciding to opt out of Social Security. This decision, once made, is irrevocable. The byword is once in always in, once out always out. Of course, at some point the government could give those who opted out a second chance.

Many young ministers are convinced that the Social Security program will ultimately fail. Each individual must make a judgment. Some financial seminar leaders fan this flame of doubt about the system's long-term viability. No doubt there will be changes over the years, but most experts agree that it will probably never disappear altogether. Ministers must count the cost of opting out and weigh it against the possible gain in such a decision. Let's consider the pros and cons.

What You Give Up When You Opt Out

If Pastor John Doe opts out of Social Security, the disadvantages are that he gives up survivors' benefits to spouse and children, disability benefits to himself if he becomes sick or injured, and Medicare and retirement benefits if he reaches his older years. College education benefits to children, with certain exceptions such as disability, have been eliminated. (Consult your local Social Security office for details regarding your specific situation). The advantages include continuing monthly income plus periodic cost of living raises to spouse and children until the youngest child is age sixteen. Such a cumulative monthly income can become a sizable amount. Medicare benefits, perhaps the biggest advantage of all, would be difficult and expensive to replace with a commercial plan. The widow can begin collecting income again at age sixty-two if she has not remarried or does not earn more than the government allows.

Suppose twenty-five-year-old Pastor Ray Brown dies and leaves his wife, age twenty-three, and a child, age one. His average indexed monthly earnings (AIME) have been $2,000 per month. Remember, his parsonage or housing allowance has been included in his AIME all along so he has been reporting the value of the parsonage and paying Social Security tax on it. If the pastor is fully insured, his widow would receive $1,281, under current benefit amounts, until the child is age sixteen. Multiplying $1,281 per month times the number of months in fifteen years, or 180 months, results in $230,580 received by the widow and child, provided she did not work and earn more than is allowed. There are stated limitations on the amount one can earn and still draw Social Security survivor's benefits. These amounts change every year. Consult your local Social Security office for these amounts.

Another example. Pastor A. B. Smith is twenty-five, has twin sons (age one), and has an AIME of $2,500 per month. If he dies, his spouse would receive $1,693 per month for fifteen years. That amounts to $304,740 received by the widow during the fifteen-year period, provided she did not earn more than the allowable amount.

Still another example. A minister, age thirty, has four children, ages one, two, three, and four. His AIME is $3,000 per month. If he dies, his widow would receive $1,824 per month until the two-year-old is age sixteen; then she would receive $1,564 for one more year. That amounts to a total received by the widow and children during the next fifteen years of $325,200, provided she does not earn more than the allowable amount.

Any minister who opts out of Social Security will give up the equivalent of thousands of dollars of life insurance that would otherwise be provided by Social Security.

Far too many couples with children assume that if one spouse dies, the other can work and also draw Social Security. Many spouses of ministers are highly educated and have professions of their own. The thought of premature death is all too often shoved aside and not considered in financial planning. In deciding whether or not to opt out of Social Security, ministers would be wise to project the possible survivor's benefits available to them if one spouse dies and leaves dependent children. The surviving spouse could be working full time for half pay because of the restrictions on earned income imposed by the Social Security Administration. Furthermore, an option to stay at home and draw full Social Security includes the assurance that a parent will be there when small children come home from school. Most professional counselors agree that a parent should be available to young children.

In the case of ministers dying prematurely, leaving spouses who have not been active in their professions, there is always lag time until they can catch up, be recertified, or retrain. The job market can be limited to such a person, since younger professionals join the work force each year. All too often a young beginning professional can be hired for less than an older professional with more experience and higher income needs. Anyone doubting that need only read newspaper stories about older higher-paid persons being encouraged to retire.

9-8 What Are Qualified Services?

If you have an exemption from self-employment tax for earnings you receive for qualified services, the exemption applies only to the services performed in the exercise of your ministry. The exemption does not apply to any other self-employment income. If you do not have an exemption, amounts you receive for performing qualified services are subject to self-employment tax.

9-9 Definition of Qualified Services as Applied to Ministers

Most services you perform as a minister, priest, rabbi, etc., are qualified services. These services include:

1) Performing sacerdotal functions,
2) Conducting religious worship, and
3) Controlling, conducting, and maintaining religious organizations, boards, societies, and other integral agencies that are under the authority of a religious body that is a church or denomination.

If you direct, manage, maintain, or promote a religious organization's activities, you are considered to be in control. "A religious organization is under the authority of a religious body that is a church or denomination if it is organized for and dedicated to carrying out the principles of a faith according to the requirements governing the creation of institutions of the faith."

Other services. Certain services for nonreligious organizations may qualify, but they must be in the exercise of your ministry. Check with the IRS about your individual circumstances.

Services for nonreligious organizations. So long as your church assigns you to nonreligious services, they will probably qualify, even if those services do not include the performance of sacerdotal duties. As you can see, the elements of authority and control are important here.

For services to qualify as assigned or designated services by your church, the following must be true:

1) Your church must arrange for you to perform services for a nonreligious organization.
2) The services you perform must not be the same as those performed by other undesignated employees.
3) The services you perform must not be the same after designation as before designation.

For services to a nonreligious organization not assigned or designated by your church, only if the services involve performing sacerdotal duties or conducting religious services will they be considered qualified services.

Services that are not part of your ministry. The following are not qualified services. Your income from these services is generally subject to FICA taxes under the rules that apply to workers in general, not under SECA.

1) Services that you perform for nonreligious organizations other than the services stated earlier.
2) Services that you perform as a duly ordained, commissioned, or licensed minister of a church while employed by the United States, the District of Columbia, a foreign government, or any of their political subdivisions. This is true even if you are performing sacerdotal functions or conducting religious worship. (For example, if you perform services as a chaplain in the Armed Forces of the United States, the services are not qualified services.)
3) Services that you perform in a government-owned and operated hos-

pital are considered performed by a government employee, not by a minister as part of the ministry. However, services that you perform at a church-related hospital or health and welfare institution are considered to be part of the ministry.

Books or articles. If you write religious books and/or articles, they are considered to be part of your ministry. Any income from these efforts is considered to be self-employment income.

9-10 How to Make Sure Your Account Is on File with the Government

You can and should inquire about your Social Security account by completing a Form SSA-7004 and sending it to the Social Security Administration. They will send you a printout showing the total amount of money you earned and the amount of Social Security tax you paid for each year you have worked as a covered worker. If there is a problem, *now* is the time to get it clarified. In addition, your local Social Security office can project retirement incomes and survivor's benefits from those figures to help your financial planning process.

If you wait until retirement time, the delays could be costly to you, especially if you had been counting on receiving your Social Security income immediately upon retiring. Investigations take time, and you could be greatly inconvenienced until your first check arrives.

Worse, if a covered spouse dies prematurely, and the surviving spouse knows nothing about his or her status with Social Security, the confusion and delays added to the sorrow at such a time could be burdensome. One of the first inquiries from the surviving spouse should probably be to the Social Security Administration. If there is no record of the deceased's earnings and Social Security tax payments, any delay could be even more costly and inconvenient. The Social Security Administration will not pay any death benefits unless and until the records are in order.

Make it a habit to send in the Form SSA-7004 every two or three years to keep your account current.

9-11 How to Figure Net Earnings from Self-Employment

To figure net earnings from qualified services, assuming you are not exempt from self-employment tax, subtract the allowable business expense deductions from gross earnings. For more information, see IRS Publication 533, *Self-Employment Tax.*

In figuring your net earnings from self-employment, you must include the following:

- "Salaries and fees for your qualified services"
- Money for marrying, baptizing, conducting funerals or masses, etc., less any allowable expenses reported on Schedule C or Form 2106
- Cost of meals and lodging provided for you and your dependents if paid for the convenience of your employer (This is *not* a misprint; see IRS Publication 517, page 4. Tax preparers differ on this point. Please consult with your tax adviser on this troublesome question. It is simply not clear in the government publication.)
- The fair rental allowance plus utilities paid to you, "including the cost of utilities that are furnished"
- So-called income tax offsets or income tax allowances

Example. Pastor Roger Adams receives an annual salary of $16,500 as a full-time minister. $1,500 of the salary is designated as a rental allowance to pay utilities. His church owns a parsonage that has a fair rental value of $5,200 per year. Pastor Adams is given the use of the parsonage. He is not exempt from self-employment tax. He must include $21,700, his salary including the rental allowance for utilities, and the fair rental value of the parsonage, to figure his net earnings for self-employment taxes.

It is probably safe to say that most pastors assume that the cost of utilities is not reportable for self-employment tax purposes. Many churches make the mistake of calling it a benefit or allowance, believing it to be nonreportable as income.

Even if Pastor Adams's church combined his utility costs in his housing allowance, making it a total of $6,700 plus a salary of $16,500, the taxable amount would be the same for self-employment tax. However, for income tax purposes, it is treated differently.

To figure your net earnings, omit the following from gross income:

- Offerings that others made to the church,
- Amounts contributed by your church to an annuity plan set up for you, including any salary reduction, that are not included in your gross income, and
- Pension payments or retirement allowances you receive for your past qualified services.

In the past, many ministers have been advised to have their churches withhold their tithe from their salary, thus avoiding the payment of Social Security taxes. This issue has become very controversial. Recent research on this subject has turned up almost equal opinions for and against. Some tax experts say you can; some say you cannot. My strong advice is, don't leave it to chance. Check with your local IRS office on this one. It could be costly to you if you ignore this warning and guess wrong.

9-12 Understanding Social Security Benefits Payable to Your Survivors When You Die

When you die, benefits will be paid to your spouse, regardless of age, if your spouse is taking care of your child, and if the child is under age sixteen or has a disability.

When you die, benefits will be paid to your child who is under age eighteen, or if in high school, age nineteen, or is any age and has a disability.

AIME (the average indexed monthly earnings) is a term you must understand before attempting to project any of the Social Security benefits, whether for retirement, survivor's, disability, or Medicare benefits. The number of years of earnings must be known to determine the various benefits for survivors. The Social Security employee with whom I talked about this said that there is a somewhat complicated formula involved and that it would be best if individuals called with the details of their own situations. The following figures will help to some extent, but a call to the Social Security office is best. Figures 9.1, 9.2, and 9.3 were furnished to me over the telephone by calling the Social Security toll-free number, 1-800-772-1213. These numbers are not published in pamphlets. Anyone can call and get specific answers to questions regarding these figures.

Birth Year	No. of Years	Birth Year	No. of Years	Birth Year	No. of Years
1921	27	1928	34	1935	29
1922	28	1929	35	1936	28
1923	29	1930	34	1937	27
1924	30	1931	33	1938	26
1925	31	1932	32	1939	25
1926	32	1933	31	1940	24
1927	33	1934	30	1941	23

1942	22	1949	15	1956	8
1943	21	1950	14	1957	7
1944	20	1951	13	1958	6
1945	19	1952	12	1959	5
1946	18	1953	11	1960	4
1947	17	1954	10	1961	3
1948	16	1955	9	After 1962	2

Figure 9.1

9-13 Understanding Social Security Benefits Payable to You During Your Lifetime

Someone has said that the survivor's benefits from Social Security are too little to live on and too much to throw away. With inflation a growing threat, that continues to be true. However, when there are no other benefits, the funds can indeed help people to survive.

First of all, at the death of a covered worker, the surviving spouse, if living with the deceased at the time of death, will receive a lump-sum death benefit of $255. If the deceased did not have a spouse living with him or her, the children may receive the payment if they are eligible for monthly benefits, which are based on the earnings records of the deceased. Otherwise, the benefit would not be paid. No one seems to know why this $255 death benefit has not been increased along with the other survivor's benefits over the years. When this amount was first offered as a lump-sum death benefit many, many years ago, it was probably enough to purchase a pine box. Now it would be enough for only a down payment.

There is a difference between being a *currently* insured worker and a *fully* insured worker. To qualify as currently insured, a worker must have earned six out of thirteen quarters of coverage, including the one in which death occurred. To be credited for a quarter of coverage, you must have earned $520 in 1990 and $540 in 1991.

To qualify as a fully insured worker, you need to have various numbers of completed quarters, depending on your age. You may have worked in a secular occupation and paid into Social Security prior to entering the ministry. All quarters that were credited are still cumulative in your account. Your Social Security benefits, including survivor's benefits, disability benefits, retirement benefits, and Medicare benefits, will still be available to you if you are fully insured. Anytime you have ten years or forty quarters of covered employment, you are fully insured in the Social Security program. (However, if you choose to become exempt from Social Security tax, your disability coverage will no longer be in force after five years from that exemption date.) Use Figure 9.2 to determine whether you are fully insured.

Birth Year	Quarters	Birth Year	Quarters
1920	31	1942	26
1921	32	1943	25
1922	33	1944	24
1923	34	1945	23
1924	35	1946	22
1925	36	1947	21
1926	37	1948	20
1927	38	1949	19
1928–29	39	1950	18
1930	38	1951	17
1931	37	1952	16
1932	36	1953	15
1933	35	1954	14
1934	34	1955	13
1935	33	1956	12
1936	32	1957	11
1937	31	1958	10
1938	30	1959	9
1939	29	1960	8
1940	28	1961	7
1941	27	After 1961	6

Figure 9.2

9-14 What About Maximum Earnings Subject to Self-Employment Tax?

The burden of paying for Social Security has risen far beyond anyone's expectations. The skyrocketing costs of hospitals and medical care are already out of the reach of approximately thirty-seven million Americans who have no coverage. Congress is paying increasing attention to this vast need in the U.S. In 1991 Congress mandated that all local and state government employees must enter the Social Security program if they are not currently covered by a retirement plan. (All ministers were automatically included in Social Security as of 1968 unless they were exempt or were eligible to file at that particular time.)

The self-employed minister must pay 15.3 percent of net earnings up to the present maximum of $55,500 for 1992. That percentage includes 2.9 percent for Medicare hospital insurance, or the HI tax rate. In 1991 the HI (hospital insurance) tax rate maximum on which the 2.9 percent must be paid was raised to $125,000. So, if your net self-employment income from ministerial duties is $125,000, you would pay 15.3 percent on the first $53,400 and then 2.9 percent on the remaining amount of $71,600.

Figure 9.3 shows how the taxable earnings base has risen.

Year	Base of Taxable Earnings	Average Wage	Index Factor
1951	$ 3,600	$ 2,799.16	7.18056
1952	3,600	2,973.32	6.75997
1953	3,600	3,139.44	6.40227
1954	3,600	3,155.64	6.36941
1955	4,200	3,301.44	6.08812
1956	4,200	3,532.36	5.69012
1957	4,200	3,641.72	5.51925
1958	4,200	3,673.80	5.47105
1959	4,800	3,855.80	5.21281
1960	4,800	4,007.12	5.01596
1961	4,800	4,086.76	4.91821
1962	4,800	4,291.40	4.68368
1963	4,800	4,396.64	4.57157
1964	4,800	4,576.32	4.39208
1965	4,800	4,658.72	4.31439
1966	6,600	4,938.36	4.07009
1967	6,600	5,213.44	3.85533
1968	7,800	5,571.76	3.60740
1969	7,800	5,893.76	3.41031
1970	7,800	6,186.24	3.24907
1971	7,800	6,497.08	3.09363
1972	9,000	7,133.80	2.81751
1973	10,800	7,580.16	2.65160
1974	13,200	8,030.76	2.50282

1975	14,100	8,630.92	2.32878
1976	15,300	9,226.48	2.17846
1977	16,500	9,779.44	2.05529
1978	17,700	10,556.03	1.90408
1979	22,900	11,479.46	1.75091
1980	25,900	12,513.46	1.60623
1981	29,700	13,773.10	1.45933
1982	32,400	14,531.34	1.38319
1983	35,700	15,239.24	1.31893
1984	37,800	16,135.07	1.24571
1985	39,600	16,822.51	1.19480
1986	42,000	17,321.82	1.16036
1987	43,800	18,426.51	1.09080
1988	45,000	19,334.04	1.03959
1989	48,000	20,099.55	1.00000
1990	51,300	-	1.00000
1991	53,400	-	1.00000
1992	55,500	-	1.00000

Figure 9.3

Optional Methods for Figuring Net Earnings from Self-Employment

Often a minister will own a working farm and have net self-employment income from it. You would probably qualify for your income from ministry and farm income. "In general, the optional methods for figuring net earnings from self-employment are intended to permit continued coverage for social security self-employment tax purposes when your income for the tax year is low. For more information on the farm optional method, see Publication 533, *Self-Employment Tax.*"

Nonfarm optional method. You may use this method subject to the following conditions:

1) If your nonfarm net earnings are less than $1,733.
2) If your nonfarm net earnings "are less than two-thirds of your total gross income from nonfarm self-employment."
3) If you are self-employed regularly, that is, you earned $400 or more in net self-employment earnings for "at least 2 of the 3 tax years" prior to "the one for which you use this method."

4) If you have "not previously used this method more than 4 years (there is a 5 year lifetime limit)."

These four tests allow you to "report the smaller of two-thirds of the gross income from your nonfarm business, or $1,600 as your net earnings from self-employment."

Some Benefits Broadened or Extended in 1991

If a doctor will validate that a hospice resident is terminally ill after the present limit of 210 days, the limit may be extended.

As of January 1, 1991, the maximum that doctors may charge Medicare patients was set at 125 percent of the allowable amount. In 1992 this amount dropped to 120 percent; thereafter, it will drop to 115 percent.

In the case of severe kidney disease, health care coverage provided by employers has been extended from twelve months to eighteen months.

The expiration date for employer plans that provide primary coverage for employees with disabilities who are still considered to be active individuals has been changed from December 31, 1991, through September 30, 1995. To date, the definition of *active individuals* has not been stated.

9-15 You May Have a Refund Coming from an Earned Income Credit

If your earned income and your adjusted gross income (line 31, Form 1040) are each less than $20,264 and if you have a child living with you in your primary residence in the U.S. for more than half the year during that time, you may be eligible for a refund. A worksheet for determining this question is in the instructions for Form 1040. For more information, see IRS Publication 596, *Earned Income Credit*.

9-16 What About a Husband and Wife Missionary Team?

They must

1) be duly ordained, licensed or commissioned ministers of a church.
2) have a written agreement that specifies the services "that each will perform."
3) "divide the self-employment income according to the agreement."

What if the agreement is with one spouse only? Income is reported only by the spouse named in the agreement. It cannot be divided in any way, even if both are ordained.

What about "a minister-missionary's spouse who is not duly ordained, commissioned, or licensed?" Such a person may file a claim for refund of any self-employment tax paid in error for any years for which the statutory period of limitation on refunds has not expired. This period is normally 3 years from the time the return was filed or 2 years from the time the tax was paid, whichever is later. The spouse's earnings, in this case, should not be included in the minister-missionary's self-employment income. If the minister-missionary's spouse receives pay for performing services for the organization, he or she may be an employee of the organization for social security purposes.

9-17 How much Can You Earn After Retirement and Still Draw Social Security Benefits?

This question can be confusing. It is necessary to distinguish between Social Security tax and income tax. The maximum Social Security income that can be drawn in retirement before any funds are taken away is discussed in the chapter on retirement in section 3-8. If you are sixty-five or over you can earn up to $10,200 in 1992 and not report it for Social Security tax purposes. If you are between the ages of sixty-two and sixty-five, the maximum if $7,440.

That is different from two other maximums affecting retirement benefits. You are allowed to earn up to $25,000 as a single person before your Social Security benefits become taxable. You are allowed to earn up to $32,000 if you are married and file joint returns before your Social Security benefits become taxable. If you earn more than those amounts, as applicable to your age, it is possible that you will have to report some of your Social Security income for income tax purposes. This can cause you to pay income tax, whereas the limitations in the preceding paragraph speak of money taken away. Consult your tax adviser or the IRS in regard to this question.

Unearned income does not count in determining these maximum allowable amounts of income. Several examples of unearned income are deferred compensation, pension income, interest earned on investment income, and deferred royalties or commissions. For self-employed persons, which includes almost all clergypersons, any amounts earned in excess of these maximums will be subject to

Social Security tax of 15.3 percent. For true employees, the tax rate was 7.65 percent in 1992.

9-18 How to File for Social Security Benefits

The best way to start gathering information is to call the toll-free WATS number, 1-800-829-3676, and begin asking questions. Have your Social Security number handy when you call. You will be given the address and telephone number of your nearest Social Security office.

9-19 How to Pay Estimated Tax

If you anticipate earning enough self-employment income, or any other income not subject to withholding, to pay $500 in taxes for the year, you must make estimated tax payments during the year.

Use Form 1040-ES, *Estimated Tax for Individuals*, to determine your estimated tax. On April 15 of the tax year, you must pay the entire estimated tax or the first installment, using a Form 1040-ES payment voucher. This applies whether or not you live in the U.S. or outside the U.S. and Puerto Rico. For more information on this question, see IRS Publication 505, *Tax Withholding and Estimated Tax*.

If you live overseas, some income may be excluded. See IRS Publication 54, *Tax Guide for U.S. Citizens and Resident Aliens Abroad*, and IRS Publication 570, *Tax Guide for Individuals with Income from U.S. Possessions*.

Income tax withholding. Duly ordained, licensed, or commissioned ministers, members of a religious order (who have not taken a vow of poverty), and Christian Science practitioners, who perform qualified services, must pay taxes, but their salaries generally are not subject to federal income tax withholding.

Deduction for self-employment tax. After 1989, you can deduct one-half of the self-employment taxes you pay as a business expense in figuring adjusted gross income. This is an income tax deduction only, and you deduct it on line 25 of Form 1040. It is not a deduction in figuring net earnings from self-employment subject to self-employment tax.

Also effective for tax years beginning **after 1989,** a deduction of 7.65% of your net earnings from self-employment is taken when figuring your self-employment tax. This deduction is allowed only in figuring self-employment tax, and you figure it on line 4 of your Schedule SE. It is not an income tax deduction.

9-20 What About Deducting Health Insurance Costs?

Generally speaking, most clergypersons receive these health coverages tax-free. The IRS allows churches to pay the premiums in behalf of the ministers who do not have to include the amount in their gross income. (See Regulation 1.106-1.) Organizations providing such benefits to employees are required to have a written "plan." It has been held that if a church board elects to take on the payment of such premiums and so notes its intentions in the official church board minutes, such action serves as a written plan. Even if the church has only one employee—the minister—the IRS has ruled that the cost of medical insurance paid by the church is not considered to be income to the minister (Revenue Ruling 58-90).

9-21 Are Proceeds from an Accident Considered Income to You?

If a church purchases accident and health insurance coverage for a minister who is an employee for income tax purposes, in the event of a cash settlement to the minister from an insurance company, such cash is not reportable as income. If, however, the agreement is to pay the minister over a period of time, there are different rules to consider. If such a payment should be in the offing, you would be wise to seek competent counsel about how to receive your settlement money.

9-22 Who Must File Form 1040?

If you are eligible for Social Security and are not exempt from self-employment tax, you must file an income tax return on Form 1040. (See 9-11.)

If you have other self-employment earnings of $400 or more and are exempt from qualified services earnings, you must file an income tax return on Form 1040.

If you earned $100 or more from an electing church or church-controlled organization, you must file an income tax return on Form 1040.

9-23 How to Understand Medicare and Medicaid

When you and/or your spouse reach age sixty-five, your federal health care program called Medicare begins whether or not you are still working. This program is administered by the Health Care Financing Administration of the U.S. Department of Health and Human Services. If your spouse reaches age sixty-five before you and you are eligible for monthly Social Security benefits because of your work record, your spouse qualifies for Medicare at age sixty-five. Of course, if you have been disabled prior to age sixty-five and have been receiving disability income benefits from Social Security, you may also be entitled to Medicare coverage prior to age sixty-five. For complete details of all facets of the Medicare program, see *The Medicare Handbook,* published yearly by the U.S. Department of Health and Human Services Health Care Financing Administration. For your convenience, I will quote the highlights for you.

9-24 Two Parts of Medicare

Hospital Insurance or Part A is intended to help pay for services and care administered in hospitals, skilled nursing organizations, private homes, and hospice institutions. There are covered services and noncovered services under each kind of care. Part A pays for covered services and supplies.

Medicare Part A benefits include the following:

1) **Major inpatient hospital care services,** including:

- A semiprivate room (2 to 4 beds in a room).
- All your meals, including special diets.
- Regular nursing services.
- Costs of special care units, such as intensive care or coronary care units.
- Drugs furnished by the hospital during your stay.
- Blood transfusions furnished by the hospital during your stay.
- Lab tests included in your hospital bill.
- X-rays and other radiology services, including radiation therapy, billed by the hospital.
- Medical supplies, such as casts, surgical dressing, and splints.
- Use of appliances, such as a wheelchair.
- Operating and recovery room costs.
- Rehabilitation services, such as physical therapy, occupational therapy, and speech pathology services.

2) **Inpatient care in a skilled nursing facility following a hospital stay.**
3) **Home health care.**
4) **Hospice care.**

Hospital care and skilled nursing care are limited, but Medicare helps pay for each benefit period. However, Part A protection is renewed each time a new benefit period is started. Medicare pays only for skilled nursing facility care and does not pay for care that is primarily custodial.

Some services NOT covered when you are a hospital inpatient include:

- Personal convenience items that you request such as a telephone or television in your room.
- Private duty nurses.
- Any extra charges for a private room unless it is determined to be medically necessary.

Medical Insurance or Part B helps defray expenses for doctors' services, outpatient hospital care, some medical equipment, and certain other medical services and supplies not covered under Part A of Medicare.

Medicare Part B includes:
1) Major covered doctor's services include:

- Medical and surgical services, including anesthesia.
- Diagnostic tests and procedures that are part of your treatment.
- Radiology and pathology services by doctors while you are a hospital inpatient or outpatient.
- Treatment of mental illness. (Medicare payments for outpatient treatment are limited. Consult Medicare.)
- Other services such as X rays, services of your doctor's office nurse, drugs and biologicals that cannot be self-administered, transfusions of blood and blood components, medical supplies, and physical/occupational therapy and speech pathology services.

2) Outpatient hospital care
3) Diagnosis tests
4) Durable medical equipment
5) Ambulance services
6) Many other health services and supplies which are not covered by Medicare Part A

Some doctor's services *not* covered by Medicare include:

1) Routine physical examinations and tests directly related to such examinations (except some pap smears and mammograms).
2) Most routine foot care and dental care.
3) Examinations for prescribing or fitting eyeglasses (except after cataract surgery) or hearing aids.
4) Immunizations (except pneumococcal vaccinations or immunizations required because of an injury or immediate risk of infection, and hepatitis B for certain persons at risk).
5) Cosmetic surgery, unless it is needed because of accidental injury or to improve the function of a malformed part of the body.

These are only the highlights of services offered and not offered. Check with Medicare for details.

Since Medicare is not designed to pay all of your medical costs, you would be wise to purchase a Medicare supplement from a commercial insurance company. Such an arrangement, with both Medicare and a Medicare supplement, is ideal.

How Much Must You Pay Before Medicare Part B Pays?

The annual deductible amount paid by the patient is $100, and all eligible claims apply to it.

What about reasonable charges? Medicare pays only 80 percent of approved charges, even if that is less than what has been determined by doctors and suppliers as reasonable charges.

9-25 Who Can Get Medicare Hospital Insurance (Part A)?

Generally, people age 65 and over can get premium-free Medicare Part A benefits, based on their own or their spouses' employment. (Premium-free means there are no monthly premiums. Most people do not pay premiums for Medicare Part A.) You can get premium-free Medicare Part A if you are 65 or over and:

- Receive benefits under the Social Security or Railroad Retirement system,
- Could receive benefits under Social Security or the Railroad Retirement system but have not filed for them, or
- You or your spouse had certain government employment.

If you are under 65 you can get premium-free Medicare Part A benefits if you have been a disabled beneficiary under Social Security or the Railroad Retirement Board for more than 24 months.

Certain government employees and certain members of their families can also get Medicare when they are disabled for more than 29 months. They should apply with the Social Security Administration as soon as they become disabled.

Or, you may be able to get premium-free Medicare Part A benefits if you receive continuing dialysis for permanent kidney failure or if you have had a kidney transplant.

Check with Social Security to see if you have worked long enough under Social Security or Railroad Retirement, as a government employee, or a combination of these systems to be able to get Medicare Part A benefits. Generally, if either you or your spouse worked for 10 years, you may be able to get premium-free Medicare Part A benefits.

9-26 Who Can Get Medicare Medical Insurance (Part B)?

Any person who can get premium-free Medicare Part A benefits based on work as described above can enroll for Part B, pay the monthly Part B premiums [in 1991, $29.90 for most beneficiaries], and get Part B benefits. In addition, most United States residents age 65 or over can enroll in Part B.

9-27 Buying Medicare Part A and Part B

If you do not have enough work credits to be able to get Medicare Part A benefits and you are 65 or over, you may be able to buy Medicare Parts A and B—or just Medicare Part B—by paying monthly premiums. Also, you may be able to buy Medicare Parts A and B if you are disabled and lost your premium-free Part A solely because you are working.

9-28 Should You Buy a Medicare Supplement?

Yes. The rising costs of health care make it almost a necessity. Retired persons have been known to lose all their savings because of one illness and/or hospital stay. You should use care in purchasing your supplemental coverage, however, because all companies are not alike. Choose a company carefully, noting first of all its financial strength as measured by authoritative institutions. Ask for a sample policy and check the fine print. If a sample policy is not available, go to another company.

Don't rely solely on the printed advertising and promotional material or a salesman's statements unless backed up to your satisfaction. If you don't fully understand the conditions of your policy and how it works along with Medicare, seek the advice of a knowledgeable friend or other adviser. Don't take any action until all your questions are answered to your satisfaction.

There are many other details to know about Medicare. Don't hesitate to call your local Medicare office. The staff is very willing and able to answer your questions.

Benefits for Survivors*

Social Security protects the family of a deceased worker. Survivor benefits help ease the financial burden that sometimes follows a worker's death by providing the family with a continuing cash income.

Eligibility

The deceased worker must have credit for work covered by Social Security, ranging from 1½ to 10 years depending on his or her age at death.

Who May Receive Monthly Benefits

- A widow or widower at 60 or older (50, if disabled).
- A divorced widow or widower at 60 or older (50, if disabled) if the marriage lasted at least 10 years.
- A mother or father of the worker's child under 16 or disabled, if caring for the child.
- Unmarried children up to 18 (or 19 if they are attending a primary or secondary school full time).
- Children who became disabled before reaching 22, as long as they remain disabled.
- A dependent parent or parents 62 or older.

Lump-Sum Death Payment

A one-time payment of $255 is paid in addition to the monthly cash benefits described above. The lump-sum death payment (LSDP) is paid in the following priority order:

- To a surviving spouse who lived in the same household as the deceased person at the time of death. If the LSDP is not payable in this manner, it can be paid to:
  - A surviving spouse eligible for or entitled to benefits for the month of death,
  - A child or children eligible for or entitled to benefits for the month of death.

The LSDP cannot be paid if there is no eligible spouse or child.

Applying for Benefits

You must apply in order to receive benefits. You can apply at any Social Security office and, if you wish, you can apply by telephone. The

* From U.S. Department of Health and Human Services, Social Security Administration, SSA Publication No. 05-10034, September 1989, ICN 456100.

phone number of your local Social Security office is listed in your phone book under "Social Security Administration" or "U.S. Government."

When you apply you will need the following information:

- Your Social Security number and the deceased worker's number.
- Proof of your age.
- Proof of marriage, if you are applying for widow's or widower's benefits.
- Proof of divorce, if you are applying for benefits as a divorced widow or widower.
- Proof of the worker's death. Generally, the funeral director's statement, which is sent to the nearest Social Security office, will fulfill this requirement. When this is done, a death certificate usually is not necessary.
- Children's birth certificates and Social Security numbers, if they are to receive benefits.
- Deceased worker's Form W-2 (or Federal tax return, if self-employed) for the most recent tax year.
- Proof of support if you are applying for benefits as a dependent parent or grandchild of the deceased worker.

You should also bring your checkbook or savings passbook so that Social Security can arrange to have your benefits deposited directly in your bank account. In addition to being convenient, direct deposit is a safer method of payment. Direct deposit is Social Security's customary method of paying benefits.

If You're Self-Employed*

The majority of people who pay into Social Security work for someone else. Their employer deducts Social Security taxes from their paycheck, matches that contribution, and sends wage reports and taxes to the Internal Revenue Service and Social Security. But self-employed people must fill out the forms and pay the taxes directly to the government. This factsheet explains that process.

You are self-employed if you operate a trade, business, or profession, either by yourself or as a partner. You report your earnings for Social Security when you file your Federal income tax return. If your net

* From U.S. Department of Health and Human Services, Social Security Administration, SSA Publication No. 05-10022, February 1992, ICN 454900.

earnings are $400 or more in a year, you must report your earnings on schedule SE.

Paying Social Security and Medicare Taxes

The self-employment tax rate for 1992 is 15.3 percent (the same as 1991) on self-employment income up to $55,500. However, if your net earnings exceed $55,500, you continue to pay the Medicare portion of the Social Security tax, which is 2.9 percent, up to a maximum of $130,200. But, there are two deductions that reduce your tax liability. The deductions are intended to ensure that self-employed people are treated in much the same way as employers and employees for Social Security and income tax purposes.

First, your net earnings from self-employment are reduced by an amount equal to half of your total self-employment tax. This is similar to the way employees are treated under the tax laws in that the employer's share of the Social Security tax is not considered income to the employee.

Second, you can deduct half of your self-employment tax as a business expense. This is similar to the deduction allowed to employers on the Social Security taxes they pay for their employees.

If you have wages as well as self-employment earnings, the Social Security tax on your wages is figured first. If your wages are less than $55,500 in 1992, you pay the self-employment tax on the difference between your wages and the maximum, or on your net earnings, if less. If your wages are more than $55,500 but less than $130,200, you'll have to report your net earnings and pay the Medicare portion of the Social Security tax on the difference between your wages and your net earnings up to $130,200.

Earnings Credits

You need earnings credits to qualify for Social Security benefits. The number of credits you will need depends on your date of birth, but no one needs more than 40. You can earn up to 4 credits per year.

If your net earnings are $2,280 or more, you earn 4 earnings credits (1 for each $570). (If your net earnings are less than $570, you still may earn 1 or more credits by using the optional method described on the back of this factsheet.)

All of your earnings covered by Social Security are used in figuring your Social Security benefit. So, it's important that you report all of your earnings up to the maximum as required by law.

Figuring Your Net Earnings

Net earnings for Social Security are your gross earnings from your trade or business, minus all of your allowable business deductions and depreciation.

The following kinds of income do not count for Social Security, so do not include them in figuring your net earnings:

- Dividends from shares of stock and interest on bonds, unless you receive them as a dealer in stocks and securities.
- Interest from loans, unless your business is lending money.
- Rentals from real estate, unless you are a real estate dealer or regularly provide services mostly for the convenience of the occupant.
- Income received from a limited partnership as a limited partner.

Optional Method

If your actual net earnings are less than $400, your earnings can still count for Social Security under an optional method of reporting. The optional method can be used if your gross earnings are $600 or more or when your profit is less than $1,600.

You can use the optional method no more than five times. Your actual net must have been $400 or more in at least 2 of the last 3 years, and your net earnings must be less than two-thirds of your gross income.

Here's how it works:

- If your gross income from self-employment is between $600 and $2,400, you may report two-thirds of your gross or your actual net earnings if $400 or more.
- If your gross income is $2,400 or more and the actual net earnings are $1,600 or less, you report either $1,600 or your actual net.

Special Note For Farmers: If you are a farmer, you can use the optional method every year. You do not need to have had actual net earnings of at least $400 in any preceding year.

How to Report Earnings

You must complete the following Federal tax forms by April 15 following any year in which you have net earnings of $400 or more:

- Form 1040 *(Income Tax Return)*
- Schedule C *(Business Profit or Loss)*
- Schedule SE *(Social Security Self-Employment Tax)*

These forms can be obtained from the Internal Revenue Service and most banks and post offices.

Send the tax return and schedules along with your self-employment tax to the Internal Revenue Service.

Even if you do not owe any income tax, you must complete Form 1040 and Schedule SE to pay self-employment Social Security tax. This is true even if you already get Social Security benefits.

Church Workers

If you are considered self-employed because of your work for a church or church-controlled organization, you must report earnings of $100 or more. For more information, ask Social Security for the factsheet, *If You Work For A Nonprofit Organization* (Publication No. 05-10027).

Family Business Arrangements

Family members may operate a business together. A husband and a wife may be partners or joint venturers. If you operate a business together as partners, you should each report your share of the business profits as net earnings on separate schedules, even if you file a joint income tax return. The amount each of you should report depends upon your agreement.

How Your Retirement Benefit Is Figured*

As you make financial plans for your future, one of the questions you'll probably ask is, "How much will I get from Social Security?" For most people, the answer can be found in a personal benefit estimate statement available free from Social Security. (You can call or visit any Social Security office to get the form you need to request this statement.) It tells you how much you can expect when you retire, but also provides estimates of the disability benefits you might be eligible for and any benefits payable to your family if you should die.

The benefit estimate statement is a helpful and useful tool. But many people still wonder how their benefit is figured. This factsheet answers that question.

* From U.S. Department of Health and Human Services, Social Security Administration, SSA Publication No. 05-10070, February 1992, ICN 467100.

Steps in Figuring a Social Security Retirement Benefit

Basically, all Social Security benefits are based on earnings averaged over most of a worker's lifetime. This is different from many other pension plans that are usually based on a relatively small number of years of earnings.

Although a computer does all the work, the method for figuring retirement benefits goes like this. (Disability and survivor benefits are figured a little bit differently.)

Step 1—First, your earnings covered by Social Security are listed starting with 1951.

Step 2—Next, your earnings are indexed, or adjusted, to take account of changes in average wages since the year you received the earnings. For example, average earnings for 1989 are 5 times greater than average earnings were for 1958. To make 1958 earnings comparable with current earnings, they are multiplied by 5. Earnings are indexed for each year up to the year you reach age 60. The indexing factor becomes smaller the closer you get to the present. Actual earnings you have after 60 are used.

Step 3—From this list, the highest years of earnings are selected to figure your benefits. For nearly everyone retiring now and in the future, 35 years of earnings are used to figure retirement benefits. If you haven't worked for 35 years, we'll add years of "zero" earnings to your record to total 35 years.

Step 4—The earnings for these years are totaled and divided by 420 (the number of months in 35 years) to get your average monthly earnings. This is the number used to figure your benefit rate.

Step 5—A three-level formula is applied to your average monthly earnings to arrive at an actual benefit rate. For example, for people born in 1927:

- We multiply the first $339 of your monthly earnings by 90 percent.
- We multiply the next $1,705 of your earnings by 32 percent.
- We multiply any remaining amount by 15 percent.

The results are added together and rounded to the next lower dime. This is your basic full retirement age (currently 65) benefit rate.

A new formula is set each year for people reaching 62 that year. The percentages remain the same, but the dollar amounts change. Even if you don't retire until later, we'll figure your benefits using the formula based on the year you turned 62. (We don't use this formula if you also get or are eligible for a pension based on work where you didn't pay Social Security taxes. For more information about this, ask for a copy of

A Pension From Work Not Covered By Social Security, Publication No. 05-10045).

Cost-of-Living Increases

You're eligible for cost-of-living benefit increases starting with the year you become 62. This is true even if you don't get benefits until 65 or even 70.

This means your basic benefit is multiplied by all of the cost-of-living increases starting with the year you reach 62 up to the year you start getting benefits. Social Security benefits are paid in even dollar amounts, so your benefit is reduced to the next lower dollar.

Reduced Benefits

We told you how your full retirement benefit rate (the amount payable at 65) is figured. You can start getting benefits as early as 62, but at a reduced rate.

Your benefit is reduced by $5/9$ of 1 percent for each month you get benefits before 65. This amounts to a 20-percent reduction if you get benefits at 62. But, since benefits can only be paid for months you are eligible throughout the entire month, you can't get a benefit for the month you reach 62 unless your birthday is the 1st or 2nd of the month. So, chances are your benefit won't be reduced the whole 20 percent.

The closer you are to 65 when benefits start, the smaller the reduction. For example, the reduction is $13^1/3$ percent at 63, and $6^2/3$ percent at 64.

Any Questions?

For more information, write or visit any Social Security office or phone our toll-free number, 1-800-772-1213. You can speak to a representative any business day 7 a.m. to 7 p.m. The best times to call are early in the morning and early in the evening. And if you can, it's best to call later in the week and later in the month. When you call, have your Social Security number handy.

The Social Security Administration treats all calls confidentially—whether they're made to our toll-free number or to one of our local offices. We also want to ensure that you receive accurate and courteous service. That is why we have a second Social Security representative listen to some incoming and outgoing telephone calls.

Government Pension Offset*

A Law That Affects Social Security Spouse's or Widow's Benefits

If you worked for a Federal, State, or local government where you did not pay Social Security taxes, the pension you receive from that agency may reduce any Social Security benefits you qualify for.

There are two laws that may reduce your benefits. One of them affects the way your Social Security retirement or disability benefits are figured. For more information about that provision, contact Social Security for the factsheet, *A Pension From Work Not Covered By Social Security* (Publication No. 05-10045).

The second law affects Social Security benefits you receive as a spouse or widow. This factsheet provides answers to questions you may have about this provision.

I Receive a Government Pension. Will I Receive Any Social Security on My Spouse's Record?

Probably not. Some or all of your Social Security spouse's or widow's benefit may be offset if you receive a pension from a job where you did not pay Social Security taxes.

How Much Is the Offset?

The offset will reduce the amount of your Social Security spouse's or widow's benefits by two-thirds of the amount of your government pension. In other words, if you get a monthly civil service pension of $600, two-thirds of that, or $400, must be used to offset your Social Security spouse's or widow's benefits. If you're eligible for a $500 widow's benefit, you'll receive $100 per month from Social Security ($500 – $400 = $100).

If you take your annuity as a lump sum, the offset is figured as if you chose to receive regular monthly benefits.

Why Is There an Offset?

Social Security spouse's benefits provide income to wives and husbands who have little or no Social Security benefits of their own. Since the beginning of the Social Security program, spouse's benefits were intended for women and men who were financially dependent on their husbands or wives who worked at jobs covered by Social Security.

* From U.S. Department of Health and Human Services, Social Security Administration, SSA Publication No. 05-10007, February 1992, ICN 451453.

Before the offset provisions were enacted, many government employees qualified for a pension from their agency and for a spouse's benefit from Social Security, even though they were not dependent on their husband or wife.

Here's an example that helps clarify why there is an offset:

Bill Smith collects a Social Security benefit of $600 per month. His wife, Mary, is potentially eligible for a wife's benefit up to 50 percent of Bill's, or $300. However, Mary also worked and paid into Social Security, qualifying for her own retirement benefit of $400. She will not receive any wife's benefits because her $400 retirement benefit, in effect, "offsets" her $300 wife's benefit. (When you're eligible for two Social Security benefits, you generally get the higher of the two, not both.)

Bill's neighbor, Tom, also gets a Social Security benefit of $600 per month. But his wife, Nancy, worked for the Federal Government (instead of a job where she paid Social Security taxes) and earned a civil service pension of $800 per month. Before the government pension offset provisions were in place, Nancy would have been eligible for both her $800 civil service pension and a $300 wife's benefit on Tom's Social Security record. With the offset provisions in place, Nancy does not qualify for a wife's benefit from Social Security, so now she is treated the same as Mary.

Who Is Exempt?

- Any State, local, or military service employee whose government pension is based on a job where he or she was paying Social Security taxes on the last day of employment. (Some government entities were not initially covered by Social Security, but chose to participate in Social Security at a later date.)
- Anyone whose government pension is not based on his or her earnings.
- Anyone who received or who was eligible to receive the government pension before December 1982 and who meets all the requirements for Social Security spouse's benefits in effect in January 1977. (Essentially, this provision applies to a divorced woman whose marriage must have lasted at least 20 years and to a husband or widower who must have received one-half of his support from his wife.)
- Anyone who received or was eligible to receive the Federal, State, or local government pension before July 1, 1983, and was receiving one-half support from her or his spouse.
- Federal employees who are mandatorily covered under Social Security.

- Federal employees who chose to switch from the Civil Service Retirement System (CSRS) to the Social Security system on or before December 31, 1987. If the Office of Personnel Management allowed an employee to make a belated election to the Federal Employee Retirement System (FERS), the change could be made through June 30, 1988. Federal employees (such as legislative employees) who opt to switch to Social Security coverage after December 31, 1987, will need 5 years of Federal employment covered by Social Security to be exempt from government pension offset.

Even If I Do Not Get Cash Benefits, Can I Still Get Medicare at 65 on My Spouse's Record?

Yes.

Can I Still Get Benefits on My Own Record?

The offset applies only to Social Security benefits as a spouse or widow. However, your own benefits may be reduced due to another provision of the law. Contact Social Security for the factsheet, *A Pension From Work Not Covered by Social Security* (Publication No. 05-10045).

Any Questions?

For more information, write or visit any Social Security office or phone our toll-free number, 1-800-772-1213. You can speak to a representative any business day 7 a.m. to 7 p.m. The best times to call are early in the morning and early in the evening. And if you can, it's best to call later in the week and later in the month.

When you call, have your Social Security number handy. If you have a question about spouse's or widow's benefits on somebody else's record, we will need his or her Social Security number, too.

The Social Security Administration treats all calls confidentially— whether they're made to our toll-free number or to one of our local offices. We also want to ensure that you receive accurate and courteous service. That is why we have a second Social Security representative listen to some incoming and outgoing telephone calls.

Household Workers*

If you hire a household employee, such as a cleaning person, a cook, a gardener, or a babysitter, there's some important information you (and your employee) should know about paying Social Security taxes.

* From U.S. Department of Health and Human Services, Social Security Administration, SSA Publication No. 05-10021, February 1992, ICN 454750.

Your household employee will be eligible for Social Security and Medicare someday—but only if you deduct Social Security taxes from his or her wages and report those wages to the Internal Revenue Service and the Social Security Administration. When you report those wages and pay the taxes, your employee gains credits towards all the Social Security benefits available. Those benefits include retirement and disability payments for the household worker, benefits for his or her dependents, survivors benefits when he or she dies, and Medicare coverage.

This factsheet provides the information you and your household worker need to know about paying Social Security taxes and earning Social Security benefits.

Wages Must Be Reported

If you pay a household worker $50 or more in cash wages during a 3-month calendar quarter, you must deduct Social Security taxes and report the wages. This includes any cash you pay to cover the cost of bus fare, meals, or a room. Failure to report the wages on time may mean you'll have to pay a penalty in addition to overdue taxes.

A calendar quarter is a 3-month period that ends on March 31, June 30, September 30, or December 31. If wages average as little as $4 a week, they would exceed $50 for the quarter.

Are All Household Workers Covered?

If you pay a household worker $50 or more in cash wages during a calendar quarter, the work is covered by Social Security. However, special rules apply in the following situations:

- If you run a hotel, roominghouse, or boardinghouse, all wages you pay employees must be reported, even if they are less than $50 per quarter.
- If you hire someone to do household work on a farm operated for profit, wages must be reported if you:
  —spend more than $2,500 during a year on agricultural labor, or
  —spend less than $2,500 during a year on agricultural labor but pay the household worker $150 or more a year.

Household work done by your child 21 or over is covered by Social Security. Household work done by your child under 21 or by your spouse is not covered. Household work performed by your parent may be covered in certain situations.

Contact any Social Security office for more information.

Reporting the Wages

You should contact the Internal Revenue Service (IRS) for the necessary reporting forms. IRS will also give you information on how to complete them and when to file them. Meanwhile, here are a few highlights you may want to know:

- Keeping Records—For Social Security purposes, you need the name, address, and Social Security number of each household worker and the amount of wages paid. Copy the Social Security number directly from the individual's Social Security card. If an employee does not have a card, he or she should apply for one at any Social Security office.
- Deducting Social Security Taxes—The 1992 Social Security tax rate, for both employees and employers, is 7.65 percent on wages up to $55,500. If you pay your employee more than $55,500, then you must deduct the Medicare hospital insurance portion of the tax, or 1.45 percent (and pay the same rate yourself) on his or her wages over $55,500 up to $130,200.
- Quarterly Reports—Within a month after a quarter ends, you must send to IRS both the taxes and a report of the wages you paid. This is done by using IRS Form 942 *(Employer's Quarterly Tax Return for Household Employees)*.
- W-2 After Year Ends—You must also give your household employee copies B, C, and 2 of IRS form W-2 *(Wage and Tax Statement)* by January 31 after the year in which wages were paid. Send copy A to the Social Security Administration by the last day of February. You can obtain this form and the instructions for completing it by contacting any IRS office.

How Your Household Worker Earns Credit for Social Security

In 1992, a person earns 1 credit for each $570 of reported earnings, up to a maximum of 4 credits for the year. The amount needed for 1 credit will increase automatically in future years as average wages for all workers increase.

How many credits workers (including household workers) need to qualify for Social Security depends on their age and the kind of benefit they might be eligible for. Most people need 40 credits (10 years of work) to qualify for benefits. Younger people need fewer credits to be eligible for disability benefits, or for their family members to be eligible for survivors benefits if they should die.

Remember: If you do not report the wages for your employee, he or she may not have enough credit for Social Security benefits, or the amount of the benefit may be less.

For More Information

For more information, visit or write any Social Security office, or phone our toll-free number, 1-800-772-1213. You can speak to a teleservice representative weekdays between 7 a.m. and 7 p.m. every business day.

The Social Security Administration treats all calls confidentially—whether they're made to our toll-free number or to one of our local offices. We also want to ensure that you receive accurate and courteous service. That is why we have a second Social Security representative listen to some incoming and outgoing telephone calls.

Social Security and Your Right to Representation*

You can choose to have a representative help you when you do business with Social Security. We will work with your representative, just as we would with you.

Your representative cannot charge or collect a fee from you without first getting written approval from the Social Security Administration, even if your claim is denied. However, your representative may accept money in advance as long as he or she holds it in a trust or escrow account.

What a Representative Can Do

Once appointed, your representative can act for you in most Social Security matters. For example, he or she can:

- get information from your Social Security file;
- give us evidence or information to support your claim;
- come with you, or for you, to any interview, conference, or hearing you have with us;
- request a reconsideration, hearing, or Appeals Council review; and
- help you and your witnesses prepare for a hearing and question any witnesses.

Your representative also will receive a copy of the decision(s) we make on your claim(s).

* From U.S. Department of Health and Human Services, Social Security Administration, SSA Publication No. 05-10075, August 1991, ICN 468000.

Choosing a Representative

You can choose an attorney or other qualified person to represent you. You also can have more than one representative.

Some organizations can help you find an attorney or give you free legal services if you qualify. Some attorneys don't charge unless you receive benefits. Your Social Security office has a list of organizations that can help you find a representative.

You can appoint one or more persons in a firm, corporation, or other organization as your representative(s), but you may not appoint the firm, corporation, or organization itself. You also may not appoint a person who has been suspended or disqualified from representing others before the Social Security Administration or who may not, by law, act as a representative.

Once you choose a representative, you must tell us in writing as soon as possible. To do this, you can get a Form SSA-1696-U4, *Appointment of Representative,* from any Social Security office.

You must give the name of the person you are appointing and sign your name. If the person is not an attorney, he or she must, in writing, give his or her name; state that he or she accepts the appointment; and sign the form.

What Your Representative May Charge

To charge you a fee for his or her services, your representative first must file either a fee agreement or a fee petition with us. Your representative cannot charge you more than the fee amount we approved. If either you or your representative disagree with the fee we approved, you or your representative can ask us to look at it again.

A representative who charges or collects a fee without our approval, or charges or collects too much, may be suspended or disqualified from representing anyone before the Social Security Administration. He or she also may face criminal prosecution.

Filing a Fee Agreement

If you and your representative have a written fee agreement, your representative may ask us to approve it any time before we decide your claim. Usually, we'll approve the agreement and tell you in writing how much your representative may charge you as long as:

- you both signed the agreement;
- the fee you agreed on is no more than 25 percent of past-due benefits, or $4,000, whichever is less; and
- your claim was approved and resulted in past-due benefits.

If we don't approve the fee agreement, we will tell you and your representative in writing that your representative must file a fee petition.

Filing a Fee Petition

Your representative may give us a fee petition when he or she has finished working on your claim(s). This written request, accounting for the fee, describes in detail the amount of time spent on each service provided. Your representative must give you a copy of the fee petition and each attachment. If you disagree with the information shown, contact us within 20 days. We will consider the reasonable value of the services provided and tell you in writing the amount of the fee we approve.

How Much You Pay

The amount of the fee we decide your representative may charge is the most you owe him or her, except for out-of-pocket expenses. It might be different from the amount you agreed to pay.

If an attorney represents you, we usually withhold 25 percent of your past-due benefits to pay toward the fee for you. Later, we pay the attorney's fee from this money and send you any money left over.

You must pay your representative directly:

- the rest you owe
  —if the amount of the fee is more than the amount of money we withheld and paid your attorney for you.
- all of the fee you owe
  —if we did not withhold past-due benefits; for example, when your representative is not an attorney or the benefits are Supplemental Security Income; or
  —if we withheld but later paid you the money because your attorney did not either ask for our approval until after 60 days of the date of your notice of award or tell us on time that he or she planned to ask for a fee.
- for out-of-pocket expenses your representative incurs or expects to incur
  —for example, the cost of getting your doctor's or hospital records. Our approval is not needed for such expenses.

If Someone Else Pays Your Representative

Even when someone else will pay the fee for you (for example, an insurance company) we must approve the fee unless:

- it's a nonprofit organization or Federal, State, county, or city agency that will pay the fee and any expenses from government funds, and
- your representative gives us a written statement that you will not have to pay any fee or expenses.

If You Go Before a Federal Court

The court can allow a reasonable fee for your attorney. The fee usually will not exceed 25 percent of all past-due benefits which result from the court's decision. Your attorney cannot charge any additional fee for services before the court.

For More Information

For more information or to apply for benefits, call or visit Social Security. The address and telephone number are listed in the telephone book under "Social Security Administration" or "U.S. Government."

Military Service and Social Security*

People who serve in the military services on active duty or on active duty for training have paid into Social Security since 1957. Inactive duty service in the armed forces reserves (such as weekend drills) has been covered by Social Security since 1988. People who served in the military before 1957 did not pay into Social Security directly, but their records are credited with special earnings for Social Security purposes that count towards any benefits that might be payable. Additional earnings credits are given to military personnel depending on when they served. This factsheet explains how and when these special earnings are credited and provides other general information military personnel need to know about the benefits available from Social Security.

Paying Social Security and Medicare Taxes

While you're in the military service (from 1957 on), you pay Social Security taxes the same way civilian employees do. Those taxes are deducted from your pay and an equal amount is paid by the U.S. Government as your employer. In 1992, the tax rate is 7.65 percent up to a maximum of $55,500. If you earn more than that, you continue to pay the Medicare portion of the tax, or 1.45 percent, up to a maximum of $130,200.

---

* From U.S. Department of Health and Human Services, Social Security Administration, SSA Publication No. 05-10017, March 1992, ICN 452760.

Social Security "Credits"

By paying Social Security taxes, you earn "credits" that are used to determine your eligibility for Social Security. In 1992, you are given 1 credit for each $570 in earnings, but 4 credits is the maximum that can be earned in one year. In other words, any one who earns at least $2,280 a year ($570 times 4) earns the maximum number of Social Security credits. How many credits you need to qualify for Social Security depends on your age and the type of benefit you might be eligible for. Nobody needs more than 40 credits (10 years of work or military service) to be eligible for Social Security. In some situations, you can qualify with less than 40 credits.

Earnings Added to Military Records for Social Security Purposes

The "credits" mentioned in the previous section determine if you are eligible for Social Security. But how much you get from Social Security depends on your earnings averaged over much of your working lifetime. Generally, the higher your earnings, the higher your Social Security benefit will be.

Under certain circumstances, special earnings can be credited to your military pay record for Social Security purposes. These extra earnings may help you qualify for Social Security or increase the amount of your Social Security benefit. The extra earnings credits are granted for periods of active duty or active duty for training. (No additional earnings are granted for inactive duty training.)

Here's when the additional earnings are granted:

Service In 1978 and Later

For every $300 in active duty basic pay, you are credited with an additional $100 in earnings up to a maximum of $1,200 a year. If you enlisted after September 7, 1980, and didn't complete at least 24 months of active duty or your full tour, you may not be able to receive the additional earnings. Check with Social Security for details.

Service 1957 Through 1977

You are credited with $300 in additional earnings for each calendar quarter in which you received active duty basic pay.

Service 1940 Through 1956

If you were in the military during this period, you did not pay Social Security taxes. However, your Social Security record may be credited with an additional $160 a month in earnings for military service from

September 16, 1940, through December 31, 1956, under the following circumstances:

- you were honorably discharged after 90 or more days of service or you were released because of a disability or injury received in the line of duty; or
- you are still on active duty; or
- you are applying for survivors benefits and the veteran died while on active duty.

You can not receive these special earnings if you're already receiving a military pension based on the same years of service. But there is one exception to this rule: If you were on active duty after 1956, you can still get the special earnings for 1951 through 1956 even if you're receiving a military retirement based on service during that period.

Applying for Social Security Benefits

There are many kinds of benefits available from Social Security, including retirement and disability payments, benefits for your dependents, and survivors benefits for members of your family if you should die. There's also Medicare coverage and Supplemental Security Income (SSI) payments. For more information about these benefits, ask Social Security for a copy of the publication, *Understanding Social Security* (Publication No. 05-10024).

When you apply for Social Security benefits, you'll be asked for proof of your military service (DD Form 214), or information regarding your Reserve or National Guard service.

If You Get Both Social Security and Military Retirement

You can get both Social Security benefits and military retirement. Generally, there is no offset of Social Security benefits because of your military retirement. You'll get your full Social Security benefit based on your earnings. However, your Social Security benefit may be reduced if you also receive a government pension based on a job in which you didn't pay Social Security taxes. Ask Social Security for a copy of the factsheet, *A Pension From Work Not Covered By Social Security* (Publication No. 05-10045).

Social Security survivors benefits may affect benefits payable under the optional Department of Defense Survivors Benefit Plan. Check with the Department of Defense or your military retirement advisor for more information.

SSI for Children

SSI is a program that pays monthly benefits to people with low incomes and limited assets. If you have a child who gets SSI, those payments may continue if you're transferred outside the United States while in military service and the child goes with you. Your child must have received SSI the month before you reported.

A Word About Medicare

If you have health care protection from the Veterans Administration (VA) or under the CHAMPUS or CHAMPVA program, your health benefits may change or end when you become eligible for Medicare. You should contact the VA, the Department of Defense, or a military health benefits advisor for more information.

For More Information

If you'd like more information, call our toll-free telephone number, 1-800-772-1213 between 7 a.m. and 7 p.m. business days.

The Social Security Administration treats all calls confidentially—whether they're made to our toll-free number or to one of our local offices. But, we also want to ensure that you receive accurate and courteous service. That's why we have a second Social Security representative listen to some incoming and outgoing telephone calls.

A Pension from Work Not Covered by Social Security*

How It Affects Your Social Security Retirement or Disability Benefits

If you work for a government agency where you don't pay Social Security taxes, the pension you get from that agency may reduce your Social Security benefits.

There are two laws that may reduce your benefits. One law, called "government pension offset," applies only if you are eligible for Social Security benefits as a spouse or widow(er). For more information about that provision, contact Social Security for the factsheet, *Government Pension Offset* (Publication No. 05-10007).

The other law affects the way your retirement or disability benefits are figured. Under this law, the formula that we use to figure your

* From U.S. Department of Health and Human Services, Social Security Administration, SSA Publication No. 05-10045, March 1992, ICN 460275.

benefit amount is modified, giving you a lower Social Security benefit. This factsheet explains how the law works.

Who Is Affected?

This provision primarily affects people who spent most of their careers working for a government agency, but who also worked at other jobs where they paid Social Security taxes long enough to qualify for retirement or disability benefits.

The modified formula applies to you if you reach 62 or become disabled after 1985 and first become eligible after 1985 for a monthly pension based in whole or in part on work where you did not pay Social Security taxes. You are considered eligible to receive a pension if you meet the requirements of the pension, even if you continue to work.

The modified formula will be used in figuring your Social Security benefit beginning with the first month you get both a Social Security benefit and the other pension.

Why Is a Different Formula Used?

Social Security benefits replace a percentage of a worker's pre-retirement earnings. The formula used to compute Social Security benefits includes factors that ensure that lower-paid workers get a higher percentage return than their more well-to-do counterparts. For example, lower-paid workers could conceivably get a Social Security benefit that equals up to 90 percent of their pre-retirement earnings. Highly paid workers receive rates of return that are considerably less. (The average is about 42 percent.)

Before the law was changed in 1983, government employees had their benefits computed as if they were long-term, low-wage workers. Thus, they received the advantage of the higher percentage Social Security benefits in addition to their government pension. The modified formula eliminates this windfall.

How Does It Work?

Social Security benefits are based on the worker's average monthly earnings adjusted for inflation. When we figure your benefits, we separate your average earnings into three amounts and multiply the figures using three factors. For example, for a worker who turns 65 in 1992, the first $339 of average monthly earnings is multiplied by 90 percent; the next $1,705 is multiplied by 32 percent; and the remainder by 15 percent.

In the modified formula, the 90 percent factor is reduced. The reduction was phased in for workers who reached age 62 or became disabled between 1986 and 1989. For those who reach 62 or become disabled in 1990 or later, the 90 percent factor is reduced to 40 percent.

However, if you have 30 or more years of "substantial" Social Security earnings (see the table on the back), we use the regular formula to figure your benefit. If you have 21–29 years of substantial Social Security earnings, we use the modified formula, but the reduction is less than if you have fewer years of Social Security earnings. For people with 21–29 years of substantial Social Security earnings, the first factor in the formula is the following:

Years of Social Security Earnings	First Factor
30 or more	90 percent
29	85 percent
28	80 percent
27	75 percent
26	70 percent
25	65 percent
24	60 percent
23	55 percent
22	50 percent
21	45 percent
20 or less	40 percent

For the modified formula, you are considered to have a year of substantial earnings if your earnings equal or exceed the figures shown for each year in the chart below.

Year	Earnings
1937–50	$ 900[1]
1951–54	900
1955–58	1,050
1959–65	1,200
1966–67	1,650
1968–71	1,950
1972	2,250

[1]Total credited earnings from 1937–50 are divided by $900 to get the number of years of coverage (maximum of 14 years).

1973	2,700
1974	3,300
1975	3,525
1976	3,825
1977	4,125
1978	4,425
1979	4,725
1980	5,100
1981	5,550
1982	6,075
1983	6,675
1984	7,050
1985	7,425
1986	7,875
1987	8,175
1988	8,400
1989	8,925
1990	9,525
1991	9,900
1992	10,350

Some Exceptions

The modified formula does not apply to survivors benefits. It also does not apply to you if:

- You are a Federal worker hired after December 31, 1983;
- You were employed on January 1, 1984, by a nonprofit organization that was mandatorily covered under Social Security on that date;
- Your only pension is based solely on railroad employment;
- Your only work where you did not pay Social Security taxes was before 1957; or
- You have 30 or more years of substantial earnings under Social Security (as explained earlier).

Guarantee

A guarantee is provided to protect workers with relatively low pensions. It provides that the reduction in the Social Security benefit under the modified formula cannot be more than one-half of that part of the pension attributable to earnings after 1956 not covered by Social Security.

CHAPTER 10

◆————————————————————————◆

Commercial Life Insurance and Annuities

10-1 How Much Life Insurance Should You Own?

The needs of each person and/or family differ but all should schedule periodic planning sessions. Both spouses should be involved in this ongoing planning process.

First of all, it is necessary to *set your goals.* Second, it is absolutely necessary to *make a commitment* to these goals. Third, it is necessary to *stick to the plan,* no matter what else happens. The goals should be realistic and adjusted regularly as income changes over the years. The only item that might take precedence over these three goals, for ministers at least, would be tithing. Almost all tithers know that they must make their tithe immediately upon receiving income. If they are tempted to say, "Let's look at the bills first and then decide what to give," they probably will not tithe. Tithing is an act of faith.

In the same manner, after the tithe money is set aside, the amount allocated to these three goals should be taken out of the checkbook. Then, you should live on what is left. Perhaps this approach seems too idealistic. The truth is, such commitment to regular and timely allocation of funds, the same as in tithing, is the only way you can achieve the three goals listed. Both require a measure of faith.

Any reputable life insurance agent or financial planner can help you determine your goals. You would probably be wise to choose someone who specializes in helping clergypersons in these areas. The individual should understand your complicated tax status, your housing allowance, pay package designs, and specific advantages and disadvantages of certain retirement plans available to ministers.

How much life insurance should you own? It depends on how long you would like your spouse to receive income in the event of your premature death. Or you may have special responsibilities, such as a child with a disability or a parent with a need for long-term nursing care. You may have a special interest in a mission project. You may want to leave a bequest to your seminary or university. If you wish to be sure that your children have a college education, perhaps at a very expensive institution, that would have to be included in your goals. Your spouse may be unable to work outside the home in the event of your premature death. Each family has different goals. You must consider all of these contingencies, and more, in setting your goals.

During the process of setting your goals, you must coordinate all possible sources of income available in all three situations: premature death, disability, or retirement. You must know how much the surviving spouse would receive from Social Security. It makes sense to educate yourself *now*.

For example, in setting the goal of providing income for a surviving spouse, you should know that if the spouse works outside the home and has minor children still living at home, the spouse can earn only a limited income without losing the income from Social Security. (See chapter 9.) The problem of a surviving spouse learning after the death of the covered worker that the expected income from Social Security will not materialize could have been avoided with proper planning beforehand.

Group insurance and existing life insurance should be included in the planning process as well as Social Security benefits and existing retirement plans. All should be coordinated in the planning process so that valid projections can be made to check progress year by year.

A Shocking Exercise

James Palmer is a twenty-five-year-old pastor whose salary is $14,000. He is furnished a parsonage, the value of which is $5,000 per year. In addition, he receives a pension deposit of $4,000 and paid hospitalization costing $4,000. His total pay package is $27,000. Palmer has a spouse and two children.

Let's assume Pastor Palmer's pay package remains the same all the way to his age sixty-five. The total amount he would receive in cash and benefits would be $1,080,000! Reality would suggest that he would receive at least one and one-half or two times that amount. That is $1,620,000 or $2,160,000 from age twenty-five to age sixty-five. How much life insurance should he own? At his level of income the question becomes moot. The real question is, How much can he *afford?* Periodic and thoughtful attention to prioritized needs will be a valuable course for any pastor to follow over the years.

It is equally dangerous to buy too little or too much life insurance. Overbuying life insurance can deprive a family of current needs. Underbuying can produce the same results if the insured dies. So the question of how much life insurance a family must own must be approached with dead seriousness, no pun intended.

10-2 What Kind of Life Insurance Should You Own?

There have been revolutionary changes in the life insurance industry since 1980. Formerly, life insurance was not considered to be a good investment. It paid low interest rates on the funds accumulating in the policies, the prices were high, and the policies were considered to be inflexible. All that has changed. Most companies now have life insurance policies that pay current interest rates and, in fact, often pay more on the investment portion of the policy than banks pay. Some policies offer variable death benefits and variable premiums that rise and fall along with the economy. Most companies have lowered their rates since people are living longer and not as many death claims have to be paid. Some life insurance rates are as much as 40 percent lower than former rates on similar policies offered at the same age.

10-3 What About Term Insurance?

Term insurance has been available almost as long as any other type of coverage. The big difference now is that term insurance is much lower in cost than what was available prior to 1980. You can buy annual renewable term, five-year term, ten-year term, fifteen-year term, twenty-year term, term to age sixty-five, term to age one hundred, decreasing term for different numbers of years, and on and on.

The purposes of term insurance are to provide inexpensive temporary coverage and to protect future insurability, that is, to assure the term policyholder that in the event of becoming uninsurable, the term can be converted without evidence of insurability to a permanent form of life insurance. For example, if a person has a five-year term plan and is in the last year of the contract, then becomes terminally ill, the term policy can be converted to a permanent policy at standard rates to prevent it from lapsing. This conversion privilege is guaranteed in most companies. So long as the premiums are paid, either directly or by waiver of premium, the claim will be paid if the insured dies.

10-4 What About Buying Term Instead of Permanent Life Insurance and Investing the Difference?

At the younger ages, the cost of term insurance is enticingly low. There are two schools of thought regarding how long you should keep term instead of permanent life insurance, i.e., the kind that builds cash values. Term insurance requires a much lower premium per thousand than permanent insurance but doesn't build cash values. The difference between the premium for the term and the permanent insurance is then available for investment, rather than going into the premium for the permanent insurance. The theory behind buying term and investing the difference is that, if you follow this theory, you should accumulate more capital in your later years. However, this theory doesn't always work, and for some it can never work. Let's look at some examples.

Example. Let's follow an example of Pastor John Jones buying term life insurance and investing the difference. This thirty-year-old pastor has a wife and two children. His gross income from ministry is $25,000. He lives in a parsonage furnished by his church and has two used cars. He has his doctorate in ministry from a seminary. He has been pastor of the First Methodist Church for five years. His yearly raises have averaged about 4 percent. Jones's wife does not work outside the home.

Pastor Jones went to a financial planning seminar and came away sold on the idea of buying term insurance and investing the difference. At this point in his life, he owns a small permanent policy. Upon returning from the seminar, he collected the term rates from several companies and found that he was classified as a preferred-risk nonsmoker, eligible for the lowest rates. He was amazed to learn that he could purchase $250,000 of twenty-year convertible term for as low as $27 per month at age thirty with a level premium and a level death benefit. He then inquired what the cost would be for term that would remain in force until age sixty-five. When he heard the quotes for term to age sixty-five and beyond, he began to have second thoughts. The cost to renew his term policy at age fifty-one would be $91 per month. At age sixty the cost would be $173 per month. At age 70 the cost would be $407 per month, and it kept rising after that. It was plain to him that term, kept too long, would become prohibitive for a person at his income level. But he could handle the cost of term insurance for the next twenty years. By then his children would be grown and he wouldn't need that much life insurance, he reasoned.

Then Pastor Jones asked himself another question. Why should he plan to provide for only five years for his family in the event of his premature death? What would his wife and children do at the end of five years when the funds ran out? For such a low premium he could provide $250,000 instead of the $125,000 suggested by the seminar leader, and even that wouldn't be enough to take care of his wife in her old age. What if she were disabled or couldn't find a job after the children were on their own? And what about college costs? How would she live the rest of her life? He calculated that if his income continued to average only $25,000 per year from his age thirty to his age sixty-five, $875,000 ($25,000 × 35) would go through his hands if he lived. If he counted the value received by living in the parsonage as an additional $5,000, his total annual income would be $30,000. If he received $30,000 per year from age thirty to age sixty-five, assuming no further raises, he would receive total income of $1,050,000 (salary ($25,000) + value of living in parsonage ($5,000) = $1,050,000 ($30,000 × 35). He asked himself why he should short-change his wife. Jones quickly saw the wisdom of replacing his old $25,000 permanent policy and buying the $250,000 term policy. Besides, it would cost only $2 more per month than he was paying for his old policy. In addition, he would receive a refund of his cash value of $1,200. Was it a good idea?

Let's analyze this thinking. This plan could well be the right thing for Pastor Jones to do at his age. He is covering his family's need for immediate income if he dies prematurely. He has been paying so little for his insurance that, even after replacing his old policy, there is little or nothing left over for investment. But to make his "buy term and invest the difference" work, he must invest. He decides he can squeeze an additional $50 per month out of his budget for investment. That makes a total of $77 per month he is committing to his new financial plan, including the $27 he will pay for term insurance. He must assume the following:

1) Whatever investment vehicle he buys must continue to rise with inflation and never decrease.
2) His investment must be safe.
3) He must always make his $50 monthly deposit.
4) He must never withdraw funds during the next thirty-five years if he anticipates receiving any meaningful amount of income from such a low monthly deposit. A withdrawal from a tax-sheltered retirement plan, such as a tax-sheltered annuity or an IRA, must be reported as ordinary income and a 10 percent penalty paid if the withdrawal occurs prior to age 59½. Certain exceptions such as disability might apply. (See chapters 4 and 5 for details.) But even with non-tax-sheltered investments, he must not withdraw funds from his account so that it will grow steadily. If he deposits $50 per month faithfully for thirty-five years, a TSA plan would provide a projected retirement income of $689 per month, beginning at age sixty-five, for life.

If Pastor Jones sticks to his plan, let's follow the projected results after twenty years:

$27 per month for 20 years for term insurance	$ 6,480
$50 per month for a TSA plan	12,000
Total outlay during 20-year period	$18,480
Gross value of TSA in 20 years (age 50), assuming a 6.95% interest rate	$25,375

At age fifty, Pastor Jones wants to review his progress to determine the net increase in his financial plan. Since deposits into a TSA, purchased by a clergyperson under Section 403(b), are excluded from federal, state, local, and Social Security taxes, Jones will have tax savings as follows:

Total gross deposits ($6,480 + $12,000)	$18,480
Less tax savings on TSA:	
15.3% Social Security × $12,000	$ 1,836
15.0% federal income tax × $12,000	1,800
5.0% state income tax × $12,000	600
Total tax savings during 20 years	$ 4,236

To arrive at Pastor Jones's net gain at the end of twenty years, we compute the following:

Total value of the TSA in 20 years	$25,375
Net cost of TSA ($12,000 – $4,236)	7,764
Net gain from TSA in 20 years	$17,611
Total cost for term insurance	6,480
Total net gain from his financial plan for 20-year period	$11,131

At his age fifty-one, Pastor Jones must choose wisely. He is now faced with a large increase in his term life insurance premium if he is to continue the coverage. The seminar leader told him that he could drop his term insurance when his investment was high enough to replace it. In this example, if Pastor Jones dropped his term insurance and died at age fifty-one, his survivors would receive the following:

Term life insurance	-0-
Gross amount of TSA to survivors	$25,375
Less tax-free widow's allowance	5,000
Net taxable amount to widow	$20,375
Less federal tax at 15% + state tax at 5%	$ 4,075
Less total deposits: $12,000 into the TSA + $6,480 into the term policy	$18,480
Net gain: $25,375 – $4,075 – $18,480	$ 3,820
+ tax savings	4,236
Total net gain from plan	$ 7,131

If Pastor Jones had kept his term life and died at age fifty, his survivors would have received the proceeds from $250,000 of term insurance tax-free in addition to the proceeds from the TSA. Making these decisions would be easy if he knew when he was going to die. Often it is tempting to go without adequate life insurance if one is blessed with excellent health. Some people decide to take the risk. Will Rogers said, "If a man dies once without life insurance, that ought to teach him."

Clearly, this example should show that a combination of term life and an investment costing $77 per month will not provide enough death benefit and retirement income by Jones's age fifty to be on schedule.

Let's assume Pastor Jones is well aware of the shortcomings of this scenario. So in his planning session at age thirty, he considers the results of increasing his TSA deposits yearly rather than projecting only $50 per month. It is reasonable to assume that he could increase these deposits, especially after his children are grown. So he decides to purchase a TSA at age thirty that projects an annual 5 percent increase in deposits all the way to age sixty-five. At that rate he is increasing his monthly deposit by only $12 in the fifth year. But since he needs to continue his term life insurance, he now must pay a total monthly premium of approximately $91 for the next twenty years if he keeps the policy to age sixty. First let's look at the results at age sixty:

Total term premiums paid from ages 30 to 60	$17,400
Total TSA deposits assuming 5% yearly increase	37,394
Total outlay to age 60	$54,794
Gross value of TSA at age 60	$92,630

Now let's consider the tax savings Jones enjoyed because his TSA deposits were excluded from income:

Total gross deposits ($17,400 + $37,394)	$54,794
Less tax savings on TSA:	
15.3% Social Security × $37,394	$ 5,721
15.0% federal income tax × $37,394	5,609
5.0% state income tax × $37,394	1,870
Total tax savings to age 60	$13,200

To arrive at Pastor Jones's net gain as of age sixty, we compute the following:

Total value of the TSA at age 60	$92,630
Net cost of TSA ($54,794 – $13,200)	41,594
Net gain from TSA at age 60	$51,036

Pastor Jones's income tax bracket will probably rise to 28 percent after several years in his profession, but for these purposes, we will continue to assume an income tax bracket of only 15 percent.

At age sixty, Pastor Jones must consider, once again, whether or not to keep his term insurance in force. He has several options. First, he can continue, but his premium at age sixty will be approximately $173 per month until age seventy when it escalates to $407.

He can elect to reduce the face amount of his term policy, which probably is the wisest option in this scenario. The last option would be to drop his term policy altogether. After all, his TSA is now worth $92,630 and would be payable at his death. But once again, he faces the results of inflation and income tax.

Now, using Pastor Jones's strategy, let's look at the projected results at age sixty-five, assuming he keeps his term:

Total term premiums paid from ages 30 to 65	$ 16,380
Total TSA deposits from ages 30 to 65	51,040
Total outlay to age 65	$ 67,420
Gross value of TSA at age 65	$145,773

Now for the tax savings as of age sixty-five:

Total gross deposits ($51,040 + $16,380)	$67,420
Less tax savings on TSA:	
15.3% Social Security × $51,040	$ 7,809
15.0% federal income tax × $51,040	7,656
5.0% state income tax × $51,040	2,552
Total tax savings to age 65	$18,017

To arrive at Pastor Jones's net gain at age sixty-five, we compute the following:

Total value of the TSA at age 65	$145,773
Net cost of TSA ($51,040 − $18,017)	33,023
Net gain from TSA at age 65	$112,750

If Pastor Jones had elected to use investments other than the tax-sheltered annuity, such as mutual funds, stocks, or bonds, they probably would have been subject to fluctuations. That's certainly an option for him, but most clergypersons do not have the time or the means for it. They are too busy helping others, and their income levels aren't usually high enough to allow them to take too many risks. Furthermore, the TSA is so far superior and safe that pastors should use it to the fullest extent for which they are eligible before considering any other long-range investment. Then if they have other funds to invest, they could consider other investment options. (The TSA is covered in detail in chapter 4.)

10-5 What About Using Permanent Life Insurance Instead of Term?

Whole life. Whole life insurance has changed dramatically since 1980. The term *whole life* is nomenclature required by state insurance commissioners. Every company must have such a policy. It means "life, paid up at age one hundred." Whole life is a basic policy that, if paid to age one hundred, would be paid up at that age. An applicant who wanted a shorter premium-paying time could buy a life, paid up at age sixty-five, for example. The same actuarial cost would have to be squeezed into a shorter period of time to be paid up at age sixty-five. The premiums and the cash values would be much higher. The death benefit is the same for each. One is not a better bargain than the other unless the insured had purchased whole life instead of life, paid up at age sixty-five, and had died prematurely. Obviously, the amount of premiums paid would be less.

Single premium whole life. One of the most interesting and attractive life insurance policies to come along in many years is the single premium whole life (SPWL) policy. When it first came on the market, it offered the following advantages:

- Lifetime protection
- A single premium
- Tax-free death benefit
- Tax-deferred growth
- Current interest rates
- Guaranteed minimum interest rates
- A bailout privilege (If interest rates drop more than 1 percent, the insured can withdraw all cash values without penalty.)
- Guaranteed return of premium
- Cash value loans at 2 percent interest rate

This new plan looked too good to be true to many people. But it was true that such a plan could successfully compete with certificates of deposit as well as stocks, bonds, and mutual funds. It appeared safer to many people, especially with the liquid nature of the cash value and the return-of-premium guarantee. There was a penalty charged for early withdrawal during the first five to seven years, but it was not prohibitive.

This plan attracted thousands of buyers. One company took out a full two-page ad in the *Wall Street Journal* praising the SPWL contract. Buyers were able to dump huge amounts of premiums into these policies and, after one year, borrow the cash value at little or no interest. Since loans on life insurance policies are not considered to be income, they did not have to be reported to the IRS. If the insured died owing a loan on the cash value, there would always be enough death benefit to cancel the loan and, in addition, pay a considerable tax-free amount to the beneficiary. The result was that the entire equity in the policy could pass tax-free during the lifetime and after the death of the policyholder. Such frenzy caught the attention of the IRS and Congress. Indeed, the plan proved to be too good to be true. The IRS clamped down on the SPWL in 1986, taxing anyone withdrawing or borrowing the cash value prior to age $59^{1}/_{2}$.

Policyholders still could withdraw or borrow the cash value, but it would be fully taxable and subject to penalties as well. After that, essentially only two categories of buyers could benefit from purchasing the SPWL: (1) people over age $59^{1}/_{2}$ and (2) younger ones who intended to wait until after age $59^{1}/_{2}$ to withdraw the cash value. It was still a good tax-sheltered vehicle, even for those younger buyers willing to wait until after age $59^{1}/_{2}$, since the yearly buildup of cash value was not taxable if left in the policy.

The SPWL, when compared with a CD over the long haul, usually developed much higher equity because of the tax-sheltered nature of the contract. For those who have the necessary lump-sum premium dollars, the SPWL can be the safest, most effective method of buying life insurance on themselves, their children, and their grandchildren. So long as the cash value is left alone in the contract prior to age $59^{1}/_{2}$, no taxable event occurs, and there is no income to report during that period while the cash value is growing.

10-6 The Life Insurance Revolution of the 1980s

The "old" whole life fell into disfavor ten to fifteen years ago because the premiums seemed too high and the interest rates earned on the cash values seemed too low. With new mortality tables showing that people were living longer, rates came down. When interest rates reached 15 to 18 percent, the public demanded higher interest rates on their life insurance cash values. Thousands of policyholders borrowed from their old life insurance policy cash values, paying interest of 5 to 6 percent, and invested their cash at 15 to 18 percent in money markets. No one knew at the time if interest rates would remain high or decrease. Apparently, it didn't matter because there was a frenzy of borrowing and reinvesting of life insurance cash values.

Financial Seminars Encouraged Borrowing of Cash Values

Financial seminars abounded, urging people to free up their cash values. Meantime, after borrowing their cash values, those policy-holders were paying their premiums *plus* the interest on their loans. The seminar leaders caused policyholders to become angry at life insurance companies when they asked, "Why should you pay interest on your own money? Not to worry. With such a spread between your interest cost and your profit, it's a no-brainer."

The flames of discontent were also fanned by people who sold securities and other investments that competed for the life insurance premium dollar. Many financial seminar leaders stated, "Why should you let the life insurance companies skim the cream off the top of your investment money? That's not smart. You can invest your own money." It had great emotional appeal to large segments of the public.

Many New Life Insurance Companies Were Formed

Jumping into the breach, new specialty companies were formed with the express purpose of replacing existing life insurance policies issued by other companies. Their salespersons were not trained with traditional life insurance attitudes and values. It was simply a case of "seek and destroy" old whole life policies. It is fair to say that in some cases, replacing the old policies was advantageous. As with most tidal waves, some things got cleaned up, but many things of value were washed away.

Replacing Old Policies Became Commonplace

Policyholders with very large loans on their old whole life policies, who probably never would have been able to repay their loans, were probably better off when those policies were replaced with the new, lower-cost, current interest policies. But always, there is a piper to be paid. The salespersons handling the replacement had to be paid, and the policyholder, who had to start over with a new policy at an older age, was the one who paid the new commission.

Many policyholders asked, "Why doesn't my existing life insurance company offer to replace my old policy with a new one? Why should I have to change companies to get a better policy? I've been with my present company for many years. Why is it treating me this way?" These questions would seem to be legitimate to anyone not familiar with the financial structure of life insurance companies in those days. The answer is that it would be like the U.S. selling its own gold, thereby leaving its protective surplus depleted. It was a very real dilemma for policyholders and companies. Most companies were caught off guard by the fast-rising interest rates.

The emotional appeal fomented by the new companies caused mounting and widespread resentment toward the existing companies. The tidal wave of policy replacements and cancellations was out of control.

Old Life Insurance Cash Value Loans Were Canceled

A nationwide wave of replacement was imminent. With such a potential market, many new stock companies were created, offering cheap term insurance to the public. Those policies, with very low rates, immediately became attractive to people who had borrowed from their cash values and were paying even higher costs for their old permanent policies because of the interest they were paying on their loans. If they were insurable, those people could replace their old policies that had maximum loans and, at the same time, cancel their loans when they canceled their old policies. It was too good to be true for some with very large loans.

The companies had no salespersons of their own and eventually forced a repricing of term in most companies and caused a series of new permanent policies to be created. But what had once been a guaranteed, safe entity became subject to some of the same pitfalls of any other investment. And there was one other snare. Policyholders with cash values in excess of their total premiums paid found they had a taxable event when they canceled their loans. They had to pay income tax on any amount over and above their cost basis. In computing their equity, they had to include the amount they had already borrowed and then subtract their total premiums. If they got back more than they had paid, including their loan, the balance was taxable.

The new companies vaulted into action before the existing companies could meet the competition. Policyholders left their existing companies by the thousands, assuming that they were transferring to a better policy in a company at least equally good. In the past, most policyholders took for granted that life insurance was very safe because of all the guarantees: the premium, the death benefit, and the cash values. But as events would reveal, not all the new companies were stable enough to last when interest rates inevitably declined.

The Trap of Minimum Deposit Life Insurance

For years prior to that, many policyholders had been using the minimum deposit method of paying their premiums. Back then, the interest paid on a loan from an insurance policy was tax deductible, but the IRS stopped that. Still, the appeal of the yearly increase in cash value was so attractive to the policyholders, it enabled them to pay only the difference between the rise in cash value and the premium.

For example, if a life insurance annual premium was $1,000 and the increase in the cash value that year was $500, the policyholder could borrow that increase and pay an additional $500 on his annual premium, plus interest on the loan, and pay a minimum deposit, thus saving cash outlay. He was told "the policy will pay for itself." The policyholder usually did not understand that if he canceled his policy, any excess over his cost basis was taxable. Many persons were shocked when that happened, but the replacement frenzy could not be stopped. It led to new types of life insurance, such as universal life.

10-7 The Birth of Universal Life Insurance

For many years prior to 1980, the idea of life insurance policies with variable death benefits, cash values, and premiums designed to be sensitive to the fluctuations of the economy had been gaining momentum. The new products offering these features became known as variable life, universal life, and interest-sensitive life. Whereas the old conservative types of life insurance were backed up with large, low-yield, safe surpluses in each company, the companies began buying investments that could fluctuate more, and while they were relatively safe, they were not quite as safe.

Importance of Financial Strength of Life Insurance Companies

Universal life and interest-sensitive life in quality companies are fine products. Now, however, more and more attention is given to the financial strength of life insurance companies than ever before. At this writing, some life insurance companies, including some of the old stalwarts, are having trouble with their investment portfolios. Life insurance buyers are becoming much more selective. In the past, people shopped for the cheapest term premium they could find, regardless of which company was offering it; now, shoppers are looking more closely at the financial strength of these companies. Stability of companies is even more important to potential buyers of permanent life insurance such as universal life and interest-sensitive life.

Universal life comes in several different packages. The cash values, death benefits, and interest rates are three possible variables but not all companies use all three. Some companies offer a guaranteed death benefit and guaranteed premium but include a variable interest rate. Some offer the guaranteed death benefit but vary the premium and interest rate.

10-8 If You Happen to Be Wealthy

Quite often, ministers are the beneficiaries of large estates. Others come into the ministry late in life after they have accumulated substantial amounts of capital. Those who have significant equity must be good stewards so that they can distribute their funds during their lifetimes and at death. Otherwise, state and federal governments will probably be the beneficiaries of much of their estates.

It is not only possible to save estate taxes; it is a necessity to plan for such savings. Certainly, you should seek competent legal counsel to help with your estate planning. Ideally, you should have a team of advisers, including your attorney, your CPA, your investment adviser and/or trust officer, and an insurance consultant.

One of the best courses of action available to you under current tax law is the option to make gifts. You and your spouse may give up to $10,000 per year per child for as many years as you wish. In addition, you and your spouse may each be able to give a total cumulative gift throughout your lifetime as high as $600,000. With proper planning you will not incur federal estate taxes on these amounts. Much can be done not only to preserve wealth but to create more wealth if that is your goal. Many charitable foundations have been created from such gifts. Using life insurance in these instances can produce dramatic results to beneficiaries in creating and distributing wealth and in saving estate taxes.

A strong case can be made for using some of these gift funds to buy life insurance. The living donor can enjoy a tax deduction while the life insurance is in force on his or her life with the children (via a trust) as beneficiaries in the event of the donor's premature death.

The tax savings can be phenomenal. Other vehicles to discuss with your team of advisers are the irrevocable life insurance trust, the charitable remainder trust, the generation-skipping trust, and last-to-die life insurance policies.

The possible estate shrinkage can be minimized only if people with wealth will take the time to plan. So many people of wealth become too busy with the daily things of life and procrastinate until it is too late. According to *Your Estate Research Service* (1990 Longman Group USA, Inc.), the estate of J. P. Morgan shrunk 69 percent at his death. The estate of the founder of Ernst & Ernst, the famous accounting firm, shrunk by 56 percent at his death. His gross estate was $12,642,431, but his taxes and estate settlement costs were $7,124,112, leaving a net estate of $5,518,319. The estate of John D. Rockefeller, Sr., shrunk by 64 percent when he died. Elvis Presley's estate shrunk by 73 percent at his death. Adequate life insurance to pay the estate taxes would have preserved most of the assets in each of these estates.

Obviously, most ministers will not have estates of such magnitude. However, if you are fortunate enough to be wealthy, you can legally avoid taxes if you take the time to plan. Life insurance is one of the few remaining vehicles that can accomplish much in the way of estate conservation and tax avoidance.

10-9 What If You Are Rated Extra or Have Been Turned Down When Trying to Buy Life Insurance?

Almost anyone can buy *some* life insurance for a price. Blanket offers on television invite people, no matter what their state of health, to apply. However, the rate must be exorbitant. Policies offered by some companies pay no death benefit except the return of the first three years' premiums, plus interest, if death occurs during the first three years. Thereafter, the death benefit as displayed in the policy is payable in full at death. The premiums continue of course. These, also, are very high premiums.

Most companies will entertain applications from persons with a problematic medical history. Medical science has helped a great deal in improving life expectancy. Yet, most companies hope to receive applications primarily from healthy people. They can issue the policies fast and go on to the next application. When an application with indications of health impairments arrives in a home office underwriting department, the underwriter has to document the history of the applicant, all of which takes time, effort, and money. Many companies will not follow this process too far. They will go so far and no farther, arbitrarily declining the application or rating it higher than they feel may be necessary just to be sure. Such an action gets on the record of the applicant and follows the person forever.

Only by fully documenting an applicant's medical history can mistakes be corrected. If one company does not fully investigate an applicant's medical history and another one does, there is always the chance that insurance can be purchased on a favorable basis. After all, underwriting is not an exact science, and underwriters cannot be blamed for wanting to protect the assets of their companies. Therefore, there is a place for specialty companies willing to take the time and spend the money to fully document a problematic medical history, or "special risk," sometimes resulting in a favorable issue of a policy.

All underwriters fear the unknown. They appreciate full documentation of an applicant's medical history. The question becomes one of economics: Should an underwriter spend enough money on the efforts to document the medical history of an applicant or let it go to another company to make the attempt?

Special Risk Companies Sometimes Better

Special risk applications in these specialty companies tend to cost more to process than applications routinely handled by companies primarily insuring standard or preferred risks. When a company underwriter writes a doctor seeking the medical history of an applicant, the doctor charges a fee. If several doctors are involved, the company may need a statement from each one. The fees can mount up. Also, studies such as EKGs and X rays may be ordered and paid for by the company. Obviously, these costs must somehow be included in the premiums charged.

Other factors enter in the underwriting of special risks that have a bearing on whether or not some persons can buy coverage. For example, some companies have no full-time agents, thus eliminating the cost of hiring, training, and keeping a field force. They are known as brokerage companies, and they attract applications from agents with high commissions, competitive policies, and good service. The agents, in fact, are the customers of the life insurance companies, just as are the applicants. Some of these companies have a higher profit margin with which to absorb the higher cost of underwriting these special risk applicants.

Many full-time agents of established companies send in their applications to their primary company first. If the applications are issued, they follow through and place those policies in the primary company. If an applicant is turned down, or rated, that applicant is sometimes submitted to a specialty company for underwriting. The specialty company often can justify spending the extra dollars to underwrite an application, and it is not unusual for a suspected impaired risk to be issued a policy on a more favorable basis than the agent's primary company.

How Reinsurance Works

One other factor is that of reinsurance. Reinsurance comes into play when a company receives an application and does not want to assume the entire risk, for whatever reason. For example, company A receives an application for more than it wants to insure. It then buys reinsurance on the overage from company B. These reinsurance treaties can be too complex to explain in detail here. Suffice it to say that the specialty companies sometimes have wider reinsurance outlets and are sometimes able to shop for a more favorable offer.

So, if you have been turned down or rated, in your opinion, too highly, any competent agent, who is not a "captive" agent (one who is not allowed to broker in companies other than his or her primary company), should be able to obtain some alternate offers from specialty companies. Be advised that it is best to stick with one agent if you begin to shop for life insurance. Any action you take usually finds its way to a central information gathering facility and will be made available to any company entertaining an application at any time in the future. If you allow more than one agent to write applications on your life, in the hope of shopping the market, you may be doing yourself a disservice. Each company will wonder just how much life insurance you are applying for. Many will arbitrarily decline such applications, especially for large amounts.

CHAPTER 11

How to Design Your Pay Package

11-1 Your Church Board Should Include Both Young and Old

Ideally, every church board should include members who represent a fair cross section of the congregation. As older board members approach the end of their tenure, younger ones should be groomed to replace them. Most human institutions need the wisdom and conservatism of mature persons along with the fresh enthusiasm of younger ones. The church is no exception. The expressed differences of viewpoints can lead to fair compromises and adequate pay packages for ministers. A church should carefully consider the abilities and backgrounds of board members who will be responsible for setting the pastor's pay.

11-2 How Much Should a Pastor's Pay Package Be?

When churches hire consultants to help determine a pastor's pay, they always want to know the following:

- What is the average income of the town or city?
- What is the average income of the congregation?
- What is the salary range of entry-age schoolteachers in your town or area?
- What is the salary range for teachers with master's degrees?
- What is the salary range for the superintendent of schools?
- What is the history of pay packages to former pastors?
- What is the average salary range of other churches, according to size, in your town?
- What are the pastor's educational attainments?

- What is the pastor's work experience?
- What are the pastor's specific needs that may be unusual?
- What are the pastor's age and energy level?
- Is there anything about the pastor's family that could be a factor?
- In reviewing a current pastor's pay package, does the congregation really want to keep the person long-range?
- If an associate or assistant pastor is being reviewed or considered for employment, can a livable pay package be agreed upon and still keep the senior pastor's pay package in the same relative range? This could be a problem.

Quite often, pastors enter the ministry later in life at a point when income needs are the highest they will experience. Finding churches with pay package levels high enough to justify the needs of such assistant pastors will not be easy. If you are in this category, carefully consider this dilemma before you make any final decision. You may have children ready for college or already in college. Your needs will likely never be greater. Reality dictates that you will almost never earn more than the senior pastor.

If you are entering the ministry later in life, you should make it clear to everyone at the outset of your negotiations that your intentions are to ultimately go on to senior pastor status with another church. Knowing that up front, your senior pastor might well help you find your church when the time comes. Your senior pastor might be nearing retirement age, and you might be a candidate to move up to senior pastor. On the other hand, some churches have a stated policy never to promote an assistant pastor to the position of senior pastor.

One of the most common benchmarks in determining pastors' pay package levels is the comparison between them and schoolteachers and administrators. Their educational attainments are similar in that most have master's degrees, and many pastors have their doctorate as well. An entry-age teacher begins a career at a salary level lower than one with a master's degree; one with a master's degree usually has a pay level lower than one with a Ph.D. Reason should suggest that churches might successfully and fairly apply the same process in their quest to set the pastor's pay scale commensurate with educational attainments.

Since most churches do not hire a consultant to determine the pastor's pay level, it will be up to you, the pastor, to do your homework in preparation for the annual salary review. (Heed the same advice when you apply to a different church.) *Know* what you and your family will need to live on. Of course, if you are fresh out of seminary, your options will be limited. But if you have much to offer a church and you have paid your dues, so to speak, it may not be fair to your family to settle for a pay package that is not adequate for your needs.

Honestly consider these questions:

- Can you and your family really live on the proposed pay package?
- What are the prospects for pay increases in the future?
- What is expected of the spouse?

11-3 Why You Need One or More Advocates on Your Church Board

A support group can be a most helpful and encouraging relationship. I suggest that you have a support team of persons interested in you, your ministry, and your family as you make your decision about accepting a call to a church. There is still wisdom in the multitude of counselors. A young, inexperienced minister, in particular, would be advised to have at least one mature mentor, preferably a pastor, with whom to discuss the call to a church. Seminaries do not go into much detail in preparing ministers to discuss pay packages and tax matters. Most ministers go out into the field ill prepared to talk about money.

Once you get into a church, you would be wise to discern who among the elders seems knowledgeable, up-to-date on economics, and perhaps sympathetic to the needs of your family. If you can develop a trusting relationship with one or more such persons on your board, they might become your advocates during the course of your ministry in that particular church. If possible, you should seek the advice of other knowledgeable advocates outside your congregation as well.

11-4 Educating Your Church Board About Pay Packages

You will have to educate your church board members in regard to your pay package. Church board members come and go. Most, quite understandably, begin their tour of board duty knowing nothing about setting a pastor's pay package, especially such a complicated subject as housing allowance.

Usually, church budget reports are prepared on computer printouts showing the proposed budget for last year, the actual budget for last year, the proposed budget for this year, since this year isn't over, along with a proposed budget for next year. Under the column "Pastor's Pay Package," every conceivable item is listed including pension deposit, utilities, hospitalization, book allowance, conventions, and continuing education. Then there is the bottom line, showing the gross cost. The tendency is to look only at the bottom line and not at the salary and housing, the two items considered to be actual compensation. However, if it isn't reportable to the IRS, it is *not* compensation.

Once you have done all your homework in determining your income needs, you're ready to discuss your new pay package with your board members. All such efforts should be covered with constant prayer, individually and with your board. Good business practices should not be ignored, but your relationship with your church board is more than a business contract. It should be a joint effort to lovingly determine a fair and adequate package of salary and fringe benefits. The spirit of the law, not the letter, should be followed.

Running a church is not like running a business. Another dimension, a spiritual dimension, must be kept in mind at all times. Fortunate are the church and the minister where fairness and brotherly love abound when money is discussed. Fortunate is the church in which both the minister *and* the spouse feel good about the pay package.

11-5 Be Prepared for the Denominational "Minimum Salary" Syndrome

Whether you are a pastor in the field or a denominational executive, I urge you not to consider the denomination's stated "minimum salary" to mean "average salary." The denominational headquarters publishes the minimum salary and sends it to all the churches in the fellowship. But something gets lost in the shuffle. Even though the official published minimum figure is known by all, not all pastors receive even that amount because the local churches sometimes see that minimum figure as an average salary level. Many local churches do not comply with it, and some, of course, cannot afford to pay it. So it is an area to watch and be sensitive to.

11-6 Ask Your Board Members If They Could Live on Your Pay Package

Gently and courteously asking your board members if they could live on the pay package they've proposed for you might be a worthy question. It could be risky, of course. But congregations must be shown, from time to time, that they have a responsibility before God to pay their ministers adequately. That's why some board members need to be realistic about the current costs of living.

11-7 Pastoral Pay Packages and Guilt

Psychologists and counselors to pastors have known for years that many pastors live with a tremendous burden of guilt about money. For example, Pastor John Jones knows that he does not measure up to the expectations of the entire congregation. The reason he knows? He gets telephone calls criticizing something he has done or not done, said or not said. Sometimes he gets phone calls from very angry people who "unload" on him. Some probably are justified; some are not. There is no way that Pastor Jones can please each and every person in the congregation. But he tries to do just that. Pastor Jones is on the horns of a very real dilemma, for some people in every congregation impose unrealistic expectations on the pastor. Pastor Jones tries to please, sees that he cannot measure up, tries harder, becomes frustrated, then angry, represses his anger (because pastors are not supposed to get angry), and then becomes very guilty about all his apparent failures.

This guilt carries over to his attitude toward his pay package. He believes that if his congregation expects him to live on less than he needs, he should somehow do it. If he can't, the process outlined above unfolds. If, in any facet of life, pastors fall short of what is expected of them by congregations, guilt, depression, and silent suffering follow.

But if this process outlined is true for you, and there is a line of communication between you and your board members, or at least between you and one or two sympathetic board members, you should seek an opportunity to share your feelings. If you feel you can't talk to anyone in your church, you would be wise to seek the counsel of someone you trust outside the church rather than suffer in silence.

Do not let these feelings go without facing them and seeking a solution. Denial only complicates the situation. If you and your advisers believe you are in the wrong church, you probably should seek to use your gifts and talents in another church. Continuing to live with a heavy burden of guilt, imagined or justified, is counterproductive to ministry. It is, of course, a highly sensitive subject and should be considered with much prayer and, in some cases, with professional counseling help.

11-8 Worksheet to Develop Your Pay Package

Now you can begin the process of building your pay package. If you have a spouse, the first thing to do, prior to salary review time, is to have a planning session together and anticipate your needs for the coming year. The following budget form will help you do that.

	This Year	Next Year
Cash salary	$_____	$_____
Housing allowance (If in parsonage, list amount reported for Social Security.)	$_____	$_____
Utilities	$_____	$_____
Automobile allowance (If using reimbursement method, so indicate: Yes____ No____.)	$_____	$_____
Hospitalization	$_____	$_____
Pension contribution		
By church	$_____	$_____
By minister	$_____	$_____
Tax-sheltered annuity		
By church	$_____	$_____
By minister	$_____	$_____
IRA	$_____	$_____
Social Security payments		
By church	$_____	$_____
By minister	$_____	$_____
(It is *all* income to the minister.)		
Disability insurance		
By church	$_____	$_____
By minister	$_____	$_____
Continuing education	$_____	$_____
Book allowance	$_____	$_____
Discretionary fund (Must be accounted for)	$_____	$_____
Other	$_____	$_____
Annual total	$_____	$_____

CHAPTER 12

Financing a College Education

12-1 The Value of Starting to Save
Early for College

A family that begins saving immediately upon the birth of a child, and continues saving without interruption, moves effectively toward the goal of accumulating a healthy college fund. Consider the impact of 7 percent compound interest when you save certain amounts yearly from the birth of a child until age eighteen:

$ Per Year	Amount at 18
240	$ 8,731
300	10,914
360	13,096
420	15,279
480	17,462
600	21,827
900	43,655
1,200	54,568
2,000	72,758

There are many vehicles to use for building this college fund. CDs, savings accounts, stocks, bonds, mutual funds, and life insurance all have their place. Some are safer than others. However, the higher the interest rate you enjoy, the greater the risk you incur. Taxes take their share of most accumulating accounts. If you can live with the ups and downs of investing in the stock market or mutual funds, you must realize that it will always depend on your ability to buy low and sell high.

The economy is always cyclical. If your investment account is high when you need the money for education, you are fortunate. If it is not, you have the dilemma of when to withdraw your equity. If your child has reached school age and your investment account is not as high as you had hoped, you may wish to leave it alone for the time being, anticipating that it will eventually rise again. Mutual funds, for example, usually will correct to an upward swing, but it may be months or years too late for your college-age child. Meantime, you will have to make other arrangements for the college needs. On the other hand, your account may have risen to highs beyond your expectations. But if that is the case, the cost of living probably will have risen correspondingly with inflation, wiping out what might otherwise have been a profitable excess.

Bank savings rates will usually be several points less than you can earn in other vehicles. At this writing, for example, current bank savings rates are approximately 3 percent less than those shown in the opening example about compound interest.

As most investment counselors will tell you, the answer is to diversify, keeping in mind your specific needs, your temperament, and your ability to save. Ministers should never decide not to save. No matter how small an amount, the important thing is to start and continue without interruption. (See 4-10 for a detailed comparison of CDs and the tax-sheltered annuity.)

12-2 Sources to Contact for Student Loans and Scholarships

The money is out there if you will join in the search. During the 1991–92 school year, according to the U.S. Department of Education, more than $19 billion was distributed in grants, loans, and work-study aid. These funds are open to all qualified U.S. citizens and some eligible noncitizens regardless of race, color, sex, or national origin. Many persons assume incorrectly that they could not qualify for these loans. Don't assume. Go ahead with your investigation. You might be surprised at how much help you can get. You should start by visiting, writing, or calling the educational and applicable governmental institutions nearest you.

The public library can provide information about student aid in your state as well as private sources. At the end of this chapter (in 12-7) there is a list of sources usually found in most libraries.

Consider these sources for loans and/or scholarships:

- Professional organizations, such as the American Bar Association, the American Medical Association, various certified public accounting associations, and nursing associations
- Service clubs, such as Rotary, Kiwanis, 4-H, Jaycees, Boy and Girl Scouts, and Chamber of Commerce
- Foundations, such as YMCA, YWCA, American Legion, Veterans of Foreign Wars, and religious and many other civic groups
- Companies, corporations, and labor unions
- Veterans Administration
- National Honor Society and National Merit scholarships

Note: All quotes in this chapter, unless otherwise noted, are from *The Student Guide* detailing financial aid from the U.S. Department of Education.

12-3 The Pell Grant

The Pell Grant is awarded to first-time undergraduates for post–high school education. These grants, usually limited to five or six years for undergraduate study, do not have to be repaid. It may be possible to obtain other federal financial aid in addition to qualifying for a Pell Grant. You should discuss this idea with school administrators.

To qualify for the Pell Grant, you must attend school at least half-time. Consult your school administrator for the definition of *half-time.*

The amount of money you may be able to get in a Pell Grant depends on your Pell Grant Index (PGI) number and on your school's cost of education. This is still another question you should pose to the educational institution you choose. However, the maximum Pell Grant awarded in the 1991–92 academic year was $2,400.

To determine how you will be paid, you must complete three parts of your Student Aid Report (SAR) by a specific date. Your Pell Grant application must be received at the proper address by a date you should learn about from your school administrator. The date could change so it is not included here. Late arrivals will be declined, without exception. You will receive your money at least once per quarter, semester, or trimester. Schools are required to pay at least twice per academic year.

You will be notified in writing as to when and how much you will receive. Be sure to answer in writing.

12-4 The Supplemental Educational Opportunity Grants (SEOG) and Loans

You may be able to tap into three "campus-based" programs. You may qualify for one or more of them.

1. Supplemental Educational Opportunity Grants (SEOG)

First-time undergraduates with "exceptional financial need" can apply for grants up to $4,000 that do not have to be paid back. Pell Grant recipients have priority in receiving these grants.

File your application as early as possible because the funds are limited and given out on a first-come basis until they are all allocated.

There are several ways to receive the SEOG money. It can be paid directly into your school account or to you directly or by both methods. Your school must pay you at least once each semester. If your SEOG total is less than $500, your school can elect to pay you only once each year.

2. The College Work-Study (CWS) Program

This program makes it possible for first-time undergraduates and graduate students to apply for funds if they are in financial need and allows them to work simultaneously so long as they receive at least the minimum wage. Working for commission is not allowed. You must be paid directly by your school once each month.

The program allows you to work either off or on campus. Generally, you will work at something that is in the public interest. Your work-study program should be "related to your course of study."

Your financial aid administrator determines the number of hours you are allowed to work. Your total activities will be taken into account. And, finally, "the amount you earn can't exceed your total CWS award."

Co-op programs. In addition, many employers offer co-op programs. Often, it is a way for a company to offer work in the student's chosen field of study and provide a job after the student graduates. The student works out a schedule with the sponsoring company that allows him or her to attend school a semester, then work a semester, repeating the process until graduation. It is an effective program that allows a student to have career-related work experience even before graduation. It is equally advantageous to employers because they can closely observe the students in action, thus enabling them to choose the most qualified students after graduation.

3. The Perkins Loan

This program is available to first-time undergraduate and graduate students "with exceptional financial need." Undergraduate students with a Pell Grant will be given priority. Perkins Loans are from your school and must be repaid. The interest charge is 5 percent.

The amounts available vary, depending on your individual situation. You must seek counsel from your school financial aid administrator to determine the amount. You may receive up to $4,500 "if you've completed less than 2 years of a program leading to a first bachelor's degree, or if you've enrolled in a vocational program." You may receive up to $9,000 "if you've already completed 2 years of study toward a first bachelor's degree and have achieved third-year status." You may receive up to $18,000 for graduate or professional study.

You will receive at least two payments per academic year from your school unless you receive a total of $500 or less from a Perkins Loan. Your school may then choose to pay you only once each academic year.

You must first sign a promissory note obligating you to repay the loan. If you are a "half-time" student, you will have a "grace period" of nine months after graduation before you must begin repayment. Your grace period may vary depending on how your financial aid administrator classifies you. You will have ten years to repay the loan once you begin repayment. Generally, you must pay at least $30 per month. If you miss a monthly payment or are late, appropriate penalties will be charged until your payments are current. The following exceptions can result in cancellation or partial cancellation of loans:

- If you suffer long-term illness. If this situation occurs, your financial aid administrator will guide you. Under certain circumstances, you may apply through your school for a deferment, so long as your loan is not in default. However, you must continue your payments until you receive approval for a deferment.
- If you die or become permanently disabled.
- "If you're a teacher (under certain circumstances), if you're a full-time staff member of a Head Start program, or if you're a Peace Corps or VISTA volunteer."
- If you file bankruptcy under certain circumstances.

• If you enlist in the armed forces. Contact your local recruiting office.

12-5 The Stafford Loan

For "half-time" students, low-interest loans may be made by banks, credit unions, schools, or savings and loan associations. These loans are insured by each state's guarantee agency and are reinsured by the federal government and must be repaid.

When "new borrowers" take out loans on or after July 1, 1988, they will be charged an interest rate of 8 percent during the first four years of repayment and 10 percent after that. New borrowers who received loans between July 1, 1987, and June 30, 1988, will be charged an 8 percent interest rate.

You may borrow up to $2,625 "if you're a first or second-year undergraduate student, or if you're in a program that is normally completed in 2 academic years or less."

You may borrow up to $4,000 a year "if you've completed 2 years of undergraduate study and have achieved third-year status."

You may borrow up to $7,500 a year "if you're a graduate/professional student."

You may not have a total undergraduate debt in excess of $17,500, including loans from the Guaranteed Student Loan (GSL) program. The maximum for graduate or professional students is $54,750 "including Stafford Loans and GSLs made at the undergraduate level."

To apply, you and your school must complete an application detailing your financial need, the financial aid you receive, and your academic standing. Your school must first determine if you and your school are eligible for a Pell Grant. Your school will make the final determination of the amount of your loan.

Since not all lending institutions participate in the Stafford program, you should research your state thoroughly to determine which one would be the best source for you. You can call the Federal Student Aid Information Center toll-free to obtain more information about loans at 1-800-433-3243.

You will be charged an "origination fee" of 5 percent, which will be forwarded to the federal government. In addition, the lending institution may charge you up to 3 percent for an insurance premium. The lender sends the money to your school at least twice each semester, and your school may choose to pay you directly or credit your account. "If you're a first-year undergraduate student who is also a first-time Stafford Loan borrower, you can't receive your first payment until 30 days after the first day your program begins. A 30-day wait also applies to all first-time Stafford Loan borrowers attending schools with a default rate of over 30 percent. (See your financial aid administrator for more information.)"

As for repaying your loan, you will generally have a "grace period" of six months before you must begin repaying between $50.00 and $187.01 per month, depending on the size of your loan. You must notify your lender "when you graduate, leave school, or drop below half-time."

Your lending institution may sell your loan to another lending institution, or the institution itself may be purchased by another institution. In either case, you must be notified.

Under certain circumstances, including disability, Peace Corps service, and U.S. armed services duty, you may apply for a deferment. Check for details with your financial aid administrator if you are requesting initial information about a Stafford Loan. If you already have a loan and need a deferment of your payments, check with your lender.

If you apply for a deferment of repayment, you must continue your payments until your deferment is approved so that you do not end up in default. If you don't qualify for deferment under the circumstances outlined here but get into financial difficulty, you may apply for "forbearance," which permits a temporary discontinuance of your payments.

Stafford Loans may be canceled if you die or become totally disabled or file for bankruptcy. "However, 7 years must have passed between the date your loan became due and the date you filed (not counting deferment periods). If you can prove to the bankruptcy court that repayment would cause undue hardship, your loan may be canceled before 7 years have passed."

The Department of Defense may repay certain portions of your Stafford Loan. Your local recruiting officer can give you the details about this incentive to enlist in the armed forces.

12-6 PLUS Loans and Supplemental Loans for Students (SLS)

Loans may be available—up to $4,000 per year for five years—to parents through this program, which provides additional educational funds through lending institutions. These loans are subject to changes in interest rates that cannot exceed 12 percent. Students must be dependent and enrolled at least half-time.

This program makes available amounts of up to $4,000 per academic year for half-time enrolled graduate or professional students who are independent undergraduates. These loans may be made in addition to loans received under the Stafford Loan program. Under certain circumstances, dependent undergraduates may also qualify for a Supplemental Loan.

The amount of the loan is limited to $2,500

if you're enrolled in a program that is at least ⅔ of an academic year but less than a full academic year. $1,500 is the limit if you're enrolled in a program that is less than ⅔ but at least ⅓ of an academic year. SLS loans are not made to first-year undergraduates enrolled in a program that is less than ⅓ of an academic year. You can't receive more than one SLS during any 7-month period, or the length of your school's academic year, whichever is longer.

To be eligible for the SLS,

you must have a high school diploma or a General Education Development Certificate (GED). You can't qualify by taking a test approved by the U.S. Department of Education, as is true for the other programs mentioned in *The Student Guide* of the United States Department of Education.

To apply for a PLUS or SLS, use the same procedure as outlined for the Stafford Loan. You do not have to show financial need for these programs, but you do have to qualify.

The repayment of the PLUS and SLS is between the lenders and you and/or your parents. Lenders can charge up to 3 percent for insurance premiums. Repayments must begin within sixty days after the final loan disbursement, and there is no grace period. If a deferment is requested and granted, only principal, not the interest, may be postponed. Of course, if the loan is in default, no deferment will be granted. And repayments must be continued after a deferment request until it is actually granted. "Forbearance" may also be available to stop repayments temporarily.

Both PLUS and SLS can be canceled, the same as Stafford Loans. "However, 7 years must have passed between the date the loan became due and the date you (or your parents) filed, not counting deferment periods. If you or your parents have filed for bankruptcy you or they must prove to the bankruptcy court that repayment would cause undue hardship." Before seven years have passed, the loan may then be canceled.

Just as for the Stafford Loans, you or your parents may receive some repayment incentive if you or they enlist in the armed forces. Your local recruiting office will give you details.

These are only the highlights of the various government programs. Seek the details applicable to your specific circumstances. Many ministers assume they will never be able to send their children to college. Yet, almost any person in financial need can qualify for funds for college.

12-7 Additional Sources for Scholarships and Loans

Be advised that I am not singling out the following sources as being the best. The list represents the sources available. You may be able to discover many more. You should do your homework and make your own decision. Then check with your local or state departments of education to get their opinions of the sources listed.

One of the best source books for information about loans and scholarships is *Financial Aids for Higher Education* by Oreon Keeslar, published by Wm. C. Brown Publishers, Dubuque, Iowa. It offers great detail about each school and occupation mentioned. It will help you focus on specific occupations.

Check with your various advisers, including high school guidance counselors and college financial aid administrators.

Waverly Community House, Inc.
Lammont Belin Arts Scholarships
Scholarships Selection Committee
Waverly, PA 18471
717-586-8191

College Music Teacher Career
  Information
College Music Society
1444 15th St.
Boulder, CO 80302

Creative Writing Career
  Information
National Writers Club
1450 S. Havana, Suite 60
Aurora, CO 80012

Creative Writing Career
  Information
Writers' Guild of America East
555 W. 57th St.
New York, NY 10019

The A's and B's of Academic
  Scholarship
Potameron Association
P.O. Box 3437
Alexandria, VA 22302

Teaching Abroad
Institute of International
  Education
809 United Nations Plaza
New York, NY 10017

The Scholarship Book
Prentice-Hall
Englewood Cliffs, NJ

*Peterson's College Money
  Handbook*
Peterson's Guides, Inc.
Box 2123
Princeton, NJ 08543

*Barron's Complete College
  Financing Guide*
Barron's Educational Series
250 Wireless Blvd.
Hauppauge, NY 11788

Study Abroad
Williamson Publishing
Box 185, Church Hill Rd.
Charlotte, VT 05445

Work, Study, Travel Abroad
St. Martin's Press
175 5th Ave.
New York, NY 10010

Internships
Writer's Digest Books
1507 Dana Ave.
Cincinnati, OH 45207

Index of Majors
Times Books
201 E. 50th St.
New York, NY 10022

Making It Through College
New York Life Insurance Co.
51 Madison Ave.
PR Dept.
New York, NY 10010

Fiske Guide to Colleges
Sun Features Inc.
Box 368-K
Cardiff, CA 92007

Need a Lift?
Professional Staff Congress
25 W. 434th St., 5th Floor
New York, NY 10036

Study Abroad
The United Nations Educational,
  Scientific, and Cultural
  Organization (UNESCO)
Berman Associates, UNIPUB
10033F King Highway
Lanham, MD 20706

College Financial Aid
  Emergency Kit
American Legion Education
  Program
P.O. Box 1050
Indianapolis, IN 46206

The Educational Resources
  Institute (TERI)
330 Stuart St., Suite 500
Boston, MA 02116

CHAPTER 13

◆————————————————————◆

Do You Have a Will?

13-1 Why You Should Have a Will

Only three out of ten people have legal, written wills. Almost everyone who does not have a will says, "I intend to do that soon." But far too many people procrastinate until it is too late.

Most states have laws providing for the survivors of persons who die intestate (without a will). However, the distribution of property and the treatment of minors may not be in accordance with the wishes of the deceased. Beneficiaries are often the losers by decisions made by the state courts.

There is no reason not to have a will. Making a will should be the very first thing you do if you are serious about getting your affairs in order while there is time. I urge you to seek legal counsel as soon as possible if you do not have a will.

Here are a few important reasons why you need a legal, written will:

- First, if you have a will, unless you have a very large estate, most of your estate equity can be left directly to your beneficiaries, bypassing your estate and most taxes. Furthermore, it will be distributed according your wishes.
- Second, your spouse, or whoever else you choose, can be appointed as executor or executrix in your will to serve without bond to settle your estate.
- If you have minor children, you can name guardians of your choice rather than have the court name them, which it will do if you die intestate.

- If you have minor children, own a home, and die intestate, the court has the power to sell your home and put the children's share of the home in trust for them to protect their interests. With a will, only your wishes will be carried out. Your spouse can receive the house without tax consequences in most cases if you have a proper will.

- If you have lived in more than one state and/or own property in more than one state, all states involved may claim you as a resident and impose taxes on your estate.

- A will affords you the opportunity to leave specific objects to designated individuals. For example, you may wish to leave a specific amount of money to your church or seminary, or to a grandchild for educational purposes. You can will a valuable musical instrument to just the right person. Often a person wishes to leave silverware and treasured china to one person. On the other hand, you may see the wisdom of ordering these items to be sold and the cash distributed evenly to designated recipients. Specific items of jewelry can be designated to individuals as well as books, clothing, and tools to those who, in your judgment, could best use them.

If you do not have a will, I urge you to make it a priority to obtain one.

CHAPTER 14

Investment Strategies

14-1 Ministers Need Investments Too

Because most ministers can purchase a tax-sheltered annuity, a subject covered thoroughly in chapter 4, I suggest that they buy all the TSA for which they are eligible first before investing in anything else for *long-range* purposes. The only possible exception might be an employer plan offering a system of matching funds, such as a 401(k) plan. Some schools and colleges offer matching funds for 403(b) plans.

Once you adopt these plans to the fullest, what investments do you turn to as a next step? Your options might include mutual funds, stocks, bonds, real estate, commodities, collectibles, gold, silver, platinum, art, gems, antiques, coins, and any number of other choices.

14-2 How and Where Do You Start Investing?

The first thing to consider is whether or not you will personally have the time to investigate investments. If you don't have the time, you may want to engage an investment manager. Of course, such a decision depends on many other variables, such as how much you have to invest. Most money managers require a minimum amount of investment capital. Perhaps your spouse is willing to be the manager of the investments. So, you must decide who will expend the time necessary to monitor your investments. Most ministers do not have that kind of time.

The Rule of 72

To help you decide on the investment to make, a useful tool is the rule of 72. Financial institutions use it daily. When you want to know how much time is required for money to double at any given interest rate, divide the interest rate into the number 72. For example, if you divide 72 by 7 percent, you learn that money will double at that rate in 10.285 years. At 6 percent, the answer is 12 years.

14-3 What About Investing in Real Estate?

If you choose real estate as a vehicle for investment, you must be prepared to commit a major portion of your time or that of your manager. Real estate, by and large, has been a very good way to build up equity, but it can backfire on you. If you happen to be handy with your hands, or if you have a partner who is handy, you could begin by buying a home, at a low price of course, and fixing it up either for resale or for rental purposes. Then you buy another, using the hoped-for profit from the first, and repeat the process, always with an eye on balancing the amount of debt with the amount you are paying off. Too many people do not keep enough working capital on hand as they go through this process. Furthermore, you must be prepared to receive telephone calls in the middle of a cold January night when your tenant tells you the furnace doesn't work. You or someone must be readily available for maintenance.

You must have the temperament to negotiate (some call it haggling) over price, deposits, contract details, repairs, and evictions. Unless ministers are ready to enter into such a process, which might require a decision to evict people, the plan might not work.

The best way for ministers to own real estate is to have a manager. Pay the person 6 percent of the rental income and stay in touch with the manager primarily over the telephone. If you don't think you could stand the hassle of buying, selling, and renting real estate, buy blue-chip stocks, lock them up, and forget real estate. Still, you will need some kind of management help and in no case will you be totally free from considering your investments and making decisions as the market changes.

14-4 What About Financial Planners?

Many persons call themselves financial planners. Just as in any other profession, there are good and bad ones. Most competent planners are certified by some legitimate organization. Look for the following designations after their names: CPA (certified public accountant), CLU (chartered life underwriter), CFP (chartered financial planner), ChFC (chartered financial counselor), LLB (bachelor of laws), and/or LUTCF (Life Underwriters Training Counsel Foundation). This is not to suggest that all persons without these designations are incapable of rendering adequate service. Many with long years of experience may be well prepared to serve you. However, these designations usually are important.

14-5 How Do Financial Planners Get Paid?

Professional planners are generally paid in two ways. Either they receive a fee, or they sell financial vehicles and receive commissions. Often planners will quote a fee with the understanding that if you buy something they sell, the amount of the fee will count toward the sale of the product. The most unbiased advice would probably come from fee-only consultants. They might tend to work more with persons of wealth. The minister, on the other hand, might be better off with the planner who gets paid only if the minister buys some investment or life insurance from the planner. Of course, there is always the chance that such a person will be biased or limited in what to offer you. Take your time, listen, and compare.

14-6 What About Mutual Funds?

Perhaps the best way for you to invest toward long-range goals, after you own the maximum tax-sheltered annuity allowed, is to buy no-load mutual funds and continue making monthly deposits over the years. Don't watch the accounts every day; give them time. But whatever you do, don't put money into the mutual funds that you might need in cash in the near future. If you decide to buy no-load funds, you will have to do your own research. Brokers sell only loaded funds. No-loads do not charge brokerage fees.

To make mutual funds work for you, deposit money regularly into your account, let it have plenty of time to grow, and don't withdraw it when the economy declines. Many people make the mistake of withdrawing funds when the economy becomes tight. That's when wise investors buy more rather than sell. You have no guarantee whatsoever that those mutual fund accounts will increase again, however. Some do and some don't. Sometimes, an out-and-out thief manipulates the market and walks off with multiple millions of the investing public's money. Nevertheless, if you feel you have an even playing field in the mutual fund world, you should be able to build equity over a long period of time.

Mutual funds offer *diversity*—something you should have in any investment plan. You must know what you're trying to accomplish when you choose an investment vehicle. Do you want fast growth, long-term capital increase, safety, income, tax shelter? Are you willing to speculate? Your goals must be specific. They must be monitored and flexible enough to change as you watch the economy.

If you decide that mutual funds are the vehicle for you, I would suggest you go to a large magazine rack and select several magazines, including those that rank and rate mutual funds. Study the market. Read the *Wall Street Journal* and other financial publications. Get the views of both the bulls and the bears of the mutual fund market. Without a broker, you must do your own homework. Many pastors like mutual funds that are considered to be socially conscious in that they do not invest in munitions, repressive governments, chemicals harmful to the environment, alcohol, or tobacco. Study the market, and then make your choices.

14-7 A Word About Computers

To keep track of your goals, you must have a good record-keeping system not only for your expenses, such as car expenses, but also for your investments. If you have not yet purchased a computer, I urge you to do so. It can save you countless hours of time after you become adept at using the various programs. Many such programs, starting with a home bookkeeping program, monitor investments. You cannot overdo the keeping of records that affect your income tax return.

Certainly, the ability to write and store sermons on computer disks is appealing to most ministers. It is a simple matter to include a program for home bookkeeping and one for investments or a combination of the two in one program along with a word processing program.

Last, but not least, many computer Bible programs enable you to instantaneously call to your screen passages from the entire Bible, with various translations, all the Greek and all the Hebrew, all of *Strong's Concordance,* and Bible quizzes. You can cut down your research time tremendously.

If you or any member of your family works for a college or university, such institutions have arrangements with computer manufacturers to sell computers to their employees at a discount. While that has a price advantage, the disadvantage is that you may not know how to set up and maintain the computer. If you are a new computer user, you might be wise to buy from a well-established local dealer to get ongoing help.

I recommend a computer with the following features as a minimum:

- A 40 MB (megabytes), preferably 100 MB, hard drive
- 2 MB of RAM (random access memory)
- One 3½" drive
- One 5¼" drive
- VGA (video graphics adapter) color monitor
- 286 computer or better (meaning 386 or 486, which equals faster)
- Adequate software package including a word processing program, Bible program, spread sheet, and disk utility program
- At least 16 MHz (megahertz) speed, preferably 25 MHz
- Expansion slots for modem
- CD-ROM (compact disk–read only memory) adapters, sound cards, etc.

This setup can be purchased through catalogs for about $1,000 as of this writing. Printers can be purchased from $200 up. A laser printer is preferable, ranging in price from $600 to $3,000.

You should know that it is usually much cheaper to buy a large hard disk initially rather than a small one with the intention of upgrading the hard disk later. If you discuss this point with a dealer when you're first negotiating for a computer, you will find that the price of each higher memory hard disk is just a little more. But it isn't that way if you already have a computer and want to replace your existing hard disk with a larger one. Get as much RAM and hard disk capacity as you can initially. You will probably need it. Most computer owners will tell you they keep adding programs.

Join a users' group in your area. These people are very helpful, and the advice is usually free. If you hire a computer consultant, you will have to pay anywhere from $50 to $100 per hour. Many of the users' group members are near geniuses. In almost every club of any size, you will find someone who knows all about your software or hardware.

There are users' groups for beginners and others for experts. There are groups for various professions and special interest groups too numerous to mention. There are even users' groups for ministers. To contact them in your area, ask a local dealer, or go to your public library. Or look in the various computer publications. Such lists are published routinely, breaking down areas of interest and geographic location.

With proper programs, you can record everything you will need for income tax preparation, budgets, and investments. You can track all church records, including donations and attendance. You can have a data base of all members and prospective members ready at your fingertips, showing full and complete information about a family, including your notes of conversations and calls. There is no end to the information you can store and have ready at the flick of a switch.

Furthermore, since you probably make quarterly income tax payments, and since your income may vary because of honoraria, you can track your income quarterly to be sure that you have paid enough. It is sometimes a shock if you wait until April to learn how much tax you owe. It is better to know as you go.

14-8 What About Stocks?

Many pastors cannot justify the purchase of stocks that may involve alcohol, tobacco, repressive governments, or munitions. If you buy into large conglomerates, the chances are, you will be investing in those commodities.

To those who do not find this to be a problem, you must specify your investment goals before buying stocks. Do you want income stocks, growth stocks, speculative stocks, short- or long-term gain? What is your belief about inflation? Can you or anyone else really predict what the stock market might do?

For every yea, there is a nay. That leaves you back where you started. Maybe you would be more comfortable buying mutual funds unless you have a considerable amount of money to invest in the stock market. There is an old, old saying: "The bulls get some, the bears get some, and the hogs get nothing." The best advice you can get might be to get all the advice you can absorb, make some decisions, and stick to your guns long enough to give your investment strategy a chance to work.

If you decide to get into the market, pick a competent broker and work with the person long enough to determine if you are compatible. Of course, it is better to have an incompatible broker who makes money for you than the most compatible one who loses money for you. If you believe the market is for you, do your research, find a broker, and jump in. But don't invest money you may need for basic living costs. If you lose all of your invested funds, you should not have to alter your life-style. Be careful.

If you are trying to build from scratch, you will have a different strategy than if you have capital to invest and preserve. Many fortunes have been won and lost by using OPM: other people's money. If you have little or no investment capital to begin with, you may wish to buy stocks on margin. It's risky, of course, but it is done every day.

14-9 What About Buying Stocks on Margin?

Buying stocks on margin works this way: if your credit is good, and if your luck clings to a rising market, you can profit by paying only 50 percent of the cost of your stock. As for the other 50 percent, you can get the broker to go along with a margin account, or you can borrow enough from the bank to pay the other 50 percent. The market may rise, and perhaps it will rise enough to double the value of your stock. You could sell your stock, repay your 50 percent margin account or loan, and suddenly have profit in your hand. Of course, taxes will have to be paid on a short-range or long-range capital gains basis. Ideally, you can continue this process and accumulate a sizable equity if you're slightly wise and very lucky. It is very risky. You should be prepared to pay more on your margin account or absorb losses should the market turn down. Do *not* invest funds you need to live on! I briefly explain this method here but do not recommend it.

Do you have the temperament, the time, and the money to get into this scene? Wouldn't mutual funds serve you better? Remember, also, full-time professionals are out there armed with sophisticated computer programs, buying and selling stocks, trying to anticipate the trends. Would you be a lamb among lions?

14-10 Watch Out for "Hot" Bargains

Be wary. Watch out for bargains. Don't be taken in by telephone calls from out-of-town brokers pushing stocks or bonds you never heard of. P. T. Barnum was right—"There's a sucker born every minute." But don't join the crowd of people who respond to such telephone calls day in and day out.

The second you hear that sweet friendly voice urging you to buy some vague stock "by midnight tonight," politely hang up and save yourself some misery.

14-11 What About Buying Bonds?

In days gone by, bonds were considered to be far safer than stocks. Like most everything else, that has changed. Investments tend to be committed for shorter periods of time now. The velocity of everything has increased, along with the speed our checks clear the bank. Information is available almost instantaneously, and investment decisions can be made equally fast. Our national debt has caused knowledgeable people to be less confident in bond prices. If you are attracted to corporate bonds, be sure they are AAA-rated. U.S. Treasury bonds would also be a good choice. Check with your broker about the details of buy backs and default.

14-12 What About Junk Bonds?

So-called junk bonds have sent shock waves throughout the U.S. in the last few years. They were offered when it appeared that interest rates would stay higher than they have been in many years. But interest rates did *not* remain high. In fact, they settled back down, and those junk bonds could not deliver the promised interest. Many of them collapsed, leaving bond holders holding the bag, not their equity. The difference between junk bonds and high-grade bonds can be explained in one word: safety. There is not total agreement about where the lines of safety begin and end. It is a matter of judgment, and it varies with analysts. The bulls have different tests than the bears. But there is one rule applied by all: the higher the interest rate, the higher the risk and vice versa.

14-13 Do You Want to Become Really Sophisticated About Investments?

If you really are interested in becoming well educated in the various forms of investments, ask your broker to explain the following to see whether any of these investment vehicles appeal to you: foreign shares, Fannie Mae (Federal National Mortgage Association), Freddie Mac (Federal Home Loan Mortgage Corporation), utilities, Ginnie Mae (Government National Mortgage Association), dividend reinvestment plans, zero-coupon bonds, U.S. Savings Bonds, index options, convertible securities, covered calls, adjustable-rate option municipals, unit trusts, and tax-exempt municipals. You may also want to take some investment courses at a nearby university or college.

CHAPTER 15

◆————————————————◆

Render Unto Caesar

15-1 What About Love Offerings, Allowances, Benefits, and Bonuses?

No matter what they are called, most of these so-called nontaxable items are considered by the IRS to be ordinary income. They must be considered as taxable compensation. There are exceptions, such as a *gift of insignificant value.* The IRS says anything that is *unreasonable* is not allowed. You and your tax adviser will have to determine the definition of these two terms. Far too many ministers have assumed incorrectly that these benefits are not reportable for income tax.

A general rule that applies whenever anyone donates and deducts anything of value to a church in behalf of a minister is this: the donation is considered to be income to the minister. Of course, church members are free to give whatever gifts they wish to the minister without treating them as deductible charitable gifts. Then the minister does not have to report the gifts as income. If you are in doubt about this question, have your tax attorney or CPA research IRC 501(c)(3) and IRC 102(c).

There is, however, a proper procedure for giving ministers love offerings. The conditions are strict and uncompromisable. For a love offering to be nontaxable to the minister, the following tests must be met:

1) The minister cannot ask for a love offering.
2) The idea to give a love offering to the minister must be unplanned, impulsive, and spontaneous.

3) There must be no question about the purpose of the gift. It must clearly be for the minister but not for any services rendered.
4) The donors *cannot* deduct the love offering.
5) The donations must be given out of genuine love, fondness, and/ or affection for the minister.

No doubt many church members have contributed to such offerings in the past, unaware of the nondeductibility of their gifts. Just one IRS audit of any church member's income tax records could lead to near panic in your church. If one of your members contributed to a love offering and deducted it, the IRS may well audit every other member who contributed to that love offering. In addition, if any minister received such a love gift, one that was deducted by the donors, and did not report it as income, that so-called love gift would be disallowed. Back taxes and penalties would be imposed under those circumstances. The IRS will *not* accept ignorance of the law as an excuse.

15-2 Are You and Your Church Keeping Good Records?

In the past, many churches have been sloppy in their record keeping and knowledge of the law. Because of some notorious abuses by some television evangelists, the IRS may suspect almost any church of abuses. Any fringe benefits given to ministers must be carefully planned and monitored to be sure they comply with the law. The best way to do this is to hire competent legal and financial counsel.

15-3 What Could Happen If Your Church Is Audited

An IRS audit of your church records could easily turn up misuses. If you pay a visiting evangelist more than $600, for example, you must be sure to provide a Form 1099. If your church records are audited and the IRS finds that your church did *not* give out a Form 1099, the IRS most probably will audit that evangelist to determine whether or not the person reported the income paid by your church. Then, your church will also be subject to fines for not giving out the Form 1099. When *anyone* renders service to your church, give a Form 1099 just to be safe.

15-4 Other Benefits to Handle
Properly

Be very careful about other benefits you may receive from a church, such as church payments on any of your property, club memberships, personal use of church credit cards, or personal use of church postage.

Another area to be careful about involves your church payments for insurance of various kinds. All too often a church will lump together the payment for your hospitalization and your life insurance, then treat it as nonreportable income to the minister. Many ministers and churches seem to think this procedure constitutes a benefit to the minister. The life insurance *cannot* be treated in this manner. There is much confusion about deducting the cost of group coverage up to $50,000. Many ministers assume that individual term insurance falls into this deductible category. Not so. Only group term coverage is deductible. In most states, ten lives are necessary to be considered a group. Individual term life is *not* deductible, and a church-paid premium must be reported as income by the minister.

15-5 Be Careful Not to Put Your
Tax-Exempt Status in Jeopardy

More and more churches are losing their tax-exempt status through ignorance of the law or carelessness. In addition to handling attempts to set up love offerings, benefits, bonuses, and perks for you, you must carefully monitor any nonchurch activities occurring in your church for which you receive fees or rent. Be advised you may be in violation of the law. Once again, seek the advice of competent legal counsel in regard to this question of love offerings, benefits, bonuses, and perks. In almost every case, you should treat these items as income and pay appropriate taxes.

The government has been narrowing the list of items that can be deducted. In the area of charitable contributions, you and your church board would be well advised to learn what is acceptable and what is not. *Designated giving* must be watched carefully. The general rule is that any such giving earmarked for the minister, if deducted by the donor, must be reported as income by the minister. Even if money is given to a general fund of the church and the money is forwarded in some manner to the minister, it may be considered compensation to the minister. Such questions should never be left to chance. It is always advisable to get competent legal advice.

CHAPTER 16

◆————————————————————————————◆

How to Keep Your Records

16-1 How to Handle Your Business Expense Reimbursement Plan

I cannot stress enough the importance of your developing a working relationship with a competent income tax counselor. It will probably cost you far more in the long run to complete your own income tax forms than to pay such a person to complete them for you. The tax area is constantly changing and is becoming increasingly complex. For example, the IRS has closed the door on a method of reimbursement used by many ministers. As of December 14, 1990, IRC Section 1.62-2(d)(3) specifically prohibits reimbursement of employee expenses derived from a salary reduction agreement.

Since the IRS has taken away so many deductions, the idea of setting up pastors' reimbursement accounts with churches is becoming more widespread. But it must be done in compliance with IRS rules. These expenses have to be accounted for in a proper manner. A general guideline is, if your employing church will accept and reimburse your valid expenses, so will the IRS usually accept the church's records. These records are treated in much the same manner as those of an outside salesperson whose employer furnishes a car and expenses as part of a pay package. Remember, *reimbursement is not compensation.*

16-2 The Key to Reimbursement: Accountability to the IRS

Someone in your church must keep detailed records of your business reimbursement account. The key word is *accountability.* You must complete proper expense records detailing the business purposes, names, dates, and locations connected with these purposes, and turn them in to your church with proper receipts. Then someone in the church has to keep these records and have them available at all times should the church or you get audited. It is your responsibility to turn in such records, and it is the church's responsibility to maintain them properly. Both parties are accountable to the IRS.

In the pressure of church business, such as when a parishioner is being taken to a hospital emergency room, it is not easy to pause long enough to mark down names, dates, hospital names, and mileage, but they must be kept. A word of advice: keep photocopies of all your receipts and expense records. If the church loses them, you're still responsible and accountable to substantiate your expenses to the satisfaction of the IRS.

In actual cases, people have been called in to the IRS for an audit, and after they left their receipts with the IRS, the IRS lost them. The IRS told the taxpayers that they should have kept copies in their files. The taxpayers sued the IRS and lost.

Using the reimbursement method can be very helpful to pastors, actually resulting in their legally receiving some nontaxable income. But any money left unspent at the end of the year has to be returned to the church. Prior to December 14, 1990, pastors often kept the excess, reported it as income, and paid the taxes.

Seek the help of a professional tax accountant in setting up your reimbursement account. It is important to be classified as self-employed while using the expense reimbursement method. There are limitations to the amounts of reimbursable expenses available to persons classified as employees. If you are classified as an employee, you may well lose all your possible business expense deductions.

16-3 How to Set Up a Proper Expense Reimbursement Account

In setting up an accountable business reimbursement fund, the church board must put a resolution in the official church board minutes spelling out the details, including the amount and the intent of the account. It must be clearly understood (and in writing) by the minister that any funds left unspent at the end of the year must be recovered by the church.

Ministers are allowed a period of 120 days to return these funds.

Generally speaking, they have 60 days to turn in their business expense records to be considered "substantiated." The records must be accompanied by proper receipts and details of business purposes. Salary reductions cannot be used as a means of funding the reimbursement account.

However, at the beginning of the tax year, a church and a minister can agree to lower the stated salary by an amount to be used as a reimbursement account and so stated in the minutes of the church. Once again, any funds left unspent must be returned to the church at the end of the year. Of course, any attempt to pay the minister these unspent, excess funds would cost the offending minister dearly in taxes and penalties if an audit is ordered.

16-4 The Most Advantageous Method of Pastoral Transportation

Probably the most advantageous transportation arrangement occurs when a church is willing to purchase a car for you. But you should follow several important guidelines so that the vehicle's use is not considered to be personal and, therefore, taxable to you. See Regulation 1.274-6T(a)(2).

First of all, the car must be kept on church property when not being used for church business or being serviced. That means you would have to drive your own car to the church each day, use the church-owned car for church business during the day, park it at the church at night, and drive home in your car.

You can use the car personally only for minimal reasons such as stopping between hospital calls to have lunch.

Your church board has to substantiate that your use of the car for personal reasons is only minimal.

Any employee using the church-owned car cannot live on church premises. Such a rule must be declared as church policy in the board minutes. (See Section C, Part III of IRS Form 4562 and Regulation 1.274-6T(a)(2).)

There are exceptions to these rules, but they are important enough and complicated enough for you to seek the counsel of a competent tax accountant, especially one who knows the rules applying to clergypersons.

CHAPTER 17

How to Get Out of Debt and Start Saving

17-1 How to Use Immediate Remedies to Stop the Bleeding

Someone has said that there are two ways to improve your financial situation: earn more money and eliminate debt.

If you find yourself in the debt pit, the first thing to do is to stop incurring more debt. You may need to sell something of value that you own. Usually, however, sales under these conditions are forced, and the buyer gains the most at the seller's expense. The *first rule* of commerce is to buy low and sell high.

Many people confess their inability to resist the use of charge cards. If you are in that category, resort to plastic surgery. Return the cards, or cut them up and throw them away. If you have overdue debts and you are feeling the pressure, talk to your creditors, assuring them of your intentions to pay, and then work out a repayment schedule with them. The worst thing to do is to ignore them. Next, if necessary, go to a bank, tell all to the bank officer, and seek a consolidation loan. If one is granted, pay off all your debts, and then you will have only one payment each month—assuming you make no more debts. Stick to your plan until the debt is paid off. Then you're ready to implement a plan that will help you save money.

Important rule: never make long-term loans to pay short-term debts. Some say "never say never." Let's agree on "almost never."

17-2 Do You Have a Budgeting Philosophy?

Many ministers have told me that they have never managed to live on a budget. All persons must have some idea of how and why to budget. For ministers, budgeting is even more important because it enables them to live on whatever income they receive, and in the process, they display a great witness to the public.

Economic strife and disagreements involving money cause more marital problems than almost any other cause. Budgeting experts say that even high-income earners have trouble living on their incomes if they do not have a budgeting philosophy. Many persons spend more than they earn each year, regardless of their level of income. They seem to assume that their income will continue to rise, but it doesn't always happen that way. Budgeting is wise, no matter what the level of income. Before buying something, ask yourself three questions: Do I want it? Can I afford it? Do I really need it? Talk it over with your spouse or some trusted adviser. Then decide.

17-3 Do You Have a Method for Keeping Track of Your Bills?

For most people, certainly most pastors, there is usually too much month left at the end of the money. That is the way things are for most working people, like it or not. The struggle never ends, it seems, until we die. But sometimes, our struggle is intensified because of our negligence. We don't pay enough attention to our bills, and they pile up or become overdue.

In this computer age, there is usually no lag time during which we can wait for our checks to reach the bank. Sometimes we write checks with every intention of covering them in the bank, only to have something happen to delay us a day, and suddenly, we have a penalty from the bank amounting to $10 or $20 for a bounced check. It is too costly a mistake to make.

For years prior to the age of the computer, one man was in the habit of paying his bills once each month. If he got a bill for $40, he felt free to pay only $20 within thirty days. The department stores went along with such a procedure, especially for a good customer.

One day this man decided to purchase a new refrigerator. He went to a department store that had sent him a letter a year prior to that time inviting him to charge anything in the store since his credit record was so good. Meantime, he had charged very little in that store, and he had gotten careless about paying the small amounts on time. He felt very confident as he shopped with the salesperson and finally chose a sparkling new refrigerator.

When the salesperson wrote up the order to be charged, he made a routine check over the telephone to the company's credit office. Imagine the shock and embarrassment the man experienced when the salesperson cleared his throat and told him his credit application had been denied. Immediately, the man went to the credit office and spoke with the manager, who pointed out that he had been late making payments of $12 and $13 for five months out of the year.

That was when the man learned about the cold, objective nature of computers. He learned that whether a customer was 10¢ overdue or $1,000 overdue, it did not matter to the computer. Overdue is overdue. Any amount of delinquency caused the computer to show the "bad risk" flag. The man had allowed carelessness to hamper his credit rating over just a few delinquent dollars. The significance was that he let it happen five months that year, showing a pattern of late payments. Just a few dollars had wrecked his credit rating with that store. Shaken, the man gave his word that he would watch his due dates more carefully, and soon his credit rating with that store was reestablished.

To avoid such unnecessary embarrassment, you can follow a procedure to prevent your bills from being delinquent. If you have been having a similar problem, the first thing is to vow to watch your bill due dates more carefully. Formerly, bills were due the first of each month. Now, due dates can be any day of the month. No longer can people play the "float" game in which they write checks not covered in their checking accounts. The checks are cashed and processed immediately now because of computers.

Next, buy a file folder with thirty-one sections in it. You can get a folder at any office supply store for a few dollars. When bills arrive in the mail, file them in the folder to be retrieved and mailed on a date with enough lead time to reach the destination before the due date.

The system keeps all the bills in one place in an orderly fashion that will bring each one to your attention so that it can be paid on time. This solution requires minimal trouble and worry for you. Not only does it protect your credit rating, it also saves the high cost of interest.

To help you develop a systematic payment plan for bills due, use the following budget worksheet to begin determining your budget:

Budget Worksheet

Item	Per Month
Food	$_____
Clothing	_____
Shelter	_____
Medical and dental (including hospitalization)	_____
Transportation	_____
Household effects	_____
Life insurance	_____
Education	_____
Savings and investments	_____
Personal spending	_____
Tithes and donations	_____
Social Security tax	_____
Federal income tax	_____
State income tax	_____
Any other tax (city, etc.)	_____
Vacation	_____
Gifts	_____
Debt reduction	_____
Miscellaneous	_____
Tax-sheltered annuity	_____
IRA	_____
Other_____	_____
Other_____	_____
Other_____	_____
Monthly total	$_____
Annual total	$_____

17-4 How to Live on Your Income by Using the 10/10/80 Plan

People can save for long-range purposes if they will resolve to save, commit to a plan, and save regularly without skipping deposits or invading the account.

Here is a method that can work if you will make a serious effort to follow it, no matter your level of income. Plan to use 10 percent for tithes, 10 for savings, and 80 to live on. When should you start? *Now.* These percentages aren't carved in stone, but they are suggested as a starting point. There is a "secret" to making this 10/10/80 plan work. You must take out the two 10 percents from your stream of income before you do anything else. In fact, you would do well to have it withheld from your pay. That's why payroll savings plans have withstood the test of time.

Resolve. First, you must vow, resolutely, to begin saving. Make the vow irreversible. Enter into a joint decision with someone else so that each can hold the other accountable to the vow.

Commitment. Second, you must add an ongoing commitment to your resolve to begin. Don't sit down with your bills and look them over, thinking, *Let's see if there is enough left over after I pay my bills. If there is, I'll give to church and to my savings out of what's left.* That plan simply will not work. You cannot save what is left after spending what you think you need, for there is usually nothing left, no matter how high the income level.

Regularity. This other ingredient is necessary to save money on a long-term basis. You must vow to save regularly, no matter what happens. If you do this faithfully, you are free to spend the remaining 80 percent. If you need money for something unforeseen, find it some other way. Don't take the easiest way out. You may regret it when you are older. Reread the last paragraph in 17-2.

17-5 What Constitutes Savings?

Just what constitutes savings? Every family should have some liquid savings in the savings account for emergencies. How much? Many financial planners suggest three to six months' pay. People who have never had such savings view that as an impossible goal, and well it might be for many. However, just as the journey of a thousand miles starts with the first step, so you can begin a savings plan. Far too many people never begin, reasoning that they can't save enough to make a difference, so they don't take that first step. Consider the truth of this idea: almost anyone can save $1 every day. In one year that would produce $365 in savings, plus the interest.

Let's look at what the magic of compound interest will produce at age sixty-five by saving $365 per year, assuming 7 percent interest, if you begin saving at various ages:

Age	Amount
25	$77,968
30	53,988
35	36,892
40	24,702

45	16,011
50	9,814

These amounts are from regularly saving $1 each day. Using simple arithmetic, you can project other results based on a 7 percent interest rate. For example, you can reach a goal of $155,936 at age sixty-five if you save $2 per day starting at age twenty-five and so on. Obviously, the older you are when you start your savings plan, the more you will have to deposit to produce the results you want. For example, if you save $1,200 each year, invested at 7 percent, you will have, at ages forty, forty-five, and fifty, respectively, $81,212, $52,638, and $32,266.

Distinguish between short-term and long-term savings. An emergency fund is considered to be short term. Included in long-term savings is the cash value of life insurance and any investment you view as long term, including stocks, bonds, mutual funds, and a home of your own. Obviously, the home is not to be considered a liquid fund, although many people are borrowing on their homes via the home equity loan route. This method has possible dangers. Should the interest skyrocket as it did once before, people with home equity loans will certainly suffer a shock. It is best not to invade that equity unless there is no other option. At any rate, most real estate you own can be considered long-range savings.

17-6 Savings—A Summation

If you view your savings only as a "put and take" vehicle, the amount probably never will grow. Yes, there should be an amount earmarked for the "put and take" of emergencies and opportunities, but you should not touch long-range savings. It is a matter of attitude.

You should remind yourself repeatedly of the parallel of giving to church and saving money for yourself and your family. You should not rob from either account. You can find alternatives if you put your mind to it.

So, bank savings, cash values in life insurance policies, tax-sheltered annuities, IRAs, stocks, bonds, real estate investments, and any other type of investment constitute savings, both short term and long term. To be sure, occasionally funds will have to be withdrawn from long-range savings to meet a short-range need. That is the reality of life. It is sometimes unavoidable. But if you have a plan and monitor it periodically, the promise of resolve, commitment, and regularity leads to ultimate results. If you will resolve to peck away regularly at your savings goals year after year, you will have a better chance of reaching your goals.

Your primary residence, which qualifies for a housing allowance (discussed thoroughly in chapter 2), can be your most important long-range investment. There is no guarantee that real estate values will always increase, but over the years they certainly have. If you don't already own a home, it might be a higher priority for you than you think. Many denominations discourage home ownership by ministers, but an increasing number of ministers are seeing the wisdom of buying their homes as soon as possible during their careers. Not only will they enjoy home ownership during their productive lifetimes, they will have an opportunity to build their equity as they move from church to church and town to town, taking their equity with them. Then, at retirement, they might well have a home completely paid for.

Most everyone agrees that the goal of planning is to keep debt down and allow net equity to grow. The truth is that most people have had to borrow to pay for homes, furniture, cars, and college educations. The ideal of no debt and high equity is an honorable one, but it is also very difficult to implement. The goal of saving enough to buy a car and pay cash for it is a worthy and valuable goal, but not everybody can do it. There has to be a balance of need against the ability to save.

Finally, some financial seminars in the United States, although helpful in many ways, sometimes go overboard in stressing fear of the future, fear of the coming economic crash, and they espouse a doomsday philosophy.

Too much fear of any so-called coming crash may hinder your normal, sane tendencies to maintain a reasonable amount of debt. Too little attention to your growing debt can be costly to you even if there is no coming crash.

If you are having financial difficulties, now is the time to face that fact. For many, including pastors, these are hard economic times.

You can reach your goals if you commit yourself to a workable plan and then implement your plan. If you have too much month left at the end of the money, there are only two things you can do about it: increase your income or reduce your spending. If you do either and set reasonable updated goals, eventually you will reach them.

As my father used to say, "Do it now!"

GENERAL INDEX

*Bert Akin is available for speaking
engagements and seminars for pastors
and other church groups. He can be
reached at:*

H. L. Bert Akin
7466 Valerie Lane
Hudson, Ohio 44236

Telephone: (216) 650-1328